Since Calvary

WORKS BY LEWIS BROWNE

STRANGER THAN FICTION
A short history of the Jews

THIS BELIEVING WORLD
An account of the religions of mankind

THAT MAN HEINE
A biography

THE GRAPHIC BIBLE
Genesis to Revelation in animated maps

SINCE CALVARY
An interpretation of Christian history

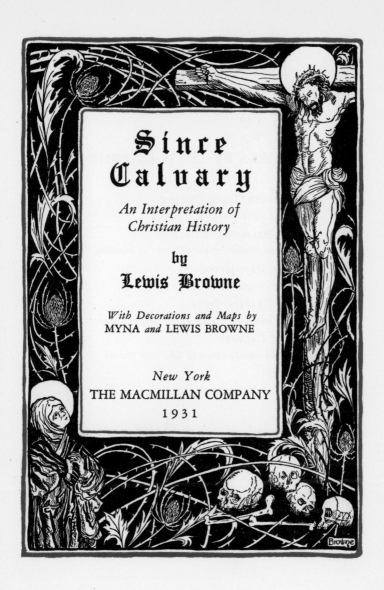

Since Calvary

An Interpretation of
Christian History

by

Lewis Browne

With Decorations and Maps by
MYNA and LEWIS BROWNE

New York
THE MACMILLAN COMPANY
1931

SET UP BY BROWN BROTHERS LINOTYPERS
PRINTED IN THE UNITED STATES OF AMERICA
BY THE FERRIS PRINTING COMPANY

To
MYNA
MY LOVELY WIFE

"As a lily among thorns,
So was my beloved. . . ."

"It is only when men have ceased to dispute whether Christianity was a revelation, that they have eyes to see what services it has rendered as a system."

LORD MORLEY.

While the author alone is responsible for what is written in this book—and also for what is left out—he cannot forego expressing his deep gratitude to Professor Francis A. Christie of Lowell, Massachusetts, and to the Reverend W. H. Murray of New York for the care with which they examined the proofs and for the many admirable suggestions they had to offer.

CONTENTS

BOOK ONE

A FAITH IS BORN: 29-70 A.D.   PAGE
1. The Disciples of Jesus: Their Character and
   Beliefs   3
2. The Resurrection and the Pentecostal Experience   9
3. The First Congregation in Jerusalem   14
4. The Education and Conversion of Saul of Tarsus   24
5. The Mysteries and the Christianity of Antioch .   30
6. Paul's Theology   39
7. Paul's Wanderings   46
8. Gentile Christianity: Its Growth and Character   50

BOOK TWO

THE ORDEAL OF CHILDHOOD: 70-323 A.D.
1. The Origin of the Gospels: Mark   59
2. Matthew. Luke. John   64
3. The Christianity of the Populace. Revelation .   73
4. Gnosticism   79
5. The Formulation of a Christian Creed . . .   84
6. The Development of a Christian Church . . .   89
7. The Persecutions   98
8. Constantine and the Triumph of the Church . .   108

BOOK THREE

THE CHURCH GROWS UP: 323-800 A.D.
1. The Arian Controversy   117
2. Julian and the Pagan Revival   128
3. More Theological Controversies   133

[xi]

CONTENTS

                                                               PAGE

4. The Rise of the Roman Papacy 142
5. Monasticism: Its Origin and Growth . . . 150
6. The Paganizing of Christianity 162
7. The Veneration of the Saints and the Virgin . 168

BOOK FOUR

THE HALCYON YEARS: 800-1415 A.D.

1. The Papacy and the World and the Flesh . . . 183
2. Corruption of the Church 190
3. The Cluniac Reform—Hildebrand 198
4. On to the Holy Land! 209
5. The Crusades 218
6. More Crusades 223
7. The Shattering of Papal Power 227
8. The Faith Wanes 234
9. The Spread of Heresy 240
10. The Franciscan and Dominican Revivals . . 246
11. Wyclif and Huss 254

BOOK FIVE

THE BREAKDOWN: 1415-1648 A.D.

1. The Economic Causes of the Reformation . . 267
2. The Cultural Awakening in Europe 272
3. The Nationalist Awakening in France and Spain 280
4. The Ducal Reformation: Lutheranism . . . 285
5. The Royal Reformation: Anglicanism . . . 298
6. The Peasants' Reformation: Anabaptism . . . 302
7. The Burghers' Reformation: Calvinism . . . 310
8. The Dynamics of Puritanism 316
9. The Catholic Revival 323
10. The Thirty Years War 331

BOOK SIX

THE ORDEAL OF SURVIVAL: 1648—

1. Catholicism Marches On 339
2. Catholicism Falters 344

[xii]

CONTENTS

		PAGE
3.	Protestantism Disintegrates	347
4.	Denominationalism Reaches America	351
5.	Credulity Triumphant: the Witch-Hunt	356
6.	The Emergence of Rationalism	362
7.	The War of the Church against Science	368
8.	The "Age of Reason"	375
9.	The Reaction Called Pietism	382
10.	Methodism	385
11.	The French Revolution	395
12.	The Reaction	401
13.	The Ordeal of the Church	413
14.	The Ordeal of the Sects	417
15.	Then Came the War	423
INDEX		429

A NOTE ON THE FOOTNOTES

With rare exceptions the footnotes in this volume are confined to bibliographical references. The reader uninterested in such details will therefore miss very little if he ignores the occasional nudges and refrains from interrupting his reading of the text.

The references, incidentally, are restricted very largely to works and translations in the English language, for they are intended solely for the lay reader. The poly-lingual scholar will have access to better bibliographies than any which could be provided in a work of this character.

BOOK ONE

A Faith Is Born
A. D. 29-70

A Faith Is Born: 29-70 A.D.

1: The Disciples of Jesus: Their Character and Beliefs. 2: The Resurrection and the Pentecostal Experience. 3: The First Congregation in Jerusalem. 4: The Education and Conversion of Saul of Tarsus. 5: The Mysteries and the Christianity of Antioch. 6: Paul's Theology. 7: Paul's Wanderings. 8: Gentile Christianity: Its Growth and Character.

E was forsaken in that hour. His disciples fled away, afraid for their lives, and only a few of the women remained behind to watch how he died. But what else could be looked for from such men? They were fisherfolk and plowmen from Galilee, and the downfall of their leader had overwhelmed them. They had believed him to be the Messiah, and had expected him to bring on the Kingdom of Heaven. Less than a week ago they had followed him up to Jerusalem in utter certainty that he would destroy this whole wicked world with a word. But instead he had suddenly been taken captive like a common felon, and mocked and scourged and hung on a cross. Moreover, he had seemed impotent to save himself. Was it any wonder, therefore, that his followers forsook him? They were dismayed. Catastrophe had fallen on them like a roof in time of earthquake, and they were left crushed and terrified.

Whither they fled we do not know for certain. They may have remained in hiding in the capital for a while.

[3]

Or they may have crept back to their homeland again. They were foreigners in Jerusalem, speaking a brogue which the city-folk mocked, and possessing neither funds nor friends. So some of them very probably straggled back to Galilee.

But no matter where they hid, they could not possibly find ease. The whole world was dark for them, for the light had died out of it. He in whom they had trusted was no more. He had been nailed to a cross by the Roman soldiery, and left to die outside Jerusalem's walls. How then could they find rest?

No one can say now—save on the controvertible basis of revelation—just who Jesus was, or what he taught. History records only what certain of his followers *believed* him to be, and what they *thought* he taught.[1] But the perplexing problem of the actual person and teaching of Jesus does not concern us here, for our specific

[1] There are, broadly speaking, four interpretations of the life of Jesus: (1) that of the traditionalists who accept the Gospel accounts as they stand; (2) that of the radicals who argue that Jesus is purely a mythical figure. J. M. Robertson (*Christianity and Mythology*), and W. Benjamin Smith (*Ecce Deus*), among many others, present this theory. Persuasive refutations are to be found in M. Goguel's *Jesus the Nazarene—Myth or History?* Eng. tr. 1926, and F. C. Conybeare's *The Historical Christ;* (3) that of the liberals who maintain that Jesus was a self-deluded Messiah—presented in Albert Schweitzer's *The Quest of the Historical Jesus,* Eng. tr. 1910 (a great book by a great man), J. Warschauer's *The Historical Life of Christ,* and Joseph Klausner's *Jesus of Nazareth,* Eng. tr. 1925; (4) that of the liberals who maintain that Jesus was no more—and no less—than a prophet, and that his followers thrust upon him the rôle of the Messiah—presented most recently in S. J. Case's *Jesus.* The stand taken by the present author is influenced by the most recent school of New Testament criticism, that of the *form und traditionsgeschichtliche Schule,* which maintains that the Gospels are valid sources only for the history of the Primitive Church, not for the life of Jesus. See R. Bultmann's *Die Erforschung der synoptischen Evangelien,* Giessen, 1925, and *Jesus,* Berlin, 1926.

interest is not in him but precisely in the beliefs about
him. Necessarily those beliefs were in large part naïve.
There must have been some among the disciples of Jesus
who recognized his prophetic grandeur, or else his homi-
lies and parables and ethical maxims would never have
been preserved. But it is clear that to most of his followers he was a healer rather than a teacher, a wonder-
worker rather than a prophet of righteousness. And it
was as such, as a doer of miracles, that these missed him
now.

Tradition has idealized the disciples, but history reveals
them to have been no more than unlettered peasants whose
minds were as full of superstitions as a pomegranate is
full of seeds. They saw demons lurking behind every
boulder, and the "evil-eye" in every strange countenance.
All life for them was an unremitting struggle to elude
the Devil. And therefore they were so terrified now.
Jesus had been their champion in the war with the Lord
of Darkness. The *shekinah,* the "Spirit," had been in the
man, making him mightier than Satan. His followers had
seen him exorcise the "unclean spirits," and cure the
afflicted and the possessed; and the sight had given them
courage. They had felt sustained and safe—so long as
Jesus was in their midst. They had even thought his
power had been transmitted to them, and they themselves
had gone abroad and routed demons. . . . But now all
that was over. Jesus was dead. He had been worsted by
the Enemy. So there could no longer be any assurance
in the hearts of his followers. They were at the mercy
once more of the powers of Satan, and dread was like a
shroud on their souls.

[5]

Nor was this all. Jesus had been even more than a wonder-worker to these men and women; he had been the veritable Messiah. Of old it had been prophesied that, when the time was fulfilled, a divinely appointed Savior would arise in the land to deliver it from the Gentiles. An extensive literature, the Apocalypses, had arisen out of this belief, and wild-eyed exhorters had long been going through the countryside to announce that the Great Hour was near. The belief in a Messiah and an apocalyptic Day of Judgment seems to have arisen first among the Zoroastrians in Persia, and had been brought over into Judaism probably after the Babylonian Exile in the sixth century B.C. It had taken root and flourished, spreading among the Jewish populace till by the first century its scarlet blooms had overgrown the whole religion.

One can well understand why so frenetic a belief should have obtained a hold on the Jews. They needed it because of their misery, especially in this latter day when they writhed in the talons of Rome. Actually there was more order now in Palestine than the land had ever known before; but this did not lessen the people's rancor. What cared they for order bought at the price of servility? They wanted to be free. And besides: even though there was order, there still remained great evil in the land. Taxgatherers terrorized over the people, extorting their last groats to build roads and garrisons for the imperial armies. Underlings from Rome, soured because they had been sent to so remote and wretched an outpost, domineered outrageously. Only outwardly was all well in Palestine; beneath the surface there was misery and hate beyond measuring. Centuries of oppression—for Israel in all its history had rarely been free of foreign domination—coupled with inordinate pride of birth, had made the Jews acutely sensitive. Their souls were so chafed and raw that they raged at the most trifling slight. And therefore they found such comfort in the thought that soon all their torments would be ended. Soon, very soon, their Redeemer would appear, and then, after a bloody struggle in which the very heavens would take part, the minions of Satan would be swallowed up in a flaming pit. Israel would be restored to glory, the Anointed One would be enthroned as suzerain over all the nations, and at his side would sit the princes of the Twelve Tribes. The righteous, whether among the quick or the dead, would be given life eternal, and there would be peace and prayer and plenty forevermore! [2]

Not all the Jews shared this dream. Some, especially among the politicians and the more venal priests, were quite pleased with things as they were. And many even of those who did expect the coming of God's Kingdom, cherished the dream in a less childish and petty form. They conceived the Messiah to be one who would bring on "a new heaven and a new earth" not alone for Israel but for all mankind. They dared declare—we find the statement in the writings of the rabbis—that "the righteous of *all* the nations will have a portion in the World

[2] The character and significance of Messianism in ancient Israel is fully discussed in Graetz's *History of the Jews*, Eng. tr. 1893, Vol. II, ch. 6. The subject is also dealt with, though far more sketchily, in the present author's short history of the Jews entitled *Stranger Than Fiction*, 1925, ch. 15. (Eng. edition, *The Story of the Jews*, ch. 14). The two succeeding chapters in that book, which deal with Jesus and Paul, should be read with caution. They present a point of view from which the author has since departed.

to Come." But the plain folk had no taste for so universal a salvation. (Plain folk never have.) They wanted the Kingdom of God to be theirs and theirs alone, and, blinded by the passion of their want, they were always ready to follow any prophet or charlatan or patriot or fool who promised to bring that Kingdom into being.

Most of the disciples of Jesus belonged unmistakably to this order. Whether Jesus himself claimed to be the Messiah is a moot question among modern historians. All we know for certain is that he believed the Kingdom to be "at hand" and that he tried to teach the people what manner of life would render them worthy to enter it. But no matter what may have been in Jesus's own mind, clearly his followers had believed him to be indeed the Anointed One. And they had further believed that as his followers they would all profit richly at his exaltation. Even when he was still an itinerant preacher going about in Galilee, they had already wrangled over the spoils they would inherit when he became King. He had appointed twelve of his followers to be his chief disciples, sending them through the countryside to spread his teaching; and these twelve had firmly expected to be princes over the twelve tribes when the Kingdom was attained. They had even disputed among themselves as to which would sit nearest the Throne, and they had repeatedly begged their leader to confide in them how long there was yet to wait.

And the collapse of these hopes was another reason for the dismay in the hearts of the fugitives. They had staked everything on Jesus, and had lost. All their fond dreams of glory and might had been shattered. Now there was nothing left for them save need and toil and sickness and terror until death dragged them down to Sheol.

2

EARING these things in mind, we are prepared for what ensued. Such men and women could not possibly go on without the faith that had been all of life to them. So, with a will not uncommon in spirits at bay, they simply turned about and clutched once more at that faith. Of a sudden it began to be whispered among them that Jesus was alive again—that though he had gone down to the grave, he was back on earth once more. Rumors flew about, at first stealthily, like bats in the dark, and then openly, like screaming gulls at dawn. The rumors were discrepant, but this only added to their convincingness. It was said that Jesus had been seen here, there, a third place. First one of the followers, then others, then a whole multitude, had seen him; and not as a mere wraith, but as a tangible body walking and talking and even partaking of food!

Romantic minds have attempted to rationalize this wonder by suggesting that Jesus may have been stolen from the cross while he was yet alive and sheltered somewhere till he was recovered. But there is no need to resort to such inventions. Seeing the dead rise up and walk among the living is a fairly common phenomenon. It has been attested to repeatedly in every generation and in every land, for so comforting a delusion suggests itself almost inevitably in certain exigencies. Belief is a dark unfathomable sea surging against the dykes of reason; and when the winds of ill fortune shatter those dykes, there is no staying the flood. The Galileans no doubt spoke the literal truth when they reported their wondrous visions. All things are possible—or plausible, at least— to people who believe. Being what they were, hapless countryfolk driven half mad by dread and disappointment, they may quite actually have seen a resurrected Jesus. And, having seen, a new spirit then entered into them. They became daring once more, and ecstatic with renewed hopefulness.

The tradition has it that Jesus continued to show himself to his followers during forty days, and that he then ascended into heaven before their very eyes. This again is beyond doubt gospel truth. Devout folk throughout history have witnessed the "assumption" of their heroes. Enoch, Elijah, Hercules, Mohammed, and countless other prophets and gods have been seen arising bodily into heaven. It required no inordinate length of credulity for those Galileans to believe that they had beheld Jesus rise up in a like way. And, having achieved this belief, their excitement became even more intense. They decided that Jesus had not left the world for good. No, obviously he would soon return again to finish what he had begun. For the present he was watching them from Heaven, waiting for the appointed hour. When it arrived, lo, then would he at last reveal his might! He would descend to the

earth amid a host of angels to open the Final Assize; and
then woe to those who had been hard of heart! They
would be cast into a burning furnace and utterly destroyed.
But the devout ones, they who had continued to have
faith, they would be exalted in glory and given bliss forevermore!

Such came to be their belief, and, cherishing it, the
Galileans became as new beings. They began to gather
again in Jerusalem, surer now than ever that the End was
imminent. A strained elation took hold of them, and
eagerly, anxiously, frenziedly they awaited their Messiah's
return. Nine days passed from the time of the ascension,
and then the believers appear to have got themselves in
final readiness. It would seem that a premonition had
come to them that he would appear on the morrow. It
was a holy day, Pentecost, and seemed peculiarly fit to be
the time for his return. Thus far his disciples may have
remained scattered throughout the city, but now they all
came together in one house. And as they stood there on
that Pentecost day and waited for the miracle, a strange
thing happened to them.

The episode is recorded in the second chapter of the
book of Acts, and enough is told for us to be able to
reconstruct the scene. Somewhere in a noisome quarter
of that crowded oriental city, in an ancient house of
crumbling stone and mud—they were poor folk, remember, and could hardly have had access to a palace—one
hundred and twenty faith-crazed peasants stand and wait.
The men are bearded, and the women are veiled; but

both alike wear the coarse, travel-stained mantles of pilgrims. Their large hands are calloused from hard labor, and their faces are scarred and drawn. It is summer, and the sun outside is a flaring brazier turned mouth down and raining heat. Flies buzz about with maddening persistence, settling on sore eyes and scabby heads. The tart pungency of sweat streaming from tight-packed bodies fouls the air till it is beyond breathing, and lungs gasp and heads ache and reel. Everyone is tense; the whole throng seems to quail and crouch, expecting the crash at any moment. And as they wait in suspense a sudden frenzy seizes them. These people belong to a stock notorious for excitability —Galilee was the scene of mad uprisings for generations —and they have just survived a stress we can hardly conceive of. They had been lifted to the skies with wild hopefulness, then plunged into despair, then lifted all over again. Now their minds are near collapse because of the strain. . . .

And their minds do collapse in that hour—or so at least is a modern reader prone to interpret what happened. Hysteria sweeps through the crowd. All at once these people begin to hear "a sound from heaven, as of a rustling mighty wind," and they see "cloven tongues as of fire" play around them. And thereupon they all take to shouting. Probably they had begun praying and singing the moment they came together, but now they are so wrought up that some of them lose all rationality and begin to scream incoherently. Meaningless cries spring from their lips, inarticulate screams and yells. It is contagious; soon they are all shouting with "tongues" and the tumult is so great that a crowd gathers around the house. People come running from the neighborhood, wondering what is wrong. And, when they learn the cause of the disturbance, certain of the onlookers are moved to derision. Hearing the crazy jabber, they cry: "Ho, those men are full of new wine!"

Modern psychologists offer a fairer and more penetrating explanation of this strange conduct of the apostles. They point out that some form of utterance is the chief means of venting excitement, but this means is narrow so long as the speech is rational, for the intellect acts as a levee and holds it in check. Therefore, when the excitement becomes too intense, the intellect has to break down—unless it is preternaturally strong. The primitive becomes manifest: speech gives way to mere sound, words to inarticulate cries, and the pent-up flood of energy then discharges itself through a wide-open channel. Glossolalia, the "gift of tongues," is consequently a natural phenomenon among simple folk in the throes of overpowering emotional stress.[3]

But such an explanation could not possibly have occurred to those who came running to see what possessed the Galileans on Pentecost day nineteen centuries ago. They decided the peasants were drunk, and simply laughed. Not all of them, however. No, many of the onlookers were apparently impressed, for we are told that "about three thousand souls" were won over to the movement there and then. Perhaps the number is an exaggeration—(the tendency to overestimate in counting converts is one that men have always been heir to)—but even if

[3] See G. B. Cutten's *Speaking With Tongues,* which contains almost all that is known on the subject—and just a little that is not known.

far fewer were won over, it was still an achievement. True, the climacteric miracle, the return of the Anointed One, had not occurred; but at least there had been a "sign." For the believers construed their frenzy to have been no less than a veritable manifestation from Heaven. They concluded that they had been impelled to shout because the Spirit had entered into them. So what lingering doubts may previously have rankled in the minds of the Galileans were thenceforth banished. The close of that day saw them unshakably convinced that Jesus had sent them a "sign" from Heaven to assure them he would soon be returning.

3

ND thus originated the sect of Those Who Wait. For a while it aroused little interest and less opposition in Jerusalem. There were many other sects active among the Jews in those days, and all of them were freely tolerated. So long as the Holy Law was observed, and forbidden food was avoided, the authorities saw no reason to complain. We read of Essenes, who wore only white, and of Nasaræi who were vegetarians, and of Hemerobaptists who believed in daily ritual ablutions. In Egypt there was at one time a sect of Jews called the Therapeutæ, and in Damascus another called the Covenanters. John the Baptist, who had been put to death a few years earlier, still had a

congregation of followers; and no doubt other such prophets had their devotees.[4]

The believers in Jesus must have formed merely one of a whole host of somewhat eccentric congregations, and in most outward respects were probably not to be distinguished from other Jews. They lacked even a distinctive name, being content to call themselves simply the Believers, or the Brethren, or Those Who Wait. They had no trace of organization, for, expecting this world to end momentarily, they saw no need for officers. They were satisfied to defer to the twelve disciples as their leaders, and to Peter, the chief of them, as their head; but otherwise they were all brethren in one family. Ritually they were strictly orthodox Jews, neglecting no jot or tittle of the Law. They observed the Sabbath, ate only permitted food, wore the fringed garments, attended the synagogue, and fulfilled their Temple duties. In one detail they even exceeded the Law's requirements, for they insisted also on the ceremonial washing which John the Baptist, a forerunner of their Master, had advocated.

But solely in their observance of the ritual were they conformists. In the essentials of life they were quite unlike their neighbors, as came to be more and more recognized. For one thing they set no store by earthly possessions, for they were sure that all the wealth of this world would soon be swept away. They did not toil or spin, for what could it avail them? Confident that in but a little moment their Redeemer would return, they were

[4] See Jackson and Lake's *Beginnings of Christianity*, Vol. I, p. 84—an important work for the student interested in the more recent research in the field.

[15]

content to live off what was already in their hands. They pooled their small wealth, drew from it each according to his needs, and waited. And this disinterestedness in worldly gain gave them a novel grace and charm. It emptied them of covetousness, and endowed them with that contentment which is only possible when covetousness is gone. They must have seemed no less than saints ,in that hard-driven world of acquisitiveness and strife.

This saintliness they believed to be altogether incumbent upon them, for by practicing it they thought to hasten the return of Jesus. In essence they were trying to *force* the coming of the Kingdom by acting as though it had already occurred. It would seem that Jesus himself had commanded them so to do, saying that in so far as they lived a life of love and selflessness the Kingdom of God was already in their midst.[5] We cannot always be certain as to the precise words of Jesus, for, as we shall soon see, the Gospels were not written until some forty and more years after his death. But it is quite clear that he taught some such perfectionist code of ethics as this first congregation of his followers tried to practice. They had hearkened eagerly to his utterances, and, with the retentive minds of unlettered folk, had remembered them well. They recalled how he had said: "Happy are you poor, for yours is the Kingdom of God"; and "no one of you who does not say good-by to all his possessions can be a disciple of mine"; and "it is easier for a camel to get through the eye of a needle than for a rich man to get

[5] Many scholars are of the opinion that the declaration in Luke 17, 21, which is usually translated, "the Kingdom of God is within you," should be rendered, "the Kingdom of God is *in your midst.*"

[16]

into the Kingdom of God." So they surrendered their belongings and ceased to strive after worldly gain. They did even more. They sought to root out all the carnal passions, striving to be as Jesus had commanded: "perfect, even as your heavenly Father is perfect." They tried to love their enemies, offer the other cheek to smiters, and pray for those who persecuted them. They must have failed at times, but they continued to try. Very earnestly did they try, because perfection, though reputedly impossible, was nevertheless imperative.

Otherworldly idealism was but one of the traits which marked the Brethren. A second was ecstatic fervor. The frenzy which had overcome them on Pentecost seems to have recurred, and day after day they prayed and sang and "spoke with tongues." The fear of the demons which harried their neighbors was unknown to these devotees. They feared nothing, for they knew beyond all doubting that the Spirit which was in them gave them full protection. And this freedom from anxiety must have attracted even more attention than their unworldliness, for heads held high and faces glowing with joy were rare sights among the poor folk of ancient Israel. Soon it began to be whispered that these Brethren possessed mysterious powers. It was said that they could exorcise demons and perform cures, and people began to resort to them in increasing numbers. Peter, the leader of the society, became so popular that, according to tradition, the townsfolk actually brought their sick into the streets through which he passed, so that his shadow might fall on them and heal them!

It was this working of miracles, not the preaching or shouting, that finally brought the apostles into conflict with the authorities. Some of the leaders were arrested and beaten, and then set free with a warning no more to "speak in the name of Jesus." But the persecution only intensified the zeal of the believers. "Rejoicing that they were counted worthy to suffer shame for his name," they became all the more active in their missionary labors. They had come to the conclusion that Jesus was delaying his return because those who strove after the perfect life were still too few in number. Accordingly they redoubled their efforts to increase their company.

They found it difficult, however, to win converts from among the natives of the city. What success they had was confined largely to the foreign pilgrims who dwelt in Jerusalem. These visitors formed a conspicuous portion of the city's population, for the Temple was a magnet attracting the more pious of the Jews from all the ends of the earth. Hellenists they were called, for, having lived all or much of their lives in foreign places, they had taken on at least the outward semblances of Hellenistic civilization. They spoke Greek and other Gentile tongues, and garbed themselves and even trimmed their beards according to the fashions of the lands whence they came. The Diaspora, the "scattering" of the Jews, was already widespread even though Israel still existed as a nation in Palestine. The emigration had begun five hundred years earlier, and crowding, hunger, and disastrous war had kept the tide flowing ever since then. By the first century there were colonies of Jews to be found all over the world. The Greek geographer, Strabo, who was born about 63 B.C., is quoted as declaring: "It is difficult to find a single place on the habitable earth that has not admitted this tribe of men, and is not possessed by them." Being a writer of travel books, Strabo may have exaggerated; but even so his statement is significant. It reveals that the Jews had come to be an obvious, perhaps even an obtrusive, element in society everywhere. They were numerous enough in Rome to influence the elections, as Cicero hints in one of his orations; and in Alexandria, the second largest city in the empire, they constituted two-fifths of the entire population. We hear of them in Spain and Parthia, in Carthage and Gaul.[6]

But no matter where they were scattered, Palestine was always home to these Jews. Everywhere else they considered themselves in exile, for their one holy Temple was in Jerusalem. They paid taxes annually to support this sanctuary, and those who were able journeyed there on pilgrimages from time to time. The more fervent even settled in Jerusalem, believing that there alone could they be completely pious.

It is not difficult to understand why many of these pilgrims were drawn into the Nazarene movement. Conditions in Jerusalem must have made them sick at heart. Far from being the holy city of their imaginings, the sensitive must have recognized it to be little more than a sacramental market place. Its priests went about their Temple tasks with the perfunctory air of hardened job-holders, and their hirelings and agents were unashamed of their

---

[6] The standard work on the subject is Jean Juster's *Les juifs dans l'empire romain.* An excellent book in English is Max Radin's *The Jews among the Greeks and Romans.*

venality. It was only natural that conditions should have come to such a pass. Jerusalem was a shrine, and it was unavoidable that a goodly proportion of its population should live not so much for God as off Him. Had the pilgrims been realists, they would have been aware of this and would have shrugged their shoulders; but had they been realists, most likely they would never have become pilgrims. It was their idealism, or their romantic piety, that had made them leave their homes and wander across seas and deserts to Jerusalem. And this same trait now drove them to cast their lot with the believers in Jesus. For the Galileans, unlettered and rustic though they might be, were at least *believers*. Religion with them was not a routine to be borne with weary acquiescence or fussy punctilio, but a vehement passion. It was the whole of life to them, absorbing all their waking hours and coloring their every thought. And the pilgrims, having trudged from the ends of the earth to find just such fervor, could not but be attracted. They listened eagerly to the preaching of the Galileans, watched how they dwelt together in love and joy, and finally were converted. They turned over all their possessions to the common treasury, and then sat down to wait with the rest.

But the wait proved longer than had been expected. Weeks went by, weeks and months, yet still the Kingdom did not come. The Brethren did not lose heart, however. They simply decided that their numbers were still not large enough to warrant the return of the Redeemer, and therefore increased their missionizing efforts. They

still held aloof from material concerns, never doubting that their treasury would hold out until the day when
a treasury would no longer be needed. They counted it a
sin to be overanxious about the things of the earth, for
Jesus himself had counseled them against it. Those of
their company who had known him could quote his very
words:

> "Do not worry about life, wondering what you
> will have to eat, or about your body, wondering what
> you will have to wear. . . . These are all things the
> nations of the world are in pursuit of, and your
> Father knows well that you need them. But you must
> strive to find his Kingdom, and you will have all these
> other things besides. . . ." [7]

Thus did the apostles quote the Master, and the new
converts were content to believe. The doctrine was a comforting one to folk of their type. Whether from Galilee
or foreign parts, they were all humble people who had
worried and stinted and scraped all their days. It must
have been a vast relief to them to throw off all earthly
cares at last and believe that the Lord would provide.
Such as had savings to surrender, especially the "widows"
who are so often mentioned in the New Testament, must
have been all the more relieved, for nothing is so burdensome as possessions to folk grown used to need. They

[7] The translation used here is taken (with the permission of the pub-
lishers) from Edgar J. Goodspeed's *New Testament—An American
Translation* (University of Chicago Press, 1923). The reader seeking in-
telligibility in the Bible text rather than sonorous and traditional phrasing will find this translation an improvement over the older ones in the
English language; at many points he will find it also more accurate.

must have been elated to be freed at last of concern over their little hoards.

But the relief gave way to misgiving after a time, as was inevitable under the circumstances. The Brethren were swiftly eating up their capital, and when they discovered their funds almost gone they began to fall out among themselves. Certain members raised the complaint that they were being discriminated against in the distribution of food. Significantly, the complaint came from the Hellenists, and was lodged against the twelve Galileans still at the head of the movement. The book of Acts, our only source for what occurred in this period, tries to slur over the incident; but enough is said to indicate what was suppressed. Apparently a rift had developed between the Palestinians and the Hellenists, and the quarrel over the doles was only incidental. We can well understand why such a rift should have come about between two groups so markedly dissimilar. The Hellenists, despite that many of them may have been half-pauperized pilgrims who could speak but a peddler's Greek, were nevertheless superior to the natives. And it must have irked them that they had no part in the leadership of the movement. Fortunately a compromise was effected, or otherwise the whole congregation might have foundered at this juncture. The "Twelve" discreetly surrendered part of their control. They asked that a committee be selected to attend to the distribution of the food, asserting that they themselves had more than enough to do as preachers and exorcisers. Accordingly "seven men of honest report, full of the Holy Ghost and wisdom"—and apparently all taken from the foreign party—were chosen as superintendents in charge of the "tables." [8]

But this compromise proved inadequate. Before long the "Seven" were not content to attend merely to administrative details. They, too, began to preach and perform miracles in the name of Jesus. And they carried on these activities in a manner which speedily got them into trouble. These Hellenist apostles seem to have been more daring than the Galileans, going so far as to extol the crucified Jesus in language which some considered sheer blasphemy. Never having known him as a man, they spoke of him as a being almost divine. They declared him greater even than Moses, and implied that his teaching transcended the very Law. Especially a certain Hellenist named Stephen spoke in this way, and the fanatic zeal with which he preached his faith began to incense the orthodox in the city. Finally he was arrested, and at the trial he turned upon his persecutors and upbraided them so violently that, even before sentence could be passed, the mob dragged him from the courtroom and stoned him to death.

The scandal precipitated an attack on the rest of the Hellenist converts. The Sanhedrin, the council of priests and rabbis which governed the religious life of Israel, decided to hunt them down and flog the blasphemy out of them. Significantly, the Twelve at the head of the native Jews in the movement, went unmolested; with them, evidently, there was no fault to be found. Only the Seven and their sympathizers were persecuted, and the

[8] For a magnified view of the significance of this rift between the Hellenists and the "pillar Apostles," the student should read F. C. Baur's *Paul the Apostle*, or any of the other writings of the so-called "Tübingen School."

campaign waged against them was so remorseless that they had to flee for their lives.

4

ND therewith a new chapter was opened in the history of the strange movement. The belief, which thus far had been confined to Jerusalem, spread now to foreign places. The fugitives carried it to Samaria, which, though situated in the heart of Palestine, was regarded as a half-heathen city; and also to Antioch in Syria, and to Damascus on the other side of the Jordan. Perhaps it was carried now even as far as Alexandria and Rome. However, the authorities in Jerusalem were not perturbed by this. So long as the heresy was weeded out of their own patch, they did not care whether or not it took root elsewhere. But there was then in Jerusalem a certain earnest young Jew who could not take the matter so lightly. Saul was his name, and he had come to the Holy City to complete his studies in the Law. He was, it would seem, a fanatical pietist, and had taken a violent part in the campaign against the Brethren in Jerusalem. Not alone had he abetted the mob that murdered Stephen, but in addition he had gone "into one house after another, dragging out men and women, (and) putting them in prison." And now, "still breathing murderous threats against the disciples of the Lord," he took it upon himself to track down those who had fled,

and destroy them in the cities where they had taken refuge.[9]

One must know the history and temper of this young man, Saul, to understand his conduct. He was himself a Hellenist, having been born in the great city of Tarsus, in Asia Minor. His father, although a Jew, had attained the distinction of Roman citizenship, and may have been a person of means. Saul was reared in the strictest piety, and his whole schooling seems to have been confined to the Scriptures and rabbinic lore. He learnt, of course, to speak Greek, for that was the language of the region; but the Holy Tongue to him was Hebrew, and whatever was not written in it—or at least, in Aramaic, its cognate —did not concern him as a student. He was, we can well imagine, a very pious lad who, having fixed on the rabbinate as his career in life, attended the synagogue regularly, prayed devoutly, and observed every precept of the Law.

But, despite all this absorption in the religion of his fathers, the boy could not possibly have remained unaffected by his environment. Tarsus was a great center of Hellenistic culture, with a university second in importance only to that of Alexandria. Even though Saul may never have attended its lecture halls, he must have heard at least rumor of what was taught in them. More probably he came under the direct influence of its teachers, for in that day it was their custom to lecture at times in the streets. The philosophers, especially of the Stoic school,

[9] The best work on Paul for the general reader is probably F. W. Farrar, *Life and Work of St. Paul.* F. J. Foakes-Jackson, *Life of St. Paul* and B. W. Bacon, *The Story of St. Paul,* are briefer but also well worth reading.

were not aloof academicians engrossed in abstruse metaphysical riddles, but zealous preachers who stood up in market places and harangued the crowds. They were concerned chiefly with the problems of moral conduct, and, as is evidenced by the ideas he later enunciated, and even by the very phrases he used, Saul must have hearkened very attentively to the words of those philosophers.[10]

And not the philosophy alone, but also the religion of the city must have etched its own thought-grooves in the boy's mind. Precisely what that religion was we cannot say to-day, for it was not a single, rigid, established thing, but rather a syncretism, composed of survivals and borrowings. One of the ancient gods of Tarsus, called Sandon, was still worshiped by the populace when Saul was a boy. Sandon was a god of vegetation, and, according to the accepted myth, he had died on a funeral pyre and had then ascended into heaven. A great festival was held in the spring of each year to celebrate the miracle, and Saul must often have witnessed the ecstasies attendant upon the rite.

Sandon, however, was not the only god worshiped in the Pagan city. Tarsus was a great port, and merchants and soldiers and slaves had brought to it a whole farrago of other gods. There was Attis imported from Phrygia, and Adonis from Syria, Osiris from Egypt, Tammuz from Mesopotamia, and Mithra from Persia. Most of these deities were strikingly akin to Sandon, since all of them were symbolic representations either of the vegetation which withers and then comes to life again, or else of the sun which goes down and comes up. And, although each

[10] See Bultmann's *Der Stil der Paulinischen Predigt*, Göttingen, 1910.

god had his own following, there was considerable merging and confusion. Having so many gods to choose from, each offering no less—and yielding no more—than the other, it was hard to remain steadfast to one.[11]

No matter how devoutly Saul may have served his own God, he could not possibly have gone without knowledge of these others worshiped in Tarsus. He may have heard tell of them even in the synagogue, for the services were often attended by Gentiles. It was a day when people groped for salvation as a man gropes for a tinder box fallen in the dark. They craved a light to show them the way out of the horror which was existence, and no ritual was too strange, no religion too old, for them to inquire into it. Indeed, the more exotic and ancient the faith, the greater was its appeal. For that reason Judaism had a large following among the Gentiles of that day. Many a synagogue in the Diaspora had its company of "God-fearers"—half-persuaded heathens who lingered just outside the door. Some of these eventually entered in—but not many. The threshold of the synagogue was too high, built as it was of the Holy Law. To be completely admitted one had to submit to circumcision, abstain from the forbidden food, observe the Sabbath, and keep the hundreds of other ritual commandments laid upon the chosen of Yahveh. It was no easy step for an alien to enter Jewry.

But though few went in, many craned their necks to peer through the door and see how the Jews worshiped. And the spirit of Saul must have been stirred by the sight of these inquirers. Knowing the colossal world-saving

[11] See W. M. Ramsay's *Cities of St. Paul,* 1908, pp. 137-156.

passion which consumed him throughout his manhood, we may take it for granted that it was already germinating in him in his youth. Physically he was of the type that is prone to be ambitious, for according to tradition he was undersized, and by his own confession he was chronically sickly. It is not unlikely, therefore, that he was already dreaming dreams of converting all mankind before he ever left his home in Tarsus. Such dreams would not have branded him mad, for they were shared by others in Israel. Judaism then was an aggressive religion, and its devotees were to be found missionizing throughout the world. Indeed, Jesus himself is reported to have complained that the elders of the synagogues "compass sea and land to make one convert." So if this devout young Jew in Tarsus cherished an ambition to win the world to the Law, he may have been merely following what was almost the fashion in Jewry.[12]

After years of study in his native city, the young man went over to Jerusalem to sit at the feet of the great rabbis there; and it was during his residence in the Holy City that he became acquainted with the believers in Jesus. His immediate reaction to them we have already seen. Apparently he realized how seductive the doctrine of a Stephen might prove if allowed to spread to the Diaspora. Slighting as it did the importance of the Holy Law, it could offer the benefits of Judaism at a price far below any which the pietists were demanding. The menace was too plain for Saul to be able to rest. Accordingly he threw

[12] On the subject of Jewish missionary activity in this period see Derwacter's *Preparing the Way for Paul.* For a discussion of the "Godfearers" and their standing in the synagogue, see Lake's *The Earlier Epistles of St. Paul,* 1911, p. 37ff.

himself with fanatic ardor into the campaign against the heretics, hounding them till they were forced to flee the city, and then setting out in their pursuit.

But thereupon a miracle was vouchsafed him. Perhaps, as some psychiatrists maintain, it was actually no more than an epileptic fit; but to Saul himself it was a miracle. It happened in this wise: Saul was nearing Damascus, bent on venting his murderous zeal on the heretics who had taken refuge there. For days already he has been trudging beneath the sun, and what with the venom in his heart and the swirling in his head, he is near to exhaustion. The terrain is as harsh and ugly as a ruffian's fist. Vivid colors are nowhere to be seen: only bleached yellows and grays and browns that return the noonday glare with a curse. Suddenly the dazed pursuer halts and sways. A flash of unnatural light blinds his eyes and he falls to the ground. And then he hears a voice cry out from heaven:

"Saul! Saul! Why do you persecute me?"

"Who are you?" the man asks in terror.

"Jesus of Nazareth!"

And in another moment, when Saul opens his eyes again, there is no one there. . . .

It is by no means established that Saul was afflicted with epilepsy, but it is plain that he was not quite normal. His own testimony reveals him to have had a peculiar psychic disposition, for, as he himself puts it, he was given to enjoying "an abundance of revelations" in some of which he knew not whether he was "in the body or out of it," but was "caught up to the third heaven," or "caught up into Paradise," where he heard "unspeakable words." In a mind thus constituted, a vision such as the one which occurred on the road to Damascus is hardly unaccountable.

Nor is the sequel to the vision unaccountable. Saul got up from the ground and continued on his way to Damascus; but when he arrived there, he did not proceed to persecute the Brethren. Instead he became one of them! And from that day to the day of his death he never deserted the movement. Indeed, he became its most fervent and vigorous apostle. As Renan has put it, Saul simply changed his fanaticisms. Where previously he had sought to root out the faith in Jesus, now he sought to spread it all over the world. And so inordinate was his energy and tremendous his zeal that he almost succeeded.

5

TO give the history of Saul's labors in detail would require far more space than we can afford here. It is enough to state that he began his new activity right there in Damascus, and prosecuted it with such aggressiveness that finally he had to be let down over the wall to escape with his life. He began to wander then, though where and to what purpose is in dispute. When next we hear with any certainty of his movements he is on his way to Antioch in response to a call for help in the missionary work already on foot there. Significant developments had occurred in Antioch.

The belief in Jesus had been carried thither by the Hellenist fugitives from Jerusalem, but, once rooted in the
Syrian city, it had proceeded to flourish strangely. To
begin with, it had managed to acquire a distinctive
name. The members of its congregation were not known
simply as the Brethren, or the Believers, but were called
"Christians." The name was not of their own choosing;
in fact, they refused to accept it at first, for it was a nickname. Hearing that the god of this strange cult was a
certain Christos—that is, Anointed One—who would
some day rule all the earth, the populace in Antioch had
decided he was some pretender to the imperial throne,
and mockingly called his followers the "Christiani." The
term was obviously a vulgarism, for it was part Greek and
part Latin, being modeled after "Cæsariani" and "Pom-
peiani" and similar political nicknames.

But if the believers in Antioch repudiated the name, it
was solely because of its connotation. That their religion
deserved a distinctive appellation they might have freely
admitted, for it had changed radically in this Gentile
environment. In the first place, it had ceased to be exclusively Jewish in its following. The Holy Law had been
thrust aside, and uncircumcised heathens had been accepted into the congregation. In the second place, the
faith itself was ceasing to be Jewish. It was rapidly taking
on the character of the Paganism whence it won its new
converts.[13]

[13] The Pagan character of emergent Christianity was first exploited
in modern times by two French scholars, Volney (*Les ruines,* 1791), and
Dupuis (*Origin des tous les cultes,* 3 vols., Paris, 1794), and was later
developed into something akin to dogma by various German writers.
Radical presentations of the subject are to be found in Paul Carus

This Paganism consisted in part of secret cults called Mysteries which taught that salvation could be won by means of magical sacraments. One had only to perform certain rites, and then redemption was unfailing. Usually these rites consisted of lustrations and sacrificial meals. Just as the denizens of the jungle believe that the consumption of a tiger's liver will implant in them a tiger's courage, so these denizens of the Greco-Roman world believed that drinking their god's blood, and eating his flesh, would endow them with their god's immortality. In order to obtain this ritual blood and flesh, a sacred animal—usually a bull or a goat or a lamb—was sacrificed and distributed to the devotees.

In some of the cults these sacramental meals were marked by the wildest turbulence, for the sacrificial animal had to be consumed in haste lest the god in it escape. But in others there seems to have been a solemn decorum. Certain of the Mysteries had outgrown their savage origins, and had hung the trappings of symbolism over the nakedness of their ancient rites. For instance, in the cult of Mithra the flesh and blood of the god was served to the celebrants in the symbolic form of bread and water or wine. This sacrament was repeated at regular intervals by the priests of the cult, and to add to the impressiveness of the ceremony there was ringing of bells, swinging of censers, and burning of lights. Partaking of this com-

---

The Pleroma, and S. Reinach, Orpheus, Eng. tr. 1930, chs. 8-9. The subject is treated more conservatively in A. A. Kennedy, St. Paul and the Mystery Religions, and S. Angus, The Mystery-Religions and Christianity. The apologia of orthodox Christianity is given (rather naïvely) in Trench's Christ the Desire of All Nations, or The Unconscious Prophecies of Heathendom, London, 1846.

munion meal was supposed to renew the divine quality contributed by the sacrament of initiation. The initiation —which seems to have consisted of immersion in the blood of a bull—had the effect of obliterating the old life and creating a new one in the believers. It was said that a man became "reborn for eternity" by virtue of his bloody baptism. But there was danger of forfeiting the boon, for the divine "spirit" within the devotee might steal away or be dissipated. It was therefore necessary to partake of the sacramental bread and wine, and thus "put on" the god freshly from time to time. If one did this, then one was assured of a share in the final victory which Mithra would win when he returned to the earth.[14]

Mithra was essentially a Messiah. The belief in him had originated in Persia, whence the Jews themselves had obtained their idea of a God-anointed hero who would come to redeem mankind. According to the legend, Mithra was born of a rock, and the only witnesses were certain shepherds who brought gifts and adored him. Chilled by the wind, the new-born god went to a fig tree, ate of its fruit, and clothed himself in its leaves. Then he set out to vanquish all the beings already existing in the world, among them the sacred bull. He was successful, and the aftermath of his labors was the creation of mankind. But thereupon the Evil One aroused himself from his sloth and set out to undo Mithra's work. He sent a drought, and then a deluge, and finally a fire to destroy the race of men. But all his efforts were of no avail. In the time of drought Mithra caused water to

[14] See Franz Cumont, *Mysteries of Mithra,* and *Oriental Religions in Roman Paganism.*

spring forth from a rock. When the deluge came there was one man who escaped in a boat with all his cattle. And after the fire ceased to rage it was discovered that only the servants of the Evil One had been destroyed.

Mithra then quitted the world temporarily. After a last supper with the Sun, the hero ascended into the seventh heaven, there to await the hour of his return. For it was an essential part of the belief of the Mithraists that their god would indeed return. He would descend to the earth when the time was fulfilled and open the Last Judgment. Calling all men from their tombs, he would condemn the wicked ones and reward those who had been faithful. The sacred bull would be slaughtered, and Mithra, mixing its fat with consecrated wine, would administer a final sacrament to the just. The Evil One and all the wicked souls on earth would be destroyed by a fire sent from Heaven; but the righteous would be glorified. In a purged and beautified world they would live on eternally, nevermore suffering want or dread, and enjoying grace to repletion.

Mithra was only one of many cult gods worshiped in the Hellenistic world.[15] In Antioch itself the more popular deity was Adonis, "the Lord." He was a savior-god like Mithra, and all who were initiated into his Mystery believed they were assured of everlasting life. Each spring his devotees gathered in sacred groves to enact a passion-play. There was weeping and wailing on the first day because the beauteous young god was supposed

---

[15] It is called Hellenistic to distinguish this world compounded of Roman, near-oriental, and Greek elements, from the Hellenic, which was purely Greek. Perhaps Hellenoid would be the better term to use.

to have just died. On the second day, amid frenzied songs
and lamentations, his corpse, represented by an image,
was ceremoniously buried. But on the third day the
mourning turned to ecstatic joy, for then proclamation was
made that Adonis had been resurrected. His image was
made to rise in the air, as though ascending into heaven,
and the people abandoned themselves to rejoicing.

One might go on and describe the cults of Osiris, Sera-
pis, Cybele, Dionysis, Attis, and the countless other deities
worshiped by the Pagans in that bewildered age; but it
would be bootless. Enough has been recounted to give
some notion of the religious ideas which had begun to
seep into the new cult in Antioch. They were ideas profoundly attractive to the common people, for they were
rooted in the belief in magic, which has always had a
fast hold on the common mind. That they should find
their way into Christianity was inevitable. So long as the
believers in Jesus would accept none but Jews, their belief
could remain more or less unchanged; but once the bar-
riers were lowered, modifications were unavoidable. The
corollary of conversion is almost always perversion—or,
at any rate, change. The new adherents who came over
from the Mysteries in Antioch brought with them their
old beliefs, for, though baptism might wash away their
sins, it could not wash away their memories. And these
memories became an integral part of the Christianity
emerging in Antioch.

No one knows how far this modification had proceeded
by the time Saul had reached Antioch. What alone is cer-

tain is that Saul—or Paul, as he soon began to call himself —far from opposing the development, gave it encouragement. Not at first, perhaps. In the beginning of his ministry in the Syrian city he seems still to have preached the need of circumcision and the importance of the Holy Law. But after a while something persuaded him to slough off his Jewish pietism, and then he became outspoken in his advocacy of the Antiochan attitude. He had come to see that so long as the belief in Jesus was weighted down with the Law of the Jews it could not possibly advance. Accordingly he cast the Law to one side, saying it was no longer binding. It would be unfair to brand him an opportunist for doing this; the man was too palpably sincere to merit such an epithet. It is true that he confessed himself ready to be "all things to all men"—but only in order to save those men. That was the one thing that counted with Saul: the world's hunger for salvation. He knew well the woes of mankind, its miseries and thwartings and devastating dreads; and he was ready to sacrifice anything, even his ancestral prejudices, that the woes might be allayed.

We who live in the twentieth century should be able to understand the world of Paul's time, for ours is peculiarly akin to it. To-day we are reaping the harvest of a civilization sown without forethought and nurtured without patience; and in the first century men were reaping a similar harvest, though in that instance of a military, not an industrial, civilization. Rome in its lust for conquest had undone itself. It had tried to unite a divided world and establish order out of chaos; but it had gone at its task with more firmness than wisdom, relying on force to achieve its ends. As a consequence there was peace, but

only on the surface, and plenty, but only for the few. Fine
roads ran throughout the length and breadth of the empire;
mighty cities clustered all around the Great Sea. Nevertheless there was hunger on earth, and terror and wretchedness and hate. The fit had survived, but so had the unfit.
The world swarmed with abject men and women who
never knew surcease of want. So many slaves were there
in the empire that laws had to be passed forbidding them
to wear distinctive garb, lest they discover their own
strength. And even of the freemen the vast majority were
destitute, toiling day and night merely to keep alive.

Nor was this the worst. Need was no new thing on
earth; it had always been, and mankind had grown inured
to it. The real evil was that mankind had lost those consolations which had once made need endurable. The rise
of Rome had upset things. Its generals had deported whole
populations, scattering them broadcast, or herding them
into mines and slums. Famine, plague, and invasion had
likewise forced hordes to migrate. Now that there were
many roads and few frontiers, the populace was untethered
and could roam almost at will. As a consequence, millions
had become homeless, for, though they may have had roofs
over their heads, they dwelt where they did not belong.
And this barbed their poverty. Hunger at home is never
so keen as hunger in exile.

But what tormented the people even more than the loss
of their homes was the loss of their gods. Rome had upset
the heavens as well as the earth. It had not intended to do
so. On the contrary, from the very first it had been the
imperial policy to leave the religions of the subject nations
severely alone. But those religions had been gravely

affected nonetheless. In the disorder attendant upon the violent reordering of the world, the gods toppled with the kings. The ancient assurances which had made life endurable were shattered and swept away, and the poor folk who most desperately needed these assurances were left in despair. Without a faith they could not live, for the exigencies of life were too harsh. They *had* to believe that there was a god who could protect them, and who would reward them all some day. Even the rich and the enlightened languished because they had been emptied of their ancient faith; but these were able to find a measure of comfort in the philosophies of the day. They could indulge in a refreshing revulsion from luxury, and take up the ascetic diet of the Cynics. Or they could sustain themselves with the cold collations of the Stoics, training their wills to withstand the lusts of the flesh and accept fate resignedly.[16]

But the poor and the benighted, the lowly ones who had been dispossessed and now wandered about like children lost in the night—they cried for a comfort less austere than that offered by the philosophers. They wanted a god, and a sure way of winning his favor. They wanted spells of proven efficacy, and dreams and enticing promises. They wanted salvation.

And it was just this that Paul yearned to bring to them. He knew well what could impart to men the kind of assurance which is salvation. He had learnt of it years earlier in his wondrous vision, and the knowledge had never grown dim. It was faith in Jesus. But not the narrow

[16] On the religious significance of Hellenistic philosophy see S. J. Case, *Evolution of Early Christianity*, ch. 8. The subject is considered in greater detail in Zeller, *Stoics, Epicureans, and Sceptics*.

trammeled faith preached by the handful who struggled along in Jerusalem. No, rather the generous and emancipated faith which was flourishing in Antioch. What alone disturbed Paul was that the Antiochan gospel lacked form and sound argument. It had developed not as a result of one man's willfullness, but in response to a whole host of environmental influences. Consequently it was disordered and not altogether certain of itself. Had Paul been like the other apostles in Antioch, probably he would not have been concerned over this disorder. But quite obviously he was not like them. He had been a student and his mind was disciplined: he could not abide to wear a faith which was in tatters. So forthwith he began to sew those tatters into a presentable garment.

6

 HE task was never completely finished. Paul's theology continued to change till the day of his death, for he kept cutting his thought to the changing pattern of his experience. Yet from first to last certain tenets did remain fixed. Basically, there was his conviction that Jesus died to redeem mankind from the "original sin" of old Adam. But this Jesus was not the carpenter of Nazareth who became an exhorter and wandered about in Galilee. Instead, he was the Christ, the only-begotten Son of God, who descended into the world and offered himself on the cross in order to appease the

[39]

wrath of his Father. The idea that Jesus was a creature of flesh and blood, knowing passion and pain; that he could flog the money-changers in a burst of wrath, or curse a fig tree in a fit of irritation; that he could be "sore amazed" and "very heavy" in the garden of Gethsemane, or cry, "My God, my God, why hast thou forsaken me?" when on the cross: these were things Paul did not know, or knowing, did not heed. He had never seen Jesus in the body; he had seen no more than a dazzling effulgence in a vision. So Jesus was not a mortal being to him; he was the Lord! Indeed, following no doubt the usage in the Antiochan congregation, Paul called him by that very name—*Kyrios,* the Lord—just as the Pagans called Adonis, or Attis, or Mithra, the Lord. "Kyrios Christos"—into this had the prophet of humility been translated. . . . Paul still believed in God, "the Father of our Lord Jesus Christ"; but it was the Son he worshiped. For the Father was distant while the Son was very near. He had actually walked the earth once, taking upon himself the whole burden of human sin and then offering himself as an atonement. So it was but meet to worship the Son.

This, then, was the first point in Paul's theology: that Jesus was the Christ, and the Lord and Savior of all men. From it followed the second: that now Jew and Gentile were on one plane. Jesus had not died for Israel alone, but for all mankind. Therefore circumcised and uncircumcised were now equally ready for salvation. The Law of Moses, which had once given to the Jews their distinction, was now no longer of any worth. It had been abrogated by Christ's death on the cross. Circumcision and dietary taboo and Sabbath restrictions no longer counted. What alone could be of avail was faith in Christ. To be saved one must receive the Spirit—nothing more. For this Spirit was not some vague impulse to righteousness; nothing of the kind. It was a very concrete and objective entity. Paul, for all that he had the intuitions of genius, was nonetheless a child of his time. The demons were as real to him as the hairs in his beard; and so were the angels. When he spoke of a believer being "in Christ," he spoke just as literally as did the Pagans of the day when they said a madman was "in the demon." Possessing the Spirit was no figure of speech to Paul; it meant quite literally that a divine power was in one, a magical power rendering one capable of living eternally.

This doctrine was no innovation on the part of Paul. The believers in Jerusalem were likewise convinced of the magical properties of the Spirit. Where he differed from them was in his doctrine as to the means of acquiring the amazing boon. Peter and the rest of the Twelve, being still strict Jews, insisted that it could be attained only through obedience to the Law of Moses and practice of the teachings of Jesus. But Paul, having become emancipated in Antioch, could not agree to such rigorous requirements. The stringent Law of Moses he now believed to be abrogated; and the perfectionist ethic of Jesus he refused to accept. Perhaps he suspected that such an ethic had not even been taught by Jesus, for Paul never once deigns to mention it. Certainly he must have felt that it was impracticable. One might be able to persuade a handful of peasants to surrender their possessions and sit down to await the return of Christ; but the conversion of the whole world to such a course of conduct was, Paul realized, quite out of the question. Accordingly he did not even trouble to refer to the renunciation of private property and the abnegation of worldly desire, which were so cardinal in the thought and practice of the Jerusalem church.

Of course, Paul was well aware of the importance of love; indeed, he proclaimed it the greatest of virtues and extolled it in words as fervent as they sound sincere. Paul was indubitably a good man. No one can read his epistles without sensing the inordinate generosity of heart and expansiveness of character which must have been innate in him. But he was also a practical man. His head, despite that it was filled with visions, was hard; he could dream, but with eyes keenly narrowed. Therefore he refused to demand the impossible. He let his converts hold on to their property; he countenanced even slavery. All he demanded of them, apparently, was belief. To confess "Kyrios Christos"—that alone was the price they must pay, it would seem.

But this belief which Paul demanded had to be manifested in very concrete ways. There were sacraments to be observed, definite rites which were utterly obligatory. The disciples in Jerusalem knew nothing of these or any other sacraments. As we have already seen, only two elements in their religion differentiated it from orthodox Judaism: an insistence upon a perfectionist ethic, and a conviction that Jesus the Messiah would soon return. To these Paul now added a third element: belief in the efficacy of certain rites. First there was Baptism, the rite of initiation into the Christian cult. This baptism, however, was not the mere

[42]

ceremony practiced in Jerusalem. It had taken on a magical character; indeed, it was almost indistinguishable from the baptism in the Mysteries. According to Paul, the sacrament was an agency capable of exorcising the demons from a man's soul, leaving room for the Spirit to enter as into a house "swept and garnished." It did not simply wash away guilt; it literally "put on" Christ. To assure that the rite did not miscarry—for the world was crowded with "unclean spirits" on the lookout for vacated souls—it came to be believed that a certain gesture must be made and a formula recited. Whoever administered the rite had to "lay on" his hands and invoke the name of "Kyrios Christos." In default of this, the rite could not possibly be efficacious.

Such was the first of the sacraments, and without receiving it one could never be truly "in Christ." But there was a second, and even more important rite: the Lord's Supper. This, unlike Baptism, had to be taken not once but repeatedly, for it served to renew the Spirit which had entered the believer on his initiation into the cult. The rite was derived in part from the congregational suppers in Jerusalem. The Brethren there seem to have eaten together from the very first, for their whole economy necessitated common tables. With the passing of the years—for almost two decades had already elapsed since the Crucifixion— these communal meals had acquired somewhat of a religious aspect, not alone because the Law of Moses demanded that certain prayers be recited at meat, but also because it was but in the nature of things for such regular gatherings to become ritualized. Primarily, however, they were still meals.

But Paul's sacrament of the Lord's Supper was derived more directly—even though perhaps less consciously—from the rites of the Mysteries. It was not at all a meal, but a memorial of the last supper eaten by Jesus. The actual food consisted of no more than a piece of bread and a cup of water or wine, and was consumed for the nourishment of the soul, not the body. For the bread and wine were symbols of the flesh and blood of Christ, and to partake of them improperly was to be "guilty of profaning the body and blood of the Lord," and also to put one's health and very life in jeopardy.[17] There was magic in the Lord's Supper; it was a holy rite which brought the worshiper and the Christ into supernatural communion.[18]

These two sacraments, Baptism and the Lord's Supper, were the outward essentials of the religion according to Paul. That a Christian must also practice charity and forgiveness, and be honest and faithful, was taken for granted. If he suppressed his passions and lived in celibacy, so much the better. Paul's epistles are full of adjurations concerning righteousness and the virtues. Save in the matter of tolerance—a most important virtue which he, unhappily, was incapable of appreciating—Paul was unsurpassed by even the noblest Pagan moralizers. But his major emphasis was always on the sacramental rather than the ethical. One thing seemed to him absolutely obligatory: to be saved one *must* observe the sacraments. Once that requirement was

[17] I Cor. 11, 30.

[18] See Case's *The Evolution of Early Christianity*, pp. 342-352. This and Otto Pfleiderer's *Christian Origins* give excellent critical accounts of the origin of Paul's theology. For a Catholic account of the origin and history of the sacrament of the Lord's Supper, see A. Fortescue, *The Mass*.

adhered to, there was nothing left to fear. The Spirit entered the soul and remained there, rendering a man proof against sin and misfortune. The believer could laugh at the demons, for they were impotent to do him harm. He could laugh even at death, for this could have no sting for him. At worst he might "fall asleep"—but even then it would be but for a moment. For Paul believed with all his heart that the Lord would soon return again. He was continually sounding the cry *mara natha,* which in Aramaic means "The Lord is coming!" Again and again he assured his converts that the "Lord is at hand," that the "fashion of this world is passing," and that "the present evil age" must soon end. That was why he was so anxious to go out and convert the world.

Paul had no concern for the future of his own people, the Jews, for he knew they would be sure to see the light before long. (Paul, like most missionaries, was an incorrigible optimist.) Indeed, it was part of his belief that Christ would never return until all the Jews were converted. What alone tormented him was the plight of the Gentiles, for he feared that if these did not receive the tidings in time, they might be lost forever. Just how they would be lost he did not say. All he affirmed was that Christ on his return would at once convoke the Final Assize. He and his Father would act as judges, the saints would be the witnesses, and the world and the demons would stand at the bar. But as to what would then ensue, Paul seemed uncertain. He was sure, of course, that the believers would all be found guiltless and allowed to enter the World to Come; but further than that his apocalyptic vision failed to carry him. Those who pressed him for information he parried with the assurance that "things which no eye ever saw and no ear ever heard and no human mind ever imagined, hath God in store for those who love him.". . . . Nor was Paul more explicit as to the fate of those who would be found guilty. He seems not to have known whether they would be converted at the last moment or consigned to perdition; or whether, if perdition awaited them, they would be straightway annihilated or consigned to eternal torture. But, despite his uncertainty as to the ultimate outcome, what he did know was enough to make him frantic with apprehension. He could not bear to stand idly by and let the world lurch on in blindness. He *must* reach out a hand; he *had* to raise his voice. For if he did not, then. . . .

7

 OADED by his passion to save mankind, Paul could not be satisfied to stay on in Antioch. He had to go out into the world with his gospel, go out to the uttermost ends of the earth while there was yet time. And this he did. For some twelve years, perhaps even longer, he continued to wander from land to land, never pausing in his effort to save mankind. How he traveled we do not know, but probably it was on foot. With staff in hand, and perhaps a crust and some leeks in his girdle, he dragged his way over the thorny mountain roads and through the rocky defiles of

Cyprus and Asia Minor and Greece. Happily for him he
was a Jew, and was therefore not altogether lost in those
foreign places. In every town, occasionally even in the
villages, he could look for kinsmen and expect shelter
and food—until the purpose of his coming was discovered.
In addition he was, by virtue of his father's position, a
Roman citizen and could count to a degree upon the pro-

THE WORLD OF PAUL'S WANDERINGS

tection of the imperial government. Significantly, he
dropped his Hebrew name Saul, while traveling, and used
instead a Roman one. He called himself Paul—just as in
our day Mr. Cohen will take the name of Cole, and Mr.
Levy will call himself Lenox.

But despite these advantages the hazards of travel were
enormous and the hardships bitter beyond words. Not
merely were there the elements to be feared, the storms at
sea and the blasting winds on land; not merely were there

pirates and robber-bands and wild beasts to be escaped. In addition Paul had to reckon with the hostility of his fellow-Jews. When he came to a city he usually made straight for the synagogue, hoping not so much to convert the Jews to his religion as the "God-fearers" who frequented the sanctuary. And those half-Judaized Pagans were often attracted to his doctrine, for it seemed to offer all the benefits of Judaism at a fraction of the customary price. Baptism was less irrevocable than circumcision; sacramental suppers were more exciting than Mosaic meals. Besides, the whole notion of a "Kyrios Christos," a Savior Lord who had died and come to life again, sounded familiar and very sensible in their ears. So they hearkened to Paul with eagerness, and, when he called on them to accept baptism, they obeyed with alacrity. And this angered the synagogue elders. They did not like to lose their Pagan sympathizers, not alone because these lent prestige to the synagogue, but perhaps also because some of them may have given money to its support. So Paul was more than once mobbed and flogged and driven from cities by his own kinsmen.

For sheer heroism and perseverance it would be difficult to find Paul's equal in all of history. His health was poor much of the time, for some unnamed malady afflicted him. Treacheries and disappointments tried his spirit continually. Yet never would he confess defeat.

"Five times I have been given one less than forty lashes by the Jews," he writes in one of his epistles. "I have been beaten three times by the Romans, I have been stoned once, I have been shipwrecked three times, a day and a night I have been adrift at sea. I have known danger from rivers, danger from the heathen, danger from false brothers. I have been through toil and hardships, through many a sleepless night, through hunger and thirst, going often without food, and naked and cold. . . ."

The man was, of course, a fanatic, a stubborn, heedless, Christ-drunk agitator; but he was superb nonetheless. He could be impatient at moments, and bitter, irascible, even petulant. Possibly he was an epileptic; certainly he was neurotic. Perhaps some sexual frustration tortured him, some unconfessed fear because of a defect in temperament or body. But despite all these flaws he remains superb. One pictures him as he went about the world, a short, stoop-shouldered, hook-nosed Jew—for so is he described in the earliest traditions—his face perhaps disfigured by the disease of which he complains, his eyes near-sighted, his head almost bald; and one is astounded that he should have been able to accomplish all he did. There were other apostles—Peter, Barnabas, John, Mark, Timothy—but these seem to have accomplished incomparably less. That is why Paul is sometimes spoken of as the founder of Christianity. Save very indirectly, Jesus did not at all create the new religion; it recreated him. Nor were his immediate disciples the creators. In a sense, even Paul was not the innovator. Nothing is clearer than that Christianity was the product of an environment rather than of a man, and that the theology which is called Pauline was really Hellenistic. The seed of Paganism entered into the womb of Israel, giving rise to a new faith; and Paul's contribution was that of severing the umbilical cord. Had he not been present at that hour, the child might possibly have perished. It might have languished for want of nursing, and might have joined the innumerable other new-born faiths that leapt up and swiftly died in that day. But Paul *was* there, and as a consequence Christianity lived.

8

AUL'S end is shrouded in mystery. In all probability he was executed in Rome as an agitator somewhen between 62 and 67 A.D. But when he died, Christianity's hold on life was already almost secure. It was, of course, still an abject and obscure cult. Even in Syria and Greece and Asia Minor, where Paul had done most of his work, the congregations were few and were confined to the towns. Elsewhere it was known only in the great ganglia of commerce—in Rome, Alexandria, Carthage, and the like. The people in the rural regions, the *pagani,* seemed so incapable of conversion that in time their name became the generic term for those who persisted in their old beliefs. In all the world there could have been hardly ten thousand believers, the majority of them drawn from the dregs of the population.[19] Very many were slaves, and the rest were for

[19] This estimate is given in Ernest F. Scott, *The First Age of Christianity,* 1926, p. 159—an excellent little volume, concise, readable, and judicious.

the most part artisans, vendors, and housewives. Some of
them could read, but not many. If there was a man of
learning in the entire church after Paul died, no record is
left of his presence. Only once do we hear of Paul trying
to proselytize among the philosophers, and that once he
failed completely. It happened when he first passed
through Athens, and the schoolmen of that ancient center,
learning that he was the bearer of a new doctrine, invited
him to address their forum. But when they heard what he
had to say, they simply shrugged their shoulders and
smiled. His speech must have sounded barbarous in their
ears, for, as is clear from his epistles, Paul's language was
peculiarly vigorous and explosive. And in addition, his
gospel must have impressed those learned men as rank
superstition. Paul could be convincing only to the woebegone and the simple, and of such was the primitive church
composed. As he himself was forced to confess, it was
"the foolish of the world" whom God chose to be his
converts.

It was only natural that Christianity should appeal
primarily to the lower classes. In the first place it was
something novel, and the novel is always attractive to
simple folk no longer moored to the old. The learned are
capable of weighing and considering before they accept a
new teaching; but not so the ignorant. They are not strong
enough to drift when they have lost their old faith; they
become panicky, and clutch at whatever is held out to
them. And Christianity was not merely held out; it was
thrust at them. Its apostles, unlike those of the other cults,
were zealots. They did not wait for inquirers to come to
them; instead they rushed out and created inquirers. They

[51]

kept running about, here, there, everywhere, now preaching, now healing, now organizing. No matter how bitter the hostility or how stolid the indifference, they kept on urging their cause. Perhaps this was because they were Jews by birth and therefore inherently intense and aggressive. Or perhaps it was because, as confirmed Christians, they were goaded by the imminence of the Doom. Whatever the reason, they could not possibly hold still. And in a world grown tired and apathetic, the sheer enthusiasm of those apostles must have been compelling.

But Christianity had won its thousands of converts not alone because of its novelty or the vigor of its advocates. Of itself it was a superior faith, for it had added the most attractive elements in the other cults to a basic attractiveness of its own. Like the philosophic schools, it stressed the need for right living, and like the Mysteries, it encouraged rich believing. It had adopted the magical sacraments and the whole mystery of a god of whose body one could partake and in whose immortality one could share. And these it had attached to a hero not mythical but very real and human. It was only a little while since Jesus had actually walked the earth as a man, and there were apostles still alive who had been his own disciples. The tendency to make a deity of Jesus had already gone far, but not far enough to rob him of his humanity. Especially among the humbler converts, whose childlike yearnings did not require a god but could be satisfied with a hero—especially among these was the belief still firm that Jesus had been a man.

Nor was this all. Jesus had been not merely a man, but

uniquely a *good* man. He had been the champion of the
poor and the lonely and the woebegone, healing them and
promising them eventual glory. And this must have vastly
intensified the appeal of Christianity to the downtrodden.
They could warm to such a hero, for he was on their side.
Had he not given his life to redeem them from their sins?
Would he not return soon to save them from their
oppressors? . . .

And there was more even than that to attract the lowly.
Christianity could offer not alone a loving Savior in
Heaven, but also generous friends here on earth. Even in
the Pauline congregation there was some attempt to live
up to at least part of Jesus's social teachings. If the
wealthier converts did not go to the extreme of giving
away all they possessed, they did give at least a little.
They may not have actually freed their slaves; but they did
at least treat them with kindness. So the destitute may have
found it to more than spiritual advantage to become Christians. Baptism assured them not alone of eternal bliss in
the World to Come, but also of an occasional crust here
and now. The communal suppers were beginning to be
known as "love feasts," and all who were believers could
come to them and eat their fill. A Christian wayfarer was
always assured of shelter on reaching a place where there
was a congregation. Once a man became a Christian he
was no longer alone in the world. Thenceforth he was
one of a large family, and he could find brethren wherever
he turned.

No wonder, therefore, that the new religion gained its
thousands from among the "foolish of the world."

The converts seem to have met more or less regularly in private houses for prayer and fellowship. The services were akin to those in the Jewish synagogue, for there was no offering of sacrifices but only prayer and preaching. But the order was quite different; indeed, there was no order whatsoever. There were as yet no established officials, and all the congregants were allowed to do as the Spirit moved them. And this liberty was very precious to them, for save in those hours of communion with their beloved Savior they were like prisoners. Shackled by want and gagged with abasement, they were helpless in this everyday world. But once in their hidden meeting places they could let themselves loose, shouting with no fear of hindrance, praying with no dread of scorn. For was not their Redeemer present?

Of course this liberty had its drawbacks, for it frequently caused turbulence and confusion in the meetings. One worshiper would sing, another would expound, a third would relate a vision, and a fourth would "speak with tongues." Nor was there any standing on ceremony, for, being impelled by the Spirit, no man could wait for another to yield the floor. The women were perhaps the worse offenders in this regard, and we find Paul writing on one occasion: "Women should keep quiet. If they want to find out about anything, they should ask their husbands at home, for it is disgraceful for a woman to speak in church."

There were other abuses against which Paul had to warn the believers, especially with regard to the sacramental suppers. In some congregations these tended to become orgies like those of the Mysteries, for they were held in hidden places after dark, and the celebrants, becoming filled with wine as well as with the Spirit, were not always able to control themselves. But such excesses were only to be expected. It was all very well for Paul to write, "God is not a God of disorder but of peace." The believers, after all, had been Pagans only yesterday, and even to-day they were still slaves. There was restraint enough in the workaday world; in their churches they were set on being free.

The rite of the Lord's Supper was celebrated once a week, though whether on the Jewish Sabbath or on the heathen Sun-day is uncertain. Probably the practice varied in the different churches, depending on whether the local membership was drawn predominantly from the synagogue or the cults. There seems to have been as yet only limited uniformity of doctrine or practice, for the religion was still very new and it had won its adherents very hastily. Paul had tried hard during his ministry to keep a tight rein on all the churches and keep them moving in what he believed to be the one true way. That was why he had returned again and again to various cities, or had sent messengers to them with lengthy letters of advice and exhortation. But it was an impossible task. Wild horses would have been easier to curb than those inspirited congregations. Having once given them their head, having once yielded to compromise, there was no holding them back.

In Jerusalem, where the original Galilean tradition still obtained, there had been little change. The Brethren there still adhered to the Holy Law, practicing circumcision and abstaining from forbidden foods like the devoutest Pharisees. They were still Jews in all outward respects, differing from their neighbors only in the excess of their righteousness and faith. Jesus to them was a mortal become immortal, a man whom God had appointed to be Israel's long-awaited Redeemer. One of his own brothers after the flesh, a very orthodox person named James, was now their leader. Years later another relation of Jesus succeeded to the leadership, the office being apparently considered hereditary. Since the Brethren were committed to living as though the Kingdom were already come, they seem to have thought it only proper to have one of the dynasty of the eventual King as their ruler in the interim.

But the churches in the Gentile lands were devoted to an altogether different doctrine. They acknowledged the primacy of the Jerusalem congregation to the extent of sending alms to it from time to time: but otherwise the foreign churches followed their own bent. They refused to accept the yoke of Jewish ritualism, having decided with Paul that "by the works of the Law shall no man be justified." Instead they staked all on the sacraments. The process begun in Antioch had gathered momentum. Jesus was ceasing to be a man who had lived and preached, and was becoming a god who had died and been reborn. He was no longer the carpenter of Nazareth but Kyrios Christos. . . .

BOOK TWO

The Ordeal of Childhood
A.D. 70-323

THE ORDEAL OF CHILDHOOD: 70-323 A.D.

1: The Origin of the Gospels: Mark. 2: Matthew. Luke. John. 3: The Christianity of the Populace. Revelation. 4: Gnosticism. 5: The Formulation of a Christian Creed. 6: The Development of a Christian Church. 7: The Persecutions. 8: Constantine and the Triumph of the Church.

IT is no wonder that men have been prone to see the workings of Providence in the rise of Christianity. No religion ever had a lowlier origin and none ever seemed less likely to survive. Buddha was a prince by birth; Lao-tze was a court librarian; Confucius was a scholar and politician; Mohammed became the ruler of a race. But Jesus was a workingman reared in a hamlet on the frontier of civilization, and the years of his ministry were so brief and obscure that none save a few peasants remembered them. Even a generation after his death his name was known only to a scattered handful of people, and these of the most despised on earth. How from such beginnings a movement could grow till it dominated half the world is perhaps inexplicable on rational grounds. No matter how painstakingly one may search the sources, and how ingeniously one may interpret the findings, in the end one must confess that the circumstances surrounding the triumph of Christianity were so complex and involved and subtly concatenated as to defy complete analysis.

But despite this fundamental inexplicability one is tempted to hazard guesses at the secret. It seems a fairly safe assumption, for instance, that part of the reason for Christianity's survival lay in its dual derivation. Though born of Judaism, it was sired by Hellenism; though cradled in Palestine, it grew up in the Greco-Roman world. Had things been otherwise, had the child remained bound to its mother, beyond doubt it would have died. Once the perfectionist ethic became too wearing and the adventist dream passed away, there would have been nothing left to keep the child alive. And this did actually happen to that element of Christianity which failed to throw off the swaddling clothes of the Law. The Jerusalem congregation managed to drag out a tortured existence for a time, but then it disintegrated into phthistic sects like that of the Ebionites, the "Poor Ones," and finally died away. Only the more adventurous element, that which freed itself from the mother's bosom and went over to its father's world, managed to survive.

But this element, too, had its ordeal. There were many children in the father's house, and there was danger that the infant might be lost among them. Indeed, by the time Paul and his colleagues were done arraying the faith in Pagan theology and weaning it on sacramental bread and wine, Christianity was hardly to be distinguished from the rest in the brood. It began to take on the character of the Mysteries, and only because the process was checked in time did Christianity escape their fate. The influence of the mother seems to have reasserted itself just in time, and the child was saved. We have no explicit record of this salient turn of events; we know of it only by inference.

The book of Acts closes abruptly with the imprisonment of Paul in Rome, and there are no chronicles of the succeeding half-century. All that emerges out of the obscurity is an undated and largely pseudonymous literature, and upon this alone are we dependent for a guess as to what ensued. Men of learning have been poring over that literature for centuries, and during the last three generations they have succeeded in searching out its true character.[1]

This literature seems to have been in part a protest against the growing tendency to make Jesus a god. It consisted originally of a number of memorabilia and biographies of Jesus, no two of them agreeing, but all of them establishing his actual humanity. Of these most ancient writings only four have come down to us, the oldest being a biography called the Gospel according to Mark. It dates probably from the year 70 A.D., and may have been written in Rome.[2] According to many modern scholars, Mark, the author, obtained his data from Peter, who is reported to have spent his last years as a missionary in Rome. It is not unlikely that Mark had served as interpreter for the Galilean, translating the peasant Aramaic of the old man into the Greek still spoken by the immigrant population in Rome. And after Peter was gone—he is said to have been killed during an anti-Christian riot in the year 64—Mark may have

[1] The story of that hard-won triumph is, incidentally, one of the most enthralling in the saga of scholarship. The layman will find it presented in a number of recent works, among them Henry S. Nash, *The History of the Higher Criticism of the New Testament,* and E. C. Moore, *The New Testament in the Christian Church.*

[2] The question of the date and character of this book is thoroughly discussed in B. W. Bacon, *The Gospel according to Mark.* The lay reader, however, may find enough information in E. J. Goodspeed's splendid little volume entitled *The Story of the New Testament.*

tried to set down what he remembered of the other's reminiscences. Necessarily the account was far from accurate, for it was secondhand and based upon recollections of recollections. Even in our own world, where happenings are recorded within an hour of their occurrence, and where there are misanthropic editors and skeptical readers, a vast amount of exaggeration and fiction creeps into our chronicles. How much the more must this have been true in the world of the first century. Peter, we must remember, had been but a fisherman in his early days; a naïve and simple man with a mind as unstable as the lake upon which he had once sailed his boat. His account of Jesus would have been colored even had he remained a mere disciple; but he had been an apostle to boot. For more than thirty years he had gone about the world trying to convince others that the Master whom he had followed was the Anointed of God. How then could he possibly have told of this Master without diverging at times from the uncolored truth?

And Mark, the chronicler, must have diverged still further. He tried not to. Indeed, he seems to have taken such pains to preserve Peter's phrasing that often the ribs of the original Aramaic idiom protrude through the Greek flesh. But it could not have been humanly possible for Mark to set down precisely what he had once heard. The memory is a treacherous agent, especially when one has a point to prove. And Mark had several points to prove. One was that the Jews, not the Romans, were really responsible for the Crucifixion. (Mark, we must remember, may have been missionizing in Rome at the time he wrote his book.) Another was that, no matter who was to blame for the Crucifixion, it had been foreordained anyway. All of Jesus's life on earth had been, according to Mark, but a prelude to the glory of the Passion. Jesus had known all along that he must die to redeem mankind, that he must offer himself as a vicarious atonement for the sins of his fellow-men. The Crucifixion, therefore, was no disgrace; on the contrary, it was Christ's climacteric achievement. This was a rationalization that Paul had thought of, and it had apparently received wide acceptance in the churches. But it was not easy to incorporate in a Gospel, for there were too many known facts that contradicted it. Had Mark been a conscious fabricator, he might have ignored those facts and have revised the whole story of Jesus. But he was, we may well believe, too honest a man for that. Besides, the true facts were still too well known in the older congregations, for it was hardly forty years since the Crucifixion. Accordingly there was nothing left for him but to interpolate the rationalization quite openly. The very forthrightness with which he made the insertions proves the utter guilelessness of the man. He obviously believed that the ratiocinations of the Hellenistic theologian were no less gospel truth than the reminiscences of the Galilean disciple, and that if they seemed to contradict each other, it was not for him to try to make them agree. The result was a document so discrepant in the eyes of a modern-minded reader that he wonders how it could ever have been believed. Yet it *was* believed, and that most vehemently. Indeed, it is believed by many millions to this day.[3]

[3] The inherent inconsistencies in the Gospel accounts of the betrayal and Crucifixion have been pointed out by critical readers ever since Celsus, the cultured Pagan who wrote against Christianity in the second century. The subject is discussed in detail in J. M. Robertson, *Jesus and Judas*, 1927, a stimulating even though an extravagantly radical treatise.

2

OT long after Mark wrote his Gospel, another biography made its appearance. This, which is known to us as the Gospel according to Matthew, may have been written not so much to correct the Marcan account as to round it out. Mark had told only of the acts of Jesus, not his teachings. He seems to have written his book primarily for a population devoted to miracle-working gods, and therefore his emphasis was on the cures Jesus had performed, and on the demons he had exorcised. The sublime maxims and parables of the Master do not appear in it—neither the Beatitudes, nor the command to love one's enemies, nor the Golden Rule, nor the Lord's Prayer, nor anything else revealing Jesus's activity as a teacher of the perfect life.

And Matthew's biography seeks to remedy this fault. It is based quite obviously on the Marcan document, for the miracles are all there, and usually they are heightened. If Mark reports that Jesus healed "many of the sick," Matthew assures his readers that the Master healed "all the sick brought from near and far." If Mark tells how Jesus cursed a fig-tree because it was bare of fruit when he was hungry, Matthew hastens to add, "And the fig-tree immediately withered away." Whereas Mark begins his tale with the baptism of Jesus at the age of thirty, Matthew goes back to before the Master's birth and shows how his very conception was miraculous. Here, for the first time, we are told that Jesus was born of a virgin—an idea totally foreign to Jewish thought, though quite familiar to the Pagans. The Greeks and the Romans had many gods and heroes whom they believed to be the sons of virgins. Even certain of their great mortals—for instance Plato and Augustus—were said to have had gods for fathers and virgins for mothers. To make such a thing credible to the Jews, a verse from Isaiah was mistranslated—Isaiah 7, 14, should read: "a *young woman* shall conceive and bear a child," not "a *virgin*"—so that the ancient prophet is made to foretell the miracle.

But together with these wonders attendant upon the birth and life of Jesus, we are given his teachings. There were, apparently, several collections of the sayings of Jesus circulating in the churches at this time, and Matthew seems to have incorporated one or more of them in his biography. It is possible that some of these sayings were not authentic, or that they had become garbled and distorted. New problems had arisen and new needs had made themselves felt since Jesus died, and there must have been a temptation to find light on them in the Master's teachings. The capacity to remember what *should* have been said is appallingly well developed in propagandists. And Matthew was unmistakably a propagandist. Like Mark, he wrote with a missionary purpose, though his field seems to have been among the Jews rather than the Pagans. For that reason he took pains throughout his book to show how the life and the death of Jesus fulfilled in every detail the ancient Jewish prophecies concerning the Messiah. He opens his biography with a long genealogical table to prove that Jesus was descended from Abraham through

King David, the traditional ancestor of the Messiah. Curiously, the descent is traced through Joseph, who, according to the very next verse, was only the stepfather of Jesus. Evidently the genealogical table was not the product of Matthew's own research, but was invented in an earlier generation, when the detail of the virgin birth had not yet become part of the growing Christology.

Matthew was writing to convert his own folk, the Jews, but it is clear that he was not one of the congregation in Jerusalem. Actually there was no longer any congregation in Jerusalem at this time, for the city had been sacked and burnt by the Romans in the year 70. The Jews, tired of waiting for a miraculous Redeemer, had taken matters into their own hands and had revolted; and the Christians in the capital, totally out of sympathy with the bloody uprising, had fled the land. They had left their kinsmen to die at the barricades and had themselves taken refuge in the hills on the other side of the Jordan. Matthew, however, was not of their company. In all probability he was by birth a Hellenist Jew, and his Gospel, written perhaps in Syria, shows that he had no sympathy with the communism which had characterized the Jerusalem church. And he seems actually to have censored and distorted the sayings of Jesus in order to sustain his argument. According to what may have been the original tradition, Jesus had declared: "Blessed are you poor," and "blessed are you who hunger now." But Matthew makes him say: "Blessed are the poor *in spirit*," and "blessed are they that hunger and thirst *after righteousness*." The bitter woes which Jesus was said to have prophesied for the rich and the contented, are omitted from Matthew's account; nor is there any mention of the widow who was praised by the Master though she had no more than a mite to contribute. All the fulminations against property are softened; wealth is never described as "unrighteous Mammon." Singly, these may seem trifling emendations, but collectively they are enormously significant. They reveal that the apostles who still sought to convert the Jews to Christ were demanding no more than the apostles who preached to the Gentiles. Gone was the old insistence upon a perfectionist ethic; an easier code was now counted enough.

What may have been more nearly the original sayings of Jesus are to be found in a third Gospel, that of Luke. It comes to us from this same period, but it was written by one who evidently had no need to combat the utopian idealism of the mother congregation. Luke wrote for Gentiles, and, perhaps because there was little danger of his being taken too literally, he could well afford to glorify poverty. But it is plain that Luke, too, colored his biography, for he, too, had a point to prove. Writing as he did for the Gentiles, he wanted to prove that Jesus came into the world to save not merely the Jews, but all men. Therefore he traces the descent of Jesus not merely from Abraham, the father of the Hebrews, but from Adam, the father of the entire human race. And he portrays Jesus as ministering not merely to the Galileans and the Judeans, but also to the half-heathen Samaritans. Luke was dependent for his data upon sources akin to those employed by Matthew— chiefly the Gospel of Mark and various collections of "sayings"—yet his picture of Jesus is strikingly different from that presented by the man writing for the Jews. It was but natural that this should be so. Luke, like the other, was a biographer with a purpose; and truth and a purpose make bad bedfellows.

But the discrepancies between Luke and Matthew, and between both and Mark, must not be exaggerated. Though each account has its distinctive character reflecting the bias of its author and the environment in which he wrote, yet all three tell very much the same tale. That is why they are usually spoken of as the Synoptic Gospels—they all "look together." They recount the life story of one who was unmistakably a man; a being of flesh and blood who could suffer pain and know despair. In many of its details the story does show traces of Pagan influence. Like Poseidon, Jesus walks on water; like Phœbus Apollo, he wields a scourge; like Asklepios, he raises the dead; like Horus, he is born in a stable; like Mithra, he is adored by shepherds; like a hundred gods he is born of a virgin. But beneath all these borrowed drapings one sees the figure of an historic being. As the Gospels unfold their tale they reveal to us a Jesus intensely human and lovable, a wise and generous and forgiving preacher who went up and down a murdered land bringing comfort to the dejected and courage to the weak. And that may well have been an underlying reason for the writing of all three Gospels. Their authors were anxious to make it plain that Jesus was first and last a man, not a god.

The common folk, who made up the vast majority of the believers, came to be devoted to those Gospels. They found them exciting and glamorous and cheering, and listened eagerly when they were read aloud. They could never hear enough of Christ's wondrous doings. He was their hero—enough unlike them to make him worshipful, yet not enough to make him unreal. He was their champion who had died for them, their Redeemer, their Savior. And the narratives which told of him became holy books in their eyes, sacred documents to be revered and cherished as though delivered by God himself.

But it is clear that only the simpler members of the church were thus taken with the Gospels. The more cultured—and by the end of the first century there were many such in the movement—were left dissatisfied. It was but in the nature of things that a cult so exotic and attractively unconventional as Christianity should eventually have begun to find converts in the upper classes. And it was likewise in the nature of things that these converts, once the naïve character of Christianity lost its novelty for them, should have become a discordant element in the cult. A peasant exhorter who had lived and died in what must have been considered a barbaric outpost of the empire, was hardly a fit object for worship in the eyes of such upper-class folk. Even had Jesus been portrayed as an aristocrat, it would not have been enough for them. These cultured converts were too grown for hero-worship, too advanced to be awed by a mere man. They wanted a god. So, despite that the Gospels of Mark and Matthew and Luke came to be recited and revered by the humbler folk in the church, the theology of Paul was far from routed. The mother's influence which reasserted itself in the biographies was powerful enough to save the

infant faith; but hardly powerful enough to take it back
from the father. Christianity remained a Hellenistic cult,
and its tendency to make a god of Jesus, though hindered,
was not crushed.

The cultured converts began to introduce a strange notion into Christian theology. They said that Jesus, despite
all the records of his life, had never really been more than
a phantom on earth. From the beginning he had been a
deity, and his appearance among men had been altogether
illusory. As Jerome lamented many years later: "The
blood of Christ was still fresh in Judea when his body was
said to be an apparition." How far this docetic notion could
be pressed is seen, for instance, in a later document entitled the *Acts of John,* in which Christ is depicted as
calmly addressing the disciples on the Mount of Olives
while the spectacle of the Crucifixion—a sheer illusion—
is being enacted on Calvary before the eyes of the multitude! [4]

The notion was not new. It had arisen centuries earlier
out of the dualistic philosophy of the Orient, and had
already attached itself to the figure of Buddha in India.
That it should attach itself also to Jesus was inevitable
under the circumstances, for it seemed to explain away to
perfection all the stories of his earthly career. But it did
not go unchallenged. Almost at once there was revulsion
against it, as is evidenced by more than one veiled reference in the later parts of the New Testament. Finally a
whole book was written to deny the devitalizing doctrine.
The book is known to us as the Gospel according to John,

---

[4] Streeter, *The Primitive Church,* p. 6, a valuable book both for its
erudition and its occasional piquant asides.

and dates probably from the early years of the second century.[5] The tradition that it was written by a disciple of Jesus is, of course, unhistorical. John, the son of Zebedee, was a Galilean laborer, an "ignorant and unlettered" man, as Acts 4, 13 describes him; and only a person of high literary gifts and developed intellect could possibly have created the Fourth Gospel. Besides, it differs so radically from the other three biographies that it could not possibly have been written save by one unacquainted or unconcerned with the earlier traditions. In it Jesus is depicted not as a peasant Messiah wandering about in a remote countryside and exhorting the villagers to repent, but rather as a Divine Being who "became flesh" for a relatively brief moment. He is not a mere descendant of King David, but the "only-begotten Son of God"; not simply a Messiah of the Jews, but the very "Bread of Life" and "Light of the World." We are told nothing of his birth or rearing. The book opens with the cryptic statement: "In the beginning was the Word, and the Word was with God, and the Word was God." This Word—or *logos,* to use the Greek—was the divine agency by which the world and all life came into existence. Yet It was not recognized by man until It incarnated Itself as Jesus and "lived for a while among us." Some three years, in all, It continued in fleshly form, and then, having submitted to death as an atonement for the sins of man, It muttered, "It is finished!" —not "My God, my God, why hast thou forsaken me?"— and returned to Heaven.

[5] Some scholars, among them Otto Pfleiderer (*Christian Origins,* p. 278), go so far as to insist that the Gospel of John could not have been written earlier than 130-140 A.D.

Clearly this picture of Jesus derives not from Galilean tradition but Hellenistic metaphysics. Its basic idea of a divine intermediary between god and man was one that had long been common in the religious speculation of the Pagans. The Persian religion taught that Vohumano, the "good thought," was the chief of the angels mediating between God and the world. Similarly in the Babylonian religion, Nabu, the "Son" of Marduk, was the instrument of divine revelation to man, as was also Thot, the "Son" of Ra, in the Egyptian religion. From these or other sources the idea had crept into Hellenistic philosophy, and a school of Stoics spoke of Hermes, the classic messenger of the gods, as the intermediary between the Logos—which was the Eternal in their theology—and mankind. Philo, the Jewish philosopher who lived in Alexandria early in the first century, had gone a step further, saying that the Logos itself was the intermediary. He spoke of it as the "first born" of the Almighty, the divine Word through which the transcendent God created the world and remained related to it. Man could be brought to God only by this Logos, for it was metaphorically—perhaps even literally— the "Shepherd of Souls," the "Light of the World," the "Cupbearer" pouring out the divine life.

This Philonic conception of the Logos seems to have made deep inroads into Christian thought by the end of the first century—so deep, indeed, that the author of the Fourth Gospel does not even question its validity. He takes it for granted that Christ is the Word, and existed from the beginning of all time. He even uses the very language of Philo, and describes Christ as the "Good Shepherd" and the "Light of Mankind." But what he does do is insist that those who believe that Christ the Word was essentially a cosmic principle, shall also believe that for a while he was a real man. That is why he recounts his details of the earthly history of Jesus. The author is most anxious to establish the fact that Jesus was completely human as well as repletely divine; that he had not simply *appeared* to be a man—which was what many of the more sophisticated converts were saying—but that he had very actually become flesh and blood, and had died and been buried. The tendency to deify Christ had gone too far to be undone completely. At most it could only be curbed now. For Christianity was no longer a simple faith cherished only by slaves and artisans. It had fallen into the hands of learned folk and had acquired a theology. The Son of Man had been eclipsed by the Son of God.

3

UT only among the learned converts had this change come about. In all probability the implications of the Fourth Gospel—and also of the Epistle to the Hebrews, the Pauline and Johannine letters, and what other theological writings are to be found in the New Testament—were as remote from the concerns of the average Christian in the first century as are the problems of higher mathematics from the concerns of the average bank clerk to-day. The rank and file in the Church was recruited from the proletariat, and it was too hungry and careworn to be sensitive to meta-physical difficulties. It did not care about Christ's origin; it was interested only in his destiny. "In the beginning was the Word"—that meant nothing to the harried folk who dragged themselves night after night to the dark, close, half-hidden meetinghouses of the cult. *Mara natha,* "the Lord is Coming!"—*that* was what they wanted to hear.

And they did hear it. The old hope of a near advent was still burning in the church, and there were exhorters aplenty to keep the fire from dying down. The Spirit had not yet seeped out of the believers, and they were still prophesying and seeing visions and speaking with "tongues." Poor thwarted souls that they were, frenetic dreaming was all that was left for them. It was well enough for the theologians to wag their heads disapprovingly, and frown, and suck at their teeth. The masses paid no heed to them, for they knew what they wanted and insisted on crying for it. They wanted the Second Advent, and their clamor for it was so loud that it penetrated even into the Christian Scriptures. The last book in the New Testament, the Revelation of John, is an apocalyptic writing of the type which must have been exceedingly popular toward the end of the first century. It is a prophecy of the doom which was soon to overtake Rome, and of the glory which would then ensue for Christendom.

To the modern reader Revelation is a bewildering book, what with its muddled talk of the Antichrist, and poly-cephalic beasts, and avenging angels, and vials of wrath. It has the distressing quality of a nightmare, or of the rav-

ings of a madman. But to an early Christian, acquainted
with the allegory of the Apocalypse, it must have been a
glorious document. Its savage fulminations against the
"Whore of Babylon" must have delighted him, for he
knew that the epithet stood for Rome. He hated Rome
now. The bias which had moved Mark to shield the Pagans
in his account of the Crucifixion, had reversed itself since
the last decade of the century. The Christians had discovered that the imperial government, far from showing
signs of adopting the cult, seemed determined to stamp it
out. As yet there had been no severe or prolonged persecution; but there had been threats aplenty, and occasionally even riots and executions. There was ample
reason, therefore, why the believers in Christ should turn
on Rome. Being for the most part proletarians, they were
quite naturally disposed to distrust the government. Being,
in addition, for the most part orientals—for even in the
capital itself the converts were largely of Greek and Syrian
extraction—they were particularly prone to distrust a government which was Roman. And, finally, being branded
criminals because of their faith, they were convinced that
a government which was hostile as well as foreign could
not but be the very Antichrist.

With what joy, therefore, must the average Christian
have read the Revelation of John! How fervently must he
have cried Amen to the author's prayer:

"Pay her back in her own coin, O Lord! Give her
[Rome] double for what she has done! In the cup
she mixed for others, mix her a double draught! The

[75]

more she indulged herself in pride and luxury, the more let her suffer torture and grief! . . ."

There was more in this book than a vision of the Hell awaiting Rome; in addition it told of the glory awaiting the Church. Once the Antichrist was defeated, and he and all his host were flung into the fiery lake, then the New Jerusalem would be let down from Heaven for the Christians. The Apocalypse describes the wonder city in glamorous detail.

> "It shone with a radiance like that of some very precious stone, like jasper, clear as crystal. . . . In length it was fifteen hundred miles (and) its breadth and height were the same. . . . The material of the wall was jasper, but the city itself was pure gold, as transparent as glass. . . . The twelve gates were twelve pearls, each gate being made of a single pearl. . . ."

And all this would be the heritage of the faithful. The craven, those who deserted Christ because of the present persecution, would never enter the New Jerusalem. On the contrary, they would "drink the wine of God's wrath . . . and be tortured with fire and brimstone before the eyes of the holy angels and the Lamb." But those who stood firm, behold they would be brought in triumph to the Holy City, and there they would know bliss forever-more! . . .[6]

Most historians of the church are wont to make small

---

[6] Porter, *Messages of the Apocalyptic Writers*, is an excellent little work on the book of Revelation.

mention of Revelation; they are inclined to dilate rather on the epistles and the Fourth Gospel. Yet no assumption is safer than that the Apocalypse is far more truly representative of popular Christian thought in the first century than are those other writings. A mystic interpretation of the beginning of all things may have interested the few philosophers in the movement; but the plain folk craved a vision of the end. They were sick of this life of sadness and labor, utterly tired of the world and its ways. They wanted to see it ended, to see the whole iniquitous scheme of things destroyed for all time to come. And, being common folk, they wanted it destroyed amid blood and thunder. The lust for vengeance was strong in their bones, for, though they had all been properly baptized, few had been profoundly converted. Their new faith had done much for them. It had given them a reason for living, and therewith a zest and recklessness and ecstasy. But it had not made over their hearts. They were still what they had always been: bitter because of the wounds life had inflicted, and hungry for a chance to strike back. It is hardly otherwise even in our day—which is why the Revelation of John is still so popular among the poor and the oppressed in Christendom. Of the three elements basic in Christian feeling—the ethical, the adventist, and the sacramental—the adventist has always been the most popular. Righteousness is difficult; piety is exacting; but frenzied hopefulness—that is easy. So in the first century, even more than in the twentieth, the same type of Christian reveled in visions of the Doom.

One pictures that ordinary Christian as he must have appeared in the first century: a slave perhaps, or a poor artisan, his face ravaged by disease, his unwashed body cloaked in rags. Since sunup he has been at his toil, and now, released at last by the coming of dark, he flees to the meeting place of his cult. It is in some crumbling house in the slums, or in some hovel squatting on mud haunches outside the city wall. Already there is a company gathered there; a throng of people quite like himself, ragged and hungry and ill. But he has no eyes for the wretchedness all about him; he does not smell the stench. This is his shrine, and these men and women are the elect of his God. So he crowds in among them, happy that in all this unfriendly world there is one place where he is known and called brother. And he listens intently to the one at the desk who reads aloud from a scroll. The reader stumbles over the words, for the tallow dip smokes, and the scroll is worn, and his knowledge of letters is faulty; but there is no complaint from the listeners. They like to receive the words thus, one by one, so as to hold them long on their tongues and draw from them all their meaning. Their eyes grow bright at the hearing of them; color flushes their cheeks.

> "Come! Gather for God's great banquet," the reader intones with passion: "and eat the bodies of kings and commanders and mighty men! . . . Gloat over her [the Whore], for God has avenged you upon her! . . . Praise the Lord! For smoke will go up from her forevermore! . . ."

And the listeners do gloat. "Praise the Lord!" they cry. "He is coming! . . . Aye, glory! He is coming, our Lord Jesus! . . ."

UT the Lord Jesus did not come. Year followed year till the first century closed, yet still he failed to return. And then the believers began reluctantly to admit that their frenzied hopes would have to be deferred. They still believed he would come, but they had to concede it might not happen for yet a while. In the meantime they saw they must gird themselves. The opponents they had once known, the Jews outside the cult and the Judaizers within it, were now no more. The Jewish nation had been destroyed, and the Jerusalem congregation, though still in existence, was powerless. But newer and more redoubtable enemies had arisen to take their places: the Paganizers who spread corruption from within, and the Romans who attacked from without. It was against these that the cult now had to protect itself. First there was need to build a stockade around the creed, for so many new teachings were creeping into Christianity that it was losing all distinctiveness. The figure of Jesus was becoming dim and wraithlike behind a fog of metaphysical speculation; his teachings were being drowned in a muddy stream of allegory. There was danger that the whole religion might become but another futile Mystery—one more tentacle of weed swaying in the flood of despair.

The danger had remained hidden so long as Christianity had continued to win converts only from the rabble of heathendom; but since it had begun to make inroads into the upper classes the peril had become flagrant. The learned converts were not content with the ill-ordered and still somewhat Jewish creed left them by the first generation of apostles. Just as Paul had tried to give coherence to the beliefs that had sprouted in Antioch, so did these later theologians try to give form to the religion that was now spreading throughout the empire. But Paul, despite all his Hellenism, had been at heart a Jew, whereas these new leaders were former Pagans. Many of them had come over to Christianity from that chaotic syncretism of philosophies and superstitions called Gnosticism, and they had brought much of their past with them.[7]

Gnosticism was not a settled belief so much as a frantic search. It was to the cultured of that day what the Mysteries were to the ignorant; indeed, it was largely an attempt to explain metaphysically those very myths which the populace took literally. Necessarily it was not intelligent but intellectual, and those who indulged in it were prone to have the overweening pride of intellectuals. They considered themselves the illuminati, for they believed they were possessed of a gnosis, a "knowledge," totally beyond the understanding of the horde. In this they were right: the gnosis was indeed incomprehensible to folk with no more than common sense in their heads. They were wrong only in thinking that this gnosis of theirs was valid. Actually it seems to have been no more than profoundly obfuscated superstition, and its only claim to validity must have lain in its putative hoariness. But that

[7] The character of Gnosticism is discussed in J. Watson, *The Philosophical Basis of Religion*, 1907, pp. 248-299, and at greater length in C. W. King, *The Gnostics and Their Remains*.

was claim enough for the wise ones of the Hellenistic age. They regarded the gnosis as something that had been revealed centuries earlier by a god or an angel, and had been handed down ever since by word of mouth in a very secret fraternity of "knowing ones." This gnosis consisted largely of abstruse and fantastic notions concerning the nature of the universe and the destiny of the soul, and, on the practical side, of certain mysterious spells and rites which would win immortality for those who could learn and practice them. Astrology, necromancy, occultism, and all the other sorry products of the impatient intellect were to be found luxuriating in Gnosticism.

One finds such things still being taught with flamboyant secretiveness by people who call themselves Rosicrucians or Speculative Freemasons or even Theosophists. Usually there is a queer gleam in the eyes of such people, a gleam which is said to be the light of esoteric wisdom, though it may really be the glint of paranoia. In our day, however, it requires a somewhat maimed intelligence to believe that some secret fraternity of illuminati is in possession of an ancient and mysterious "inner knowledge" as to the Beyond; whereas nineteen hundred years ago the best minds labored under that delusion. There was an incessant groping and ferreting about in the wilderness of mythology to find new evidences of the revelation. Most of the ancient oriental cults were ransacked for the treasure, and all of the ancient Greek philosophies. And usually it was found in them. Someone has said that a philosopher looking for the ultimate truth is like a blind man on a dark night searching in a subterranean cave for a black cat that is not there. Those Gnostics, however, were theologians rather than philosophers, and so—they found the cat!

It was but natural that in time this feverish quest should lead the searchers to Christianity. Here was one more oriental religion which talked of salvation and the World to Come: who knew but that this, too, might contain the treasure? So the Gnostics fell to with a will. They turned the Master's sayings inside out, seeking ever deeper and more startling secrets in them. With the help of allegory and cryptology, those crowbars of the intellect, they pried open every parable in the Gospels. And, as was their wont, they found that which they sought.

The Gnostics did not make very docile converts. On the contrary, almost the moment they received baptism they claimed to know more about Christ than the born Christians themselves. They scoffed at the tradition that he had been a real man living in Galilee. He had been and was still a god, they claimed, and at most he had temporarily taken on the *semblance* of a man. This he had done solely in order to impart to mankind the secrets of the Beyond, and, once this purpose was accomplished, he had ceased to manifest himself on earth. The secrets, they further declared, had been cherished by an inner circle within the church membership, and to this inner circle they themselves belonged. They were not unwilling to accept others into their circle, but only such as showed themselves fit for the great gnosis. These were initiated very solemnly into small esoteric groups within the local churches and then were permitted to take part in séances and discussions concerning which only faint rumors ever reached the outside world. Within the groups there were degrees and passwords and signs and emblems—all the trappings which fascinate the ungrown mind to this day.

Necessarily there was considerable strange teaching imparted in these circles. Gnosticism was largely of Persian origin, and on entering Christianity it at once tried to make the new religion compatible with the old Zoroastrian dualism. It declared that there were in reality two gods: first, the cruel Jehovah of the Old Testament, who exacted justice remorselessly; and, superseding him, the good Christ of the New Testament, who offered love. The Gnostics admitted no relationship between these deities save one of unremitting hostility, and they repudiated the Old Testament as vehemently as the narrowest Jews rejected the New. When Marcion, one of the insurgent teachers during this period, drew up a canon of sacred literature, he not only omitted the Jewish Scriptures, but even dared to suppress every Old Testament quotation which occurred in the Christian writings. Had these men had their way, the religion would have been torn completely from its roots and left to grow in the ooze of Pagan syncretism.

In addition to such strange teaching there was also no little bizarre conduct. Some of these illuminated souls claimed they were beyond the moral law. Christ had freed them of bondage to it, even as he had freed the ordinary Christian of bondage to the ritual law. So they behaved as they pleased, especially in their secret sessions. Many sought to peer into the Beyond by rutting in the Beneath, indulging in orgies which the horrified Church Fathers described with perhaps unnecessary fulsomeness and detail. And others of the "knowing ones" went to the opposite extreme, practicing the bitterest asceticism. There were many schools of Gnostic thought within the Church, and each had its own tradition to prove that it alone possessed the genuine esoteric teaching of Christ.

5

IT was largely the menace presented by the Gnostic incursion that betrayed the older leaders in the Church into seeking to define the faith. It drove them to resort to rules and formulæ in an effort to make orthodoxy—that is, the "correct teaching"—unmistakably plain. The recourse was fraught with great hazards, for a faith is prone to wither when exposed to the harsh glare of definitions. But either the Fathers did not realize this, or they were ready to take the risk. What alone gave them concern was the difficulty of directing the light. The one lamp which could provide the illumination was necessarily tradition, and its wick was as yet untrimmed. The literature of Christianity then in existence was exceedingly varied in character, and by a judicious selection from all these documents it was possible to prove almost anything. So the first move of the conservers was to decide just which writings were authoritative and which were not. They were unanimous, of course, in declaring the Gospels of Mark, Matthew, Luke, and John to be holy, for these contained the best refutations of the Gnostic claim that Jesus

had been but a phantom. And, since these Gospels referred repeatedly to the ancient Jewish prophecies, the orthodox had to admit that also the Old Testament was holy. The writings of Paul had already become widely known and highly respected in the Church, as had also the book of Acts; so these too were pronounced fit to be read in the churches. But as to the epistles of various other early missionaries, and the apocalypse called the Revelation of John, there was considerable dispute. Revelation was especially opposed by some of the leaders, for reasons which we can well imagine. Only its intense popularity among the plain folk seems to have secured its eventual inclusion in the canon. On the other hand certain writings which are now almost completely forgotten— for instance the *Epistle of Barnabas,* the *Shepherd of Hermas,* and the *Acts of Paul and Thecla*—were for a long while ranked as Scripture and included in the Church ritual. Not until two hundred years later was the present make-up of the New Testament definitely established.

Even then modifications were still made, though perforce of a minor nature. The autograph originals have long been lost; nor do the first copies of the scrolls exist any more. But what early manuscripts do exist give evidence that the texts suffered considerable tampering. For instance, as late as the fourth century some scribe interpolated a proof of the doctrine of the Trinity in the First Epistle of John. No doubt in piety, but nevertheless without warrant, he neatly inserted the words: "There are three that bear witness in heaven: the Father, the Word, and the Holy Spirit; and these three are one."

This is by no means the only interpolation that has been

discovered. To cite another instance, our earliest manuscripts do not include what is perhaps the most dramatic story in the New Testament, that of the adulteress whom Jesus saved from death by declaring to her judges: "Let him among you who is without sin cast the first stone at her." Originally the story may have been told of some tolerant Greek philosopher—it certainly reflects a latitudinarianism far more Greek than Hebraic—but in a later day certain Christians began to tell it of their own Master. Apparently some time had to elapse, however, before the story could become part of the Gospel record. We find it as a marginal note in some of the later manuscripts, or as an appended paragraph at the end of Luke and John. Finally it was inserted in the body of the Fourth Gospel, and there alone it remains to this day. . . .

If such changes could be made as late as the fourth century, who can tell how many more may have been made in earlier days?

But despite the continued disputes as to the contents of the New Testament, and the modifications which crept into the texts, the tradition became relatively fixed by the middle of the second century. Even then, however, dissension did not cease, for the tradition thus circumscribed was capable of various interpretations. The Scriptures in which the tradition was embodied had been written in response to different needs, and were consequently discrepant. Each was in effect a concession to pressing circumstances, and the congregations in accepting them all as their final authority were trying to build a creed on a

sandy mound of compromises. It was trying to pla-
cate the Pagans by admitting that the Son was also God,
and at the same time it was holding fast to the Jewish
belief that the Father alone was God. The position was
untenable logically and therefore had to be bolstered theo-
logically. As a result, heresies—that is, disagreements—
were unavoidable.

Theology may be none too unfairly defined as the science of reinterpreting words so that they can be made
to mean what they do not really say. By its very nature
it is an inexact science, and therefore cannot but breed
differences. Heresies succeeded each other during the
second and third and fourth centuries with the regularity
of plagues, and spread no less virulently. On the one
hand there were the Marcionites and the Gnostic groups,
some of whom insisted that the Son and the Father were
two distinct Beings. On the other hand there were the
tentatively orthodox who maintained that the Godhead
was one. These, however, were of two different and bitterly hostile schools: the Adoptionists, who said that God
had merely adopted Jesus as His divine Son; and the
Modalists, who argued that Jesus was really God Himself
in a fleeting earthly manifestation. As Noetus, a typical
Modalist, phrased it: "Christ was the Father Himself, and
the Father Himself was born and suffered and died."

A generation or two later a new complication entered
into the problem. Not merely the Father and the Son had
to be allocated their places then, but also the Spirit, the
Holy Ghost. This third element had played a conspicuous
part in the shadow-world of Christian thought from the
very beginning of the movement, and finally certain theo-

logians undertook to find out just where it belonged. Some
among them, influenced no doubt by the many Pagan religions which worshiped trinities, went so far as to say that
Father, Son, and Holy Ghost were three distinct divine en-
tities. But others, for example the Sabellianists, recoiling
from such tacit polytheism, insisted that all three were
merely manifestations of one God. The peasant exhorter
who died on a cross in Jerusalem would have stared in
dismay had these problems been posed to him. Even Paul
might have quailed. Yet in the second century they were
a source of unending strife among the theologians.

We live in so different an intellectual climate, that
it is not easy for us to be just to those theologians. Their
aim—that of defining how God is related to Himself—
seems so presumptuous, and their method—that of building towers of reason on a foundation of unreasoned faith
—seems intellectually so grotesque, that we are moved to
regard them with contempt. Yet their impulse was admirable. They wanted to force order into the confusion
of superstitions accepted by the mass; they hungered to
make rational the abysmal irrationalities inherited from
the past. They could not be content with the belief that
God was just beyond the horizon; they had to leave their
valley of faith and track Him down. It was not that their
credulity was limited, but that their curiosity was vast.
They wanted to know as well as believe, and, if they
could not escape on the wings of mysticism and peer into
the Beyond from the skies, they would at least try to
burrow their way out of their valley with the blunt shovels
of metaphysics. That they only succeeded in burying
themselves in deeper and darker confusion is a reflection

on their method, not on their motive. Fundamentally they were moved by the passion for truth, that same passion which has won for us all we know. The Quantum Theory may be nearer the truth than the doctrine of Consubstantiality, ether may be a less inadequate hypostasis than the Holy Ghost; but all alike are the findings of one search. The theologians of the second century, like the physicists of the twentieth, were intent on plumbing the infinite—a fruitless endeavor, vain by its very nature, yet precious and brave nonetheless.[8]

6

THESE same exigencies which led to the formulation of a Christian creed led also to the establishment of a hierarchy. As we have already seen, in the beginning there was almost no organization whatsoever among the Christians. They had been so sure then that Jesus would return in a moment that they had seen no reason for establishing offices and making laws. Even Paul—who is often spoken of, and quite mistakenly, as the organizer of the Church—had seen no need for an ecclesiasticism. He had on occasion appointed leaders over congregations, but when writing

[8] A fuller and far more sympathetic treatment of Church theology is to be found in any one of a number of excellent histories. G. P. Fisher, *History of Christian Doctrine,* is especially recommended. F. Loof, *Leitfaden zum Studium der Dogmengeschichte,* and Harnack, *History of Dogma,* 7 vols., are the classic works on the subject.

his epistles he had always addressed them to the congregations themselves, never to those leaders. In his day
the churches had still been small brotherhoods in which
anyone gifted with the Spirit had had the right to rise
up and declaim.

But by the end of the first century so anarchic an
arrangement was no longer tolerable. The congregations
had grown from tiny brotherhoods to loose and heterogeneous societies, and there were no longer great apostles
like Paul to whom to appeal when dissensions arose. So
the second century saw the gradual establishment of a
priesthood. The development was as ominous as it was
inevitable. Created so to speak to "bank" the fire of
Christian faith, the priesthood threatened after a time
to extinguish that fire altogether. Yet had not some form
of organization developed, the fire might have gone out
of itself immediately. Some may say that that would
have been a blessing to mankind, but the point would
be difficult to prove. In any case, whether for good or ill
—and who save God and the dogmatists on either side
is in a position to pontificate on that issue?—the development did occur. Bit by bit the control of the churches
began to drift into the hands of local boards of overseers,
or *episcopoi,* "bishops." These boards in turn often came
to be dominated by single individuals who relegated their
fellow-bishops to the position of *presbuteroi,* or "elders."
Where the congregational affairs were sufficiently extensive, a third order of officials was created—that of the
diakonoi, or "deacons." The whole development was not
consciously planned, but grew of itself in response to
immediate needs. As a consequence there was no uniformity of government in the churches, some few remain-

ing democratic societies, others yielding to rule by presbyters, and still others accepting monarchical control.[9]

Of the three forms the monarchical became in time the
most popular, especially in the West. There was as yet
no plethora of able men in the movement, and it was
not difficult for superior individuals to get control of the
various churches. And once in control they were not
easily dislodged. To brand them usurpers would hardly
be fair. Some of the men who became bishops may well
have been careerists, but most of them were unmistakably
sincere. If they took more and more power into their
hands, forcing their fellow-Christians into religious subservience, it was not out of conscious villainy but pure zeal
for Christ. Perhaps an innate will-to-power had no little
to do with their encroachments; but they would not have
admitted this. They would have insisted it was solely
for the greater glory of God that they made themselves
masters of the churches. Indeed it soon became part of
their faith that God himself had ordained them the masters. For example, Ignatius, who became bishop of Antioch in the middle of the second century, was able right
solemnly to declare:

". . . Your Bishop presides in the place of God.
. . . Without your bishop you should do nothing.
You should follow your bishop even as Jesus Christ
followed the Father. . . ."

[9] The problem of the development of the ministry is one of the most
involved and perplexing in church history. Interest in it is more than
academic because of the dispute which still goes on between certain
denominations as to the primacy of the congregational or presbyterian
or episcopalian form of government. Perhaps the best work on the subject is Harnack's *Constitution and Law of the Church in the First Two
Centuries*.

With no one in a position to challenge such declarations, it was not long before certain of the bishops began to assume sway not only over single congregations, but over all the congregations in a city, and later over all in a province. Finally one of them claimed sovereignty over all the congregations in the world. Even in the twentieth century his successor living in Rome is still asserting that claim.

At first the leaders were literally no more than overseers, controlling the finances, settling disputes, and in a general way keeping peace in the churches. But as time went on they began to assume other and more significant duties. The regular services had ceased to consist simply of extempore prophesying and shouting with "tongues." Fervor had simmered down to piety, and the vaporings of spontaneous devotion had condensed into a viscous liturgy. The illiterate could no longer lead in the services, for now there were involved prayers to recite and creeds to repeat and long passages from the Scriptures to be read. In addition, the sacramental rites had become complicated, requiring specialized knowledge for their proper administration. And thus it came about that the officials, being for the most part better educated than the rank and file, became priests as well as overseers. Beginning by taking the lead in the services, they ended by taking complete charge of them.

It was a usurpation, but one which could not be forestalled. Once the ritual was allowed to become elaborate, professionalism was unavoidable; and once professionalism was allowed to enter in, the ritual had to become even more elaborate. Before long a caste distinction began to be drawn between the *kleros,* the clergy, and the *laikos,* the laity. In earlier days a Christian had needed only to be moved by the Spirit in order to have the right to declaim in church; but now he had to be ordained first. Once ordained, he became a person apart from his fellow-men, possessing a claim not alone on the ear of the Lord but also on the support of the congregation. Perhaps he still engaged in some worldly pursuit, for the free-will offerings of food and money were not always sufficient for his needs. But before long he began to demand more than such offerings, going so far as to insist that the lay-men ought to pay a fixed tax to the Church of one-tenth of their earnings. The claim was based on good Old Testa-ment precedent, for it had been the ancient law among the Jews to give tithes to the Temple in Jerusalem. The fact that Jesus had attacked the Temple system, driving the sacerdotal hirelings out of the courtyard and prophesying the fall of the shrine, was necessarily forgotten. All that was remembered was that Jesus had praised the widow who gave her mite to the priests. . . .

It was but natural that the clergy, being now considered above the laity in character, should soon become distin-guished also in appearance. It seemed only proper that the priests in the Church should wear peculiar costume, for that was an eccentricity affected by the Pagan priests, and seemed to go with sanctity. Appropriately enough, it was ancient costume, for the Christian clergy, like every other higher caste, knew well the protective value of the antique. Just as army aviators on parade still wear spurred riding-boots, so the priests, though dwelling in walled cities, still affected the robes of desert wanderers. The elaborate wardrobe of the Catholic clergy of our day, with its profusion of mitres and cassocks and copes and surplices and pallia and stoles and chasubles and dalmatics, each to be donned and doffed in fixed order and with a punctilio of genuflexion and prayer—this was still to come. But it was already on its way, and there was none to stay the advance. The laymen, it must be realized, were far from averse to this growing sacerdotalism; on the contrary, they favored it even more, perhaps, than did the clergy. The rank and file in the Church were lowly folk: ignorant, credulous, and full of fear. It came as a vast relief to them to know that there were men greater than themselves to care for their poor souls. And the wider they could make the gulf between those men and themselves, the vaster was their relief. It added to their confidence if their priests were aloof and surrounded with mystery. Their fear became awe then, and they were happy.

One pictures a Christian service as it may have been conducted in Antioch or Alexandria in the second and third centuries. The church is a bare, candlelighted hall furnished with no more than two tables, a chair, and some benches on a dais against the eastern wall. One of the tables bears the bread and wine for the Lord's Supper, and the other is laden with the offerings of food and money brought by the faithful for the support of the clergy and the poor. In the chair, which is already coming to be called the "throne," reclines the bishop; on the benches sit the lesser priests. The congregation stands below on the earthen floor, the men on one side and the women on the other. There are inscriptions on the walls, texts from the Gospels and the Prophets; but these are of course without meaning to the illiterate worshipers. Nowhere are there pictures or idols or stained glass to gladden their eyes. Yet the people stand entranced, their hearts weak with eagerness. The first part of the service, the psalm singing and Scripture reading, they endure almost with impatience. What they await is the Communion, for it is for this that the faithful have gathered.

There is a pause and a shuffle of reluctant feet as the unworthy are commanded by the deacons to leave the sanctuary. Only the confessed Christians are permitted to remain for the Eucharist; the rest, the children and the newly converted who have not yet been baptized, must depart. (Perhaps that is why the sacrament came to be called the Mass: it opened with the *missa,* the "dismissal," of the uninitiated.) For the Lord's Supper, which in the old Jerusalem congregation had been but a common meal, is now counted a mystic and secret rite. The bread and the wine are said to be the "medicine of immortality," for Christ is known to be present in them. Not symbolically, but quite physically is he believed to be present in them, and therefore whoever consumes the magic food is believed to have a fragment of Christ in his very vitals. Little wonder then that the sacrament is reserved for the faithful alone.

The bishop takes his stand at the table, and, holding aloft the bread and the wine, proceeds very solemnly to offer thanks to the Father and the Son and the Holy Ghost. This thanksgiving is the *eucharistia* proper, and the candle flames cast eerie shadows over the thick bearded lips that intone the sacred words. The worshipers stand silent, their eyes fastened on the napkin and the cup. They crowd forward to the table, impatient for the moment when they can take the magic elements into their mouths. Finally the prayer is ended, and the deacons, fearful lest a crumb of the loaf or a drop of the wine should fall to the ground and cause hurt to the body of their god, hold the cup and the bread very firmly as they offer them to the worshipers. These sip from the goblet and either eat the bread there and then or else save it to share with a sick relative at home. And then the whole service is over. The believers salute each other with the kiss of brotherly love, and depart to their hovels in glory. They are happy now, happy and full of courage, for they have become invested with divinity. The taste of the sacred "medicine" is still on their lips; they can actually feel Christ in their vitals. So their tread is firm as they leave the church, their heads are lifted high. For are they not gods at that moment? [10]

Significantly, there were few in the Church who could see how far was the cry from the tumultuous gatherings of the first Brethren to such a service of fixed ritual and magic. The change had come about so stealthily that to all ap-

[10] Justin Martyr, *First Apology*, ch. 65, and Tertullian, *De Corona*, iii, furnish what little source material we have for a description of the service in this early period. For other aspects of the life of the believers, see Dobschütz, *Christian Life in the Primitive Church*, Eng. tr., 1904.

pearances it had never occurred. There was but one note-worthy attempt to turn back the clock, and that one was suppressed with no great difficulty. A certain convert named Montanus started a frenetic movement in Asia Minor to make the Spirit once more dominant in the cult. According to the records that have come down to us, the man went up and down the countryside, accompanied by two ecstatic females, and preached a return to the old simplicity of faith and austerity of life.[11]

But by then, the latter half of the second century, the process of organization had already advanced too far to be broken down. Montanism thrived for a time, spreading from Asia Minor as far as Carthage—where it won over the pugnacious Tertullian—and even to Rome. But then it fell victim to the very plague which it had set out to destroy. Expelled from the established Church, it developed an establishment of its own. It acquired a theology, a priesthood, and a treasury, and became but a diminutive caricature of its parent. It failed dismally of its first high purpose, and sacerdotalism waxed unflaggingly in the Church. The organization grew more intricate year by year, enmeshing the believers so that none could turn about and strike. By the beginning of the third century, Cyprian, bishop of Carthage, could calmly declare:

> "He who is not in the Church is not a Christian. . . . He can no longer have God for his Father who has not the Church for his mother. . . . There is no salvation outside the Church. . . ."

[11] See H. B. Swete, *The Holy Spirit in the Ancient Church*, ch. 4.

S has already been said, dogma and ritual were walls thrown up to shield the flame of Christian faith, and, if they shut off the clear air which would have made the flame burn brighter, they also shut off the winds which might have blown it out. And such winds did come during the second and third centuries. They were rare and fleeting at first, taking the form of local attacks and sporadic persecutions. But as the years passed and the growth of the Church went on unchecked, the assaults on the part of the government became more intense and widespread. Their occurrence was almost an anomaly, for religious toleration had always been part of the established policy of Rome. As Gibbon puts it with a characteristic touch of malice: "The various modes of worship which prevailed in the Roman world were all considered by the people as equally true, by the philosophers as equally false, and by the magistrates as equally useful." But an exception was made of Christianity, and for quite obvious reasons.

In the first place, times had changed. The empire was tottering, and war, dissension, and disease were devastating the earth. The old security was gone, and day by day the vast structure built by willfulness and cunning was seen to be crumbling away. The emperors were either soldiers of fortune who had usurped the throne, or else their degenerate heirs; and intrigue, sedition, and murder

marked every reign. The Barbarians were already numerous within the empire, supplanting the old Roman stock
in the army, the fields, and the mines. And myriads more
of them were pressing against the sagging frontiers, hungry for a chance to break in. Deforestation and neglect
had allowed the swamp lands to spread in the realm, providing new breeding places for malarial insects. The
natives, enervated by the disease, deserted their farms.
They left their plows to rust in the weed-choked furrows
and crawled off to the cities. There, herded in slums, they
lingered in fevered misery, begging, stealing, and rioting.
Even the elements seemed affected, for violent changes in
climate kept recurring with inexplicable suddenness.

And when the Romans asked themselves why all these
evils were come to them, they could find but one answer
—Christianity! Like Communism in the twentieth century,
the new religion was made the bugaboo and the scapegoat
of the age. It still had only a few adherents, yet it seemed
to be everywhere. There was a frowardness about it, a
loud insurgency, which made it seem a thousandfold its
size. (The analogy with Communism is disconcertingly
close.) Perhaps the mother-element in it, the ineradicable
Jewish element, lent it that obtrusiveness. The Church,
small, insecure, poverty-stricken, and inglorious, yet seemed
to fill the whole universe. And the Romans, beholding
it, became furious. They forgot that there had been disease and distress before this religion ever came into being;
they could not see that the seeds of the present decay had
been sown long centuries before. Dazed by their many
woes, it seemed to them that previously all had been
sunny on earth, and that only today had the skies gone

dark. And, since the emergence of Christianity had synchronized with that change, the new religion seemed palpably to blame for it.

The reasoning was false; but, like much false reasoning, it was plausible. It was easy to believe that the Christians were responsible for the night that had crept over the world, for they were all a queer and suspicious lot. They were still for the most part orientals, which alone made them unsavory to the Romans. Far worse, they were all flagrantly unpatriotic. They would not serve in the army even under duress, saying that their Lord forbade them to shed blood. Nor would they offer sacrifices to the image of the emperor, declaring that their faith would not tolerate idolatry. Intolerance seemed to be the keynote of the new religion. Its adherents had none of that generosity of belief which made the Pagans take unto themselves new deities as the desert men took new wives. Their universe could contain but one god, and every other they deemed an abomination. They refused absolutely to take part in the Pagan holidays, or attend the gladiatorial games which had become part of the Pagan ritual; indeed, they were opposed to everything that the solid Romans counted right and proper. They had as yet no contempt for women or slaves, nor hatred for criminals and foreigners. They spurned the pleasures of the flesh, refusing to wear fine raiment, or loll about in the baths, or consort with the voluptuaries. Many of them would not cohabit even with their own wives! Only with the greatest difficulty could Rome secure the six vestal virgins it needed for its ancient rites, and, even when these were secured, there were no oaths or threats powerful enough to keep them chaste for long. Yet the Church contained its hundreds of virgins, some of them so strong of will that they could actually share their beds with priests without succumbing! [12]

And the worst of it was that the Christians were unashamed of their queernesses. The Jews, who were devoted to a religion which seemed no less detestable to the average Roman, were at least silent. Having lost their homeland and been reduced to servile nomadism, they had ceased to seek proselytes and were content merely to be left alone. But the Christians were aggressive and obstreperous. They sought to spread their "pestilential superstition," as Tacitus called it, by every conceivable means. Slaves terrified their little charges with its dark threats, or excited their mistresses with its sweet promises; wives sulked and stormed till their husbands joined the faith. And the Pagans, panicky at the sight of the rising tide, lost their heads. They too became intolerant. They began to blame the Christians for everything. As Tertullian complained:

> "If the Tiber rises as high as the city walls, if the Nile fails to flood the fields, if the heavens give no rain, if there is an earthquake, a famine, or a pestilence, straightway the cry is, 'The Christians to the lions.' "

Tertullian was inclined to be extravagant in his expressions—he was one of the most vociferous Christians of the second century—but there was ample justification for

[12] Cyprian, *Epist. 4*, cited in Gibbon, ch. 15. For the general problems involved, see Uhlhorn, *Conflict of Christianity with Heathenism*, and Hardy, *Christianity and the Roman Government*.

his complaint. *Christiani ad leones!* was indeed becoming the favorite cry of the Pagan rabble. Every imaginable scandal was imputed to the Christians: that they were atheists, and worshiped an ass, and practiced lewd abominations, and ate human flesh.[13]

To a degree the Christian leaders were themselves to blame for these slanders, for in their intestine squabbles over the nature of the Godhead they did not hesitate to accuse each other of the vilest depravity and crime. (Again the Communist parallel is striking.) But even had they been less uncircumspect, the slanders would have arisen nonetheless. The Pagans *wished* to believe that the Christians were debauched and despicable, and the wish easily spawned good evidence.

Just how intensely the Christians were persecuted has long been a matter of dispute among historians. Actually there was never a general massacre, and what attacks did occur were never thorough or sustained. The first persecution occurred in the reign of Nero, somewhen between 64 and 68 A.D.; but this was brief and confined to the capital. In the year 95 there seems to have been a more widespread attack—the book of Revelation may be a reflection of it—but this, too, was brief. Then came a respite lasting some eighty years. Here and there overzealous Christians like Ignatius of Antioch went out of their way to provoke the authorities; or a governor, at his

[13] Monsignor Louis Duchesne, *Early History of the Christian Church*, Eng. tr. 1926, Vol. I, p. 146. This three-volume work, written by a great Catholic scholar, is invaluable to the student.

wits' end because of the unrest in his province, ordered that all churches be closed. But save for such local disturbances all was quiet.

Under the Emperor Marcus Aurelius there seems to have been a more or less concerted effort at persecution, but it was directed against all the new cults, and not specifically against Christianity. Aurelius was one of the sagest rulers in history, learned, and ordinarily kind and patient; but he could not abide the cult-followers. Their fervor disturbed his Stoic calm, and their credulity insulted his reason. He considered them a canker in the realm, for they "insinuated the superstitious fear of the deity into men's excitable minds." But his command that they be searched out was obeyed only in a few provinces, and even in these with slight diligence; and as soon as he died, the persecution ceased almost entirely.

His successor, the debauched and imbecile Commodus, had a mistress who was secretly a Christian, and her hold over the wretch seems to have won the Church considerable advantage.[14] But even had no such influence been exerted on him, Commodus would probably have let the Christians alone. Paradoxically, only the best rulers, the men of greatest zeal for the empire, ever attempted to crush the Church. Degenerates like Commodus, Caracalla, and Heliogabalus, who descended to unimaginable depths of depravity, never thought to molest the Christians; nor did the freebooter emperors of the type of Philip the Arabian. But earnest, well-meaning rulers

[14] See Victor Duruy's *History of Rome,* Eng tr. 1883-6, Vol. VI, p. 460. This author is inclined to a sharp Gallic skepticism, but his documentation is thorough. His work is an excellent antidote if one has imbibed too freely of orthodox history.

like Decius and Diocletian, exerted all their might to root out the new religion. Such men could see that Christianity was a menace to the empire, crumbling the enormous structure as a tree crumbles the rock out of which it grows. So they issued edicts commanding its suppression, meting out imprisonment and torture and exile and death to those who would not abjure the faith. They acted much as do the rulers of modern nations when they come across "conscientious objectors" in time of war. Rome was struggling for its very life, and its panic-stricken patriots could not possibly be tolerant.

The Decian persecution, the first of any really widespread severity, began in 250, and was terminated by the death of the emperor a year later. It was followed by a half-century of quiet during which the Church, invigorated by the blood of its own martyrs, spread as never before. Then came the last and most furious attack: that instituted by Diocletian. Even this, however, was not nearly so extensive as the martyrologies would indicate. Gibbon, whose treatment of Church history in his *Decline and Fall of the Roman Empire* is now known to be surpassingly fair in fact if not always favorable in interpretation, calculates that during the ten years of the persecution initiated by Diocletian, hardly two thousand Christians could have been put to death. Indeed, it is Gibbon's estimate that during all three centuries at the mercy of Paganism, not so many Christians were killed as there were Protestants massacred in the Netherlands alone during a single reign in the sixteenth century!

Numbers, however, are of little significance when counting the toll of persecution. Relatively few Christians may have been tortured, and fewer still put to death; but all must have suffered. If profession of the faith did not always mean imprisonment and violence, it did at least bring in its train incessant fear. The believers became a hunted pack and developed all the traits characteristic of those who are hunted. For one thing they became bitter, cherishing in their hearts a venomous hate of the Pagans which was as human as it was un-Nazarene. For instance, Tertullian, who lived through the worst of the earlier persecutions, allowed himself to write:

> "You who are fond of spectacles, prepare now for the greatest spectacle of all: the last and eternal judgment of the universe. How shall I revel, how laugh, how rejoice, how exult, when I behold so many proud monarchs and fancied gods groaning in the lowest abyss of darkness; so many magistrates who persecuted the name of the Lord, liquefying in fiercer fires than were ever kindled against the Christians; so many learned philosophers scorching with their deluded scholars in the red-hot flames; so many famous poets quaking before the tribunal not of Minos but of Christ——"

and so on and on and on.

But there were other and more praiseworthy traits engendered by the persecutions. The churches became brotherhoods once more, and the Christians—even the theologians among them—were drawn together in the fellowship of common suffering. A spirit of holy heroism took hold of the believers, moving them to dauntlessness and fortitude. At times, of course, this heroism was carried to extremes. We read of governors who sought to evade the edicts of persecution, but who were coerced into doing their duty by the Christians themselves. The more fanatical believers actually sought out martyrdom, thrusting themselves before the authorities with provoking cries and demonstrations. (Again one cannot resist drawing the Communist analogy.) Like that Ignatius of Antioch who has already been mentioned, they thought of themselves as the "wheat of God" longing to be "ground by the teeth of wild beasts into the pure bread of God." Martyrdom was regarded as a "second baptism" which assured one of a secure passage to Heaven. It became pathetically attractive; for he who went to prison for the faith was looked on as a hero all the rest of his life, and he who died for it was declared a saint. A whole literature arose in eulogy of the martyrs, and the panegyrics often verged on blasphemy. The saner leaders frowned on this suicidal fanaticism, but their adjurations were swept aside. Evidently there was a deep streak of masochism in many of the Christians, especially in the lowliest among them, who were helots inured to suffering. They seem to have taken a perverse pleasure in pain.

But the pathological cases serve only to bring out in greater relief the many more instances of genuine heroism. There is, for example, the tale of old Bishop Polycarp who was put to death in Smyrna in the year 167. He had tried hard to escape arrest, but when finally tracked down he had gone to his fate without a murmur. Commanded to cry, "Away with the godless!" he had obeyed with sorrowful earnestness, for to him the godless were not his own folk but the Pagans. But when ordered to go on and curse Christ, he had quietly replied: "Six and eighty years have I served him, and he has done me naught save good. How then can I curse my Lord and Savior?" Whereupon he was sentenced to die. Wood was gathered from the shops and the baths and piled in an open square, and the white-haired old man was made to mount the heap. But when they sought to fasten him to the stake, he said: "Nay, leave me thus. He who has strengthened me to encounter the flames will give me the power also to stand firm at the stake!" And thus, erect and unshaken to the last moment, the old man went to his death.

Many Christians died as did Polycarp, and their heroism had its effect. The whole tone of Christian life was lifted: it became nobler, purer, more sure of itself. Far from crushing the Church, the persecutions served only to give it new vigor. They were, as Tertullian phrased it, "a fan which cleanses the Lord's threshing-floor." The believers now believed all the more fervently because their belief had cost them sacrifice. To quote Tertullian once more:

> "We conquer in dying; we go forth triumphant at the very moment when we seem subdued. . . . The oftener we are mown down, the more do we grow in number. The blood of Christians is the seed of the Church!"

And thus did it come about that the Church emerged the victor. It had to be. The empire was rotted at the core and possessed neither the strength nor the will to go on with the struggle. It was torn by rival claimants to the throne, drained of its resources by wasteful landlords, sapped of its vigor by disease and despair. The Church, on the other hand, was young and full of zeal. It too had its dissensions, but in the face of hostility it presented a united front. It had achieved form and substance, calling itself "Catholic"—that is, "universal." It still lacked centralization and wealth; but it possessed faith, which was far more essential. Christianity believed in itself and its future, and all the swords ever forged could not pierce such armor. When, early in the fourth century, the final desperate thrust glanced off the Christian body, the wearied government let its sword arm fall and disgustedly surrendered.[15]

8

IOCLETIAN abdicated in 305, dividing the realm between four co-emperors, all of whom continued to harry the Christians. Churches were raided, copies of the Holy Writ were burnt, and whole congregations were arrested and sent away to slave in the mines. But it was of no avail. As fast as old meeting places were closed, new ones arose. The slave colonies became thriving centers of the movement, boasting their own bishops and elders, and holding regular services.

Finally the foremost of the imperators, Galerius, began

[15] For a detailed account of the persecutions see H. B. Workman, *Persecution in the Early Church.*

to weaken. He was afflicted with some loathsome disease which he could not shake off no matter how frantically he sacrificed to the gods of his fathers. As a last resort, therefore, he decided to call in the aid of the Christians. He still counted them detestable and dangerous to the realm, but, like most men in that credulous age, he was by no means certain that they were lacking supernatural powers. Accordingly in the year 311 he issued an edict permitting the "deluded Christians . . . freely to profess their private opinions, and to assemble in their conventicles without fear or molestation"—but with the understanding that out of gratitude for this "indulgence" they should "offer up their prayers to the deity whom they adore, for our safety and well-being . . . !" The belated measure did not save him, however. Possibly the Christians refused to pray for him, or were given too little time, for within a few days of the publication of the edict, Galerius, far from improving, grew worse and died.

At once a new struggle for the mastery of the empire began to spread misery throughout the realm; but now the Church was no longer without protection. Of the four contestants for the throne, two almost at once showed favor to the Christians. Clearly their motive was political, for they were both intrenched in the West, and were intent on undermining the position of their rivals in the East, where the population was now very largely Christian. In the year 313 these two generals, Constantine and Licinius, issued an edict which not merely tolerated Christianity, but officially established it on an equal footing with Paganism. The gratitude of the Christians knew no bounds, and the heavens resounded with fervid prayers in behalf of their protectors. No doubt they did more than pray; we may well believe that they aided Constantine and his ally by spying and sedition. And the two generals emerged victorious. One of their opponents, Maximinus, realizing at the eleventh hour that he had erred in his policy, turned on the Pagan priests who had been his counselors until then, ordered them executed, and began favoring the Christians. But, as with Galerius, the change came too late. Maximinus was defeated and put to death, and the empire was left to Constantine and Licinius.

Constantine was a tall, handsome youth, illiterate but intelligent, superstitious yet amazingly shrewd.[16] Born the son of a Roman general and a Serbian tavernkeeper's daughter, he had suffered hostility and contempt from childhood, and the will to triumph was the one passion in his being. It is clear that from the outset the favor he showed the Christians was prompted by expediency rather than conviction. He very early adopted as his symbol the first two letters of the name of Christ—which in monogram (☧) resembled a cross—stamping the sign on the shields and helmets of his soldiers, and embroidering it on his banner. It was a peculiarly ambiguous symbol, for the cross in its various forms was regarded as sacred not alone in the Church but also in many of the Pagan cults. Psychologists, especially those who belong to the Freudian school,

---

[16] The principal source on the life of Constantine is the eulogistic biography by his sycophantic contemporary, *Bishop Eusebius*. A readable modern work is G. P. Baker, *Constantine the Great and the Christian Revolution*, N. Y., 1931.

are convinced that the cross is a conventionalized erotic symbol. Certain anthropologists, on the other hand, think it a representation of the fire-making drill. Either origin would account for the universality of the symbol. We find it among the Hindus, the Buddhists, the Gauls, the Etruscans, the Egyptians, the Babylonians, the Persians, and even the American Indians. Assyrian carvings of the ninth century B.C. show the kings wearing equilateral crosses around their necks precisely like those now worn by Catholic bishops. The very monogram ⚹ is to be seen on Greek coins of the third century B.C., and on the coins of the emperor Decius, who was one of the bitterest persecutors of the Christians. So Constantine was safe in adopting the cross as his symbol. The act delighted the Christians and did not antagonize the Pagans.[17]

Constantine was eager to find favor with the Christians because he realized their power. He saw that the Church was the one cohesive force left in the empire. The ancient religion of Rome was little more than a façade maintained by a few blustering but impotent old senators. Of the philosophies the most popular now was Neo-Platonism, a dilettante's stew of theosophy and astrology spiced with metaphysics. Of the many old Mysteries still in existence, only Mithraism showed signs of continued virility; but it was inherently incapable of becoming the universal faith because its membership was restricted to males. A new

[17] On the origin and popularity of the cross see W. W. Blake, *The Cross, Ancient and Modern,* and Thomas Inman, *Ancient Pagan and Modern Christian Symbolism.* The layman will find the essentials of the subject in Philip F. Waterman, *Story of Superstition,* pp. 162-173. On Constantine's use of the symbol see Duruy, *History of Rome,* Vol. VII, pp. 475ff.

religion, Manicheism, had but recently made its way into the empire, a curious syncretism of Christianity and Zoroastrianism which had originally been preached in Persia by a prophet who was crucified for his heretical teachings; but this was hardly rooted as yet.

The one flourishing religion was unmistakably Christianity. It had absorbed much from the other religions of the day, yet it had managed to retain a character of its own. It was more popular in the eastern half of the empire, but was now spreading rapidly also in the West. At one time uncompromisingly pacifist, it had since yielded the point and had begun to accommodate itself to a military order. Originally a faith cherished by the proletariat, it had since crept up out of the slums and invaded the palaces and schools. In certain circles it had become almost fashionable, much as Communism has become fashionable in certain upper-class circles to-day. Christianity had acquired a curious appeal to the more earnest and romantic in the patrician class. It was exotic and mysterious and exciting; it promised bliss in the world to come, and afforded adventure here and now. The wily Constantine saw that in favoring the Church he was winning the sympathy not alone of a large element of the populace, but also of part of the wealthy class.

Nor was this all. The Christians were not merely numerous: to boot they seemed united. Despite that they were scattered far and wide, they were all brethren. Their bishops were continually communicating with each other, and a kindness done to a congregation in Gaul was known within a few weeks as far as Africa and Greece. The Church was veritably "an empire within the Empire," and, because it preached the virtue of loyalty and obedience, it gave promise of being enormously useful if shrewdly employed. Young Constantine probably listened without a smile when he was assured by the devout Lactantius that the establishment of Christianity would restore all the glories of the pristine age. War and dissension would cease, this eloquent Christian prophesied, for would not all men be joined in the fellowship of the Church? And how could there be left any impure desire or selfish passion, since all men would be restrained by the knowledge of the Gospel? The magistrates would have to sheathe the sword of justice, for thenceforth there would be naught on earth save piety, equity, temperance, truth, and all-pervading love. . . . Thus did the good preacher assure the ambitious young ruler, and the latter was apparently impressed.

The sardonic Gibbon, writing almost fifteen hundred years later, could not refrain from remarking that Lactantius was "much more perspicuous and positive than it becomes a discreet prophet." But Constantine, having no such retrospect to teach him better, may well have been moved by the old rhetorician's brave speech. At any rate, he made it increasingly clear as the years passed that his sympathies were all with the Church. He still refused to proclaim himself a Christian, or renounce the ancient Pagan title of Pontifex Maximus. He even allowed his coinage to bear Pagan symbols. But otherwise he showed himself unmistakably a partisan of the new religion.

Licinius, his rival, seems to have been far less astute a man. In earlier years, while still the ally of Constantine, he had followed the other's lead with regard to the Christians. But now that he was on his own he threw discretion to the winds and proceeded to persecute the Church. The change of policy must have elated Constantine, for it furnished him with a grand excuse for hostilities. Setting himself up as a holy crusader battling for the glory of Christ, he fell on the aged Licinius, put him to death, and proclaimed himself sole ruler of the empire.

And thus it came about that Christianity, a faith born among the peasantry of a remote and famine-wasted shore, became the religion of the greatest realm on earth. The cult of Those Who Wait had need to wait no longer. It had climbed aboard the chariot of a tavernkeeper's grandson and had arrived. . . .

BOOK THREE

The Church Grows Up
A. D. 323-800

THE CHURCH GROWS UP: 323-800 A.D.

1: The Arian Controversy. 2: Julian and the Pagan Revival. 3: More Theological Controversies. 4: The Rise of the Roman Papacy. 5: Monasticism: Its Origin and Growth. 6: The Paganizing of Christianity. 7: The Veneration of the Saints and the Virgin.

IN the year 323, with the echoes of battle still loud in the skies, the Church and the State were wedded. It was obviously enough a marriage of convenience, a hard bargain between a prince and a horde of clerics. Had it been avoided, all the subsequent history of mankind would have been altered; but it was not avoided—it could not be—and the price is still being paid. From the very outset the alliance was an unhappy one. Constantine proved a shrewd trader, yielding little and demanding much. He professed himself a Christian, yet still clung to the title of Pontifex Maximus, and still demanded the prerogatives of that office. He surrounded himself with bishops and presbyters, yet on occasion still consulted the soothsayers of the Pagans. Characteristically he put off baptism till already on his deathbed, for thus he thought to have a freer rein and yet extract the last ounce of Christ's mercy. Realizing that the remission of sin which came with baptism could be enjoyed only once, he refused to take advantage of the sacrament until every chance of sinning was over. . . .

He did of course do much for the Church. He issued
edicts exhorting his subjects to renounce their "ancient
error" and embrace the "truth" which had brought him
victory. Even more, he commanded that state funds be
used to rebuild the churches ruined during the persecutions, and to erect new ones where they were needed. He
himself donated huge sums to build shrines at Jerusalem,
Bethlehem, and other holy places. To give further proof
of his piety, he even took the nails of the "true" cross
which his mother had unearthed in Jerusalem, and used
them for a bit in the mouth of his charger! Christian
clerics, who now were growing exceedingly numerous,
were relieved of the burdens of taxation and conscript
duty, and were granted the perquisites of civil servants.
And Christian laymen were shown marked favor in the
distribution of political appointments. As a consequence
there was a rush to the baptismal fonts. Whole mobs of
Pagans saw the light of a sudden and began clamoring
for the bread and the wine. The anxiety of the first disciples lest their light be hidden behind a bushel was at
an end; now the bushel itself was on fire.

And the bishops, though they might have preferred it
if Constantine had been less tolerant to the Pagans, were
delighted. After centuries of ignominy and generations of
persecution, they were at last in power. They had gained
the world, and, though it had been necessary to mislay
their souls while securing the prize, they did not begrudge
the cost. It was three hundred years since Jesus had been
on earth, and his doctrine of abnegation had lost its savor.
His apostles now were not guileless fishermen but ambitious men of affairs. The last embers of the old insurgency

were stamped out, and the Christianity which had once proclaimed such godly mischief became now proper and docile.

This was all part of the marriage settlement. If Constantine had given the Church the support of the State, was it not only fair that the clerics give the State the blessing of the Church? Patriotism was now declared to be one of the holiest of Christian virtues. In former days a follower of Christ was branded a sinner if he took up arms; but now he was summarily excommunicated and denied the Lord's Supper if he laid them down. The Prince of Peace became a lord of war; unto Cæsar were rendered the things not alone of Cæsar, but also of God. The change was deplorable, but beyond avoiding. Once the Church set its face toward worldly triumph, compromise and corruption were inevitable. The history of all religions bears out one law: the price of triumph is defeat.

But despite that the Christians strained with all their might to repay Constantine for his favor, he was not satisfied. Like most ambitious men, he was a confirmed monist. He desired above all things unity: a single religion worshiping a single God who favored a single government ruled by a single emperor. But now he discovered that the foundation on which he hoped to rear this ideal structure was itself in fragments. Now that the Christians no longer had.need to fight off their persecutors, they had returned to fighting among themselves. In certain regions —for instance in Africa, where the Donatist schism had set the Christians cursing and destroying each other—the cause of conflict was largely political. Rival parties of ecclesiastics contended with each other for office, and, even though they fought with fanaticism, their underlying motive was at least comprehensible to Constantine. What exasperated the emperor were the conflicts over theology, for these seemed to him utterly without point.

In the East, for example, there raged a war of words which impressed him as unmitigatedly absurd. It had started in Alexandria, where a presbyter named Arius had dared to differ with his bishop over the precise character of the Godhead.[1] Arius was a tall, thin, sad-looking man, austere, ascetic, and highly esteemed by the consecrated virgins in the city. His contention was that Christ, having been "begotten" of God, must have had a beginning, and therefore could not be of the same substance as God, who had never had a beginning. The conception was in essence Adoptionist, and Arius had learnt it in Antioch from a renowned theologian named Lucian. In Alexandria, however, there was little sympathy for this Antiochan unitarianism, and when Arius persisted in preaching it his bishop had him driven from the city. Immediately there was a howl of protest. The local virgins, enraged that their idol should have been taken from them, gave the bishop no peace; and finally Arius was allowed to return.

[1] John W. Draper, in his very stimulating but not always cautious *History of the Intellectual Development of Europe*, New York, 1876, Vol. I, p. 285, accepts unhesitatingly the canard that Arius was embittered because he himself had not been made bishop, and that the theological controversy was only a decorous cloak for one more squabble over ecclesiastical spoils. Such an interpretation is not without its plausibility, but is of course beyond proof. For a painstaking but rather labored account of the whole subject, see Gwatkin, *The Arian Controversy*.

But then the conflict increased in fury, for the populace began to take sides. Scurrilous pamphlets were written and circulated in the churches; the pulpits rang with invectives and threats. Arius composed a long rhapsody extolling the beauties of his metaphysics, and the other side wrote ballads making sport of him. The coster-mongers and sailors and dock laborers went up and down the streets bawling the songs and engaging in bloody battles. What the whole fight was about, they did not know; but neither did they care. What alone mattered to them was that there was a fight.

The controversy spread from Alexandria to other Christian centers in the East. There was a furious inter-change of letters between bishops, and a great running to and fro of gossip-laden priests and deacons. Finally Con-stantine decided to call a council of all the bishops and settle the matter once and for all. He himself did not care which side won. All he wanted was to stamp out dissension and weld his subjects into a solid and homo-geneous mass. Accordingly in the year 325 he brought together at Nicea in Asia Minor some three hundred bishops and a whole host of lower clergy. Most of these were as ignorant of the issue as Constantine himself, for —to use the language of the church historian, Socrates— they were "simpletons." But, having been provided with free transportation by the government, they had been glad enough to make the excursion.

We can imagine what most of them must have been like; spare-boned, fiery-eyed, unwashed men, as earnest as they were ignorant, as rude as they were sincere. Once they arrived at Nicea it was not difficult to stampede them into a decision. From the outset it was obvious that the Arians were outnumbered. When the aged presbyter himself got up to speak, one of the other clerics struck him in the face, and later many rushed from the hall, fingers thrust in their ears to shut out the sound of the old man's heresies. The emperor may have had difficulty in following the debate, for it dealt with matters beyond his comprehension, and was conducted in Greek, which was a foreign tongue to him. But he must have seen at once which side was the weaker, and he seems to have set out forthwith to unite the opposition and bring the stormy parliament to a close. Constantine was still unbaptized, and still officially the Pontifex Maximus of Pagan Rome; yet none challenged his right to meddle in the council. He lectured the clerics in public—Bishop Eusebius, his lick-spittle biographer, assures us that Constantine was the greatest sermonizer in the empire—and cajoled their leaders in private; and finally he succeeded in bringing them to an agreement. Arius was condemned and Christ was voted *homoousion*—that is, of the same substance as the Father. A creed was drawn up in wordy legal fashion:

> "We believe in one God, Father, Almighty, Author
> of all things, visible and invisible; and in one Lord,
> Jesus Christ, the Son of God, the only-begotten of the
> Father, of the essence of the Father, God of God,
> Light of Light, Very God of Very God; begotten
> and not made, consubstantial with the Father. . . ."

and so forth.

And to this was added the clause: "As to those who

say: there was a time when he was not . . . to such persons the Catholic Church says anathema!"

So that was that. The problem having been settled, there was nothing left but to reward the clerics with a splendid banquet. According to Eusebius, who was one of the guests,

> "the proceedings on this occasion were sublime beyond description. The soldiers of the emperor's bodyguard were drawn up before the door of the palace with their bare swords. The men of God [the bishops] passed by them proudly into the interior of the palace. Some sat at the same table with the emperor himself; others at side tables. *One might easily have imagined one beheld a replica of the very Kingdom of Christ!"* . . .

The harsh irony of the whole scene passed unnoticed. It seemed only fitting that disciples of Jesus should be honored with a military salute and be seated with an emperor. When the banquet was over, these men of God went home happy and proud. They had done right by Christ. Arius was cast out of the Church, his teaching was branded heresy, and there was promise that henceforth none would doubt that Christ was indeed *homoousion.*

But the promise was not fulfilled. Indeed, far from establishing quiet, the Council of Nicea succeeded only in stirring up still more furious strife. The theological issue, which by now had narrowed down to the distinction between the words *homoousion* ("the same as") and *homo-iousion* ("similar to"), was being employed as an excuse for the venting of personal grudges and spites. Rival ecclesiastics accused each other of secret sympathy with the condemned Arius, sometimes adding accusations of adultery and murder for good measure. Arius did have his friends, especially among the clerics who had studied with him under Lucian in Antioch; and these were by no means inactive. They stealthily won over the eunuchs in the palace and through them succeeded in reaching the royal womenfolk. They assured Helena, the emperor's mother, that none other than the renowned Lucian of Antioch was her patron saint. His body had been washed up, they testified, at the precise spot where she was born. The old lady believed the tale—belief came easy in those days—and out of devotion to the saint who had thus signally honored her she proceeded to protect his disciple Arius. His opponents were enraged, and tried to retaliate by letting loose the report that Helena had once been a barmaid—"which," says the ever-gallant Duchesne, "considering the customs of that age in the matter of hospitality, implied a great many things." . . .

For a while Constantine refused to hear anything more of the pestiferous affair. The distraught autocrat had other and more pressing matters to attend to at the moment, for his own household had become a nest of intrigue. His Christian wife, Fausta, was accusing his Christian son, to whom she was stepmother, of attempting to assault her incestuously. Constantine, already jealous of the young man because of his popularity with the people, had him put to death; and then, discovering that

Fausta had lied, he had her, too, put to death. Rome became too uncomfortable then for the "first Christian emperor," so he moved his capital to Byzantium, later renamed Constantinople. But there in the East the friends of Arius were able to plague him the more, and finally, being worn out by their clamor, Constantine ordered that the condemned man be permitted to return. As it fell out, however, on the very eve of his restoration Arius was suddenly struck dead—whether by an act of God or an assassin no one knows.

But even this did not bring an end to the conflict, for it left the Arians in power at the palace. The orthodox party had acquired a new leader in Athanasius, a man who made up in fervor what he lacked in charity. Unlike many of his colleagues, he took the nominal cause of the controversy in dead earnest: he really believed that unless the Son was identical with the Father all mankind was damned. And by communicating this feeling to his colleagues, Athanasius was able to prolong the war. New councils were called and new fiats were handed down. Athanasius, but recently elected bishop of Alexandria, was deposed and driven into exile; yet still he continued his agitation. He went from land to land appealing to the bishops—especially to the one in Rome—and arousing the fanatical monks; he argued and pleaded and cursed and connived. Finally he got himself restored to office, only to be deposed a second time. A third and fourth time he was reinstated and deposed, but his furious spirit still could not be broken.

Constantine died, baptized in the nick of time, and the three sons who survived him, busy with their own wars, left the theologians to squabble to their hearts' content. Heresies multiplied. There were not merely lingering remnants of the older schismatic groups such as the Novations, Valentinians, Marcionites, Paulianists, Ebionites, Montanists, and Donatists; in addition there were any number of new dissident parties. The major conflict however, was still over the distinction between *homoousion* and *homoiousion*. There were of course many ecclesiastics who sought to ignore the whole issue, or else to effect a compromise. One such was a certain Leontius, for many years bishop of Antioch, whose tactics are worth recording. The quarrel between the two factions would flare up at every service during the recitation of the Doxology. The Athanasians would cry in what is now orthodox fashion: "Glory be to the Father and to the Son and to the Holy Ghost." But the Arians, offended by the polytheism which seemed to them implicit in such a formula, would shout: "Glory be to the Father, *through* the Son, *in* the Holy Ghost." And the old bishop, conscious that his lips were being watched by both sides, would begin: "Glory be to the Father—" then suddenly go off into a fit of coughing, and fail to recover his voice until at the very conclusion, he could join in—"world without end!" [2]

Men like Leontius may have constituted the majority in the Church, but they could not prevail against a zealot like Athanasius. Thirty years had passed since the Council of Nicea, but he was still fighting its battles. Finally violence had to be brought against him. One night in the winter of 356, while the doughty old man was celebrating the midnight service in the principal church in Alexandria,

[2] Duchesne, *The Early History of the Church,* Vol. II, p. 223.

the door was forced open and a disorderly rabble of soldiers and hooligans rushed into the sanctuary. The congregation consisted in large part of consecrated virgins, for only the "unco' guid" attended church at so late an hour. The ruffians leapt on them with obscene yells and obscener intentions, belaying the men and assaulting the women. Trampled under foot and crushed at the exits, the faithful left more than one corpse upon the floor. Athanasius himself, though severely bruised, managed to escape. Taking advantage of the uproar and confusion, he fled into the night and was never again seen among men.

Even then, however, there was no peace. The Arians, unchallenged at last, fell out among themselves. Two parties emerged, one so conservative that it was practically Athanasian, and the other radically Arian. There was a prolonged struggle, but eventually the conservatives, who were called the Semi-Arians, won. True Arianism was then finally rooted out of the Church; it survived only among certain tribes of Barbarians converted by Arian missionaries. Even among these it was ultimately crushed in the sixth and seventh centuries. Thenceforth for almost a millennium the doctrine of Consubstantiality —not to be confused with Consubstantiation—remained unchallenged. Wherever there were Christians, there the belief was firm that that homeless young Jew who had once wandered barefoot amid the sun-baked hills of Galilee had been none other than "God of God, Light of Light, Very God of Very God . . . begotten of the Father . . . of one essence with the Father . . . begotten but not made. . . !"

2

NE wonders how the religion was ever able to survive these dissensions among its teachers. They did impose a measure of order on Christian thought, but it was a forced order, and therefore incapable of enduring. The "second law" of thermodynamics holds good in history as well as in physics: light can produce heat, but heat cannot produce light. The disputes of the Church Fathers were always rancorous and led not to understanding but greater dark. Fortunately, the State was still friendly, so that even though the Church rent its own vitals, its numbers continued to multiply. The sons of Constantine improved on their father, for they not alone favored Christianity but also persecuted Paganism. They raised the cry, *"Cesset superstitio!"* and proceeded to prohibit the ancient sacrifices and close the heathen temples.

But more efficacious even than the zeal of the emperors was the fanaticism of the believers. The plain folk in the Church did not wait for the government to harass the unconverted; they took the law into their own hands, and pillaged, burnt, and destroyed with a ferocity largely innate in their frustrated souls and for the rest induced by their religion. One reads of dramatic episodes such as that which occurred during this period in the town of Tipasa in North Africa. A little Christian girl, feverish with zeal for her Christ, crept into the local temple, seized a bronze god, and flung it over a cliff. The Pagans, catching the child, sent her to join the idol at the bottom of the sea, and the battle which ensued turned the narrow alleys of the town into rivers of blood.

In that particular instance the Pagans happened to be numerous enough to put up a fight, but in most places they seem to have been largely helpless in the hands of their enemies. Of all the virtues possessed by the Christians, tolerance was last and least. They could not brook the thought that there were still some alive on earth who had not been saved; they preferred to slash the throats of the wretched infidels rather than let them live on in their sin. The Christian mobs tore down Pagan temples, shattered their idols, burnt their libraries, and slaughtered their priests and philosophers. There was no restraining them, so fierce was their ardor for the greater glory of Christ.

But then came a sudden change. In the year 361 the emperor Julian fought his way to the throne, and with him came a complete reversal in religious policy.[3] Julian was a nephew of Constantine and had been reared a Christian; but from his childhood he had himself leaned toward Paganism. He was a studious young man, earnest, ascetic, and given to mysticism. It has been assumed by some historians that Julian's devotion to the ancient gods, like his long beard, was an affectation; but far more probably it was genuine. He had suffered bitterly at the hands of

[3] Alice Gardner, *Julian, Philosopher and Emperor,* is good. Bidez, *Vie de l'Empereur Julien,* is more recent and thorough. Ibsen's *Emperor and Galilean* is dubious as history, but superb as dramatic interpretation.

his converted relatives, and this alone may have been enough to turn him against Christianity. In addition, his whole temperament rendered him averse to the new religion. Its doctrines impressed him as coarse and vulgar, fit only for dock laborers and fishwives; and its theology seemed to him arid and dull, lacking all charm and profundity. One rather imagines him to have been of the type that nowadays turns with revulsion from the brash Evangelicalism of the populace and throws itself into the "High Church" movement. Nor were these prejudices altogether without reason, for the Christianity with which Julian had been brought into contact was anything but lovely. When at the age of twenty his interest in the ancient gods and philosophies aroused the suspicions of his family, they sent for Ætius, one of the most celebrated of the Christian theologians, to set him right. This learned doctor was just then astonishing all Antioch with what was considered the scintillating brilliance of his disputations. We can get an inkling of the man's style of address from a little treatise which he wrote, and which begins as follows:

"If it is possible for the unbegotten God to make the begotten become unbegotten, both substances being unbegotten, they will not differ from each other as to independence. Why, then, should we say that the one is changed and the other changes it, when we will not allow that God produces [the Word] from nothing?" . . .

Such turgidity was hardly calculated to win Julian from the mysteries of Eleusis and the worship of

Apollo. And when, at the age of thirty, the fortunes of war thrust him into a position of supremacy, he lost no time in declaring his mind. On becoming emperor his first act was to call together the Christian ecclesiastics and announce to them that henceforth Church and State were divorced. There would no longer be any protection of orthodoxy, or persecution of heresy; so far as the government was concerned, all beliefs were on a plane.

It was a shrewd stroke. Julian despised Christianity and ached to see it rooted out of his realm; but he was too clever to attack it directly. Instead he delivered it over into the hands of its own theologians, confident that they themselves would destroy it. At the same time he bent every effort to revivify the languishing Paganism. He ordered that the old temples be reopened and saw to it that they were manned by priests of integrity and zeal. Unashamed to take a leaf from the Christians, he established an order of deacons in the ancient cult to visit the sick and distribute alms. Whoever sacrificed to the ancient gods was openly favored, and none who refused was allowed to remain in high office. The Christian eunuchs in the royal household were supplanted by Pagan philosophers, and the bishops presiding over the civil courts were replaced by Pagan magistrates.

The immediate consequence was a sharp turn of the tide which had set in toward the Church a generation earlier. With the baptismal waters still wet on their brows, thousands now scurried back to the temples. The Church was beset from within and without. The heretics, free now to return from exile, began to attack the orthodox clerics who had taken their offices. In some cities there were now as many as three or four bishops, all claiming the same throne and all battling to lay hold of it. And the Pagans, at liberty at last to wreak their vengeance, assaulted heterodox and orthodox Christians alike. There were uprisings and savage attacks everywhere, and if Julian did not abet the excesses, neither did he seek to avert them.

But very little was accomplished. The Church was bloodied and bruised, but its hold on the masses remained firm. Julian had not realized that religion is not a thing one can establish by fiat. His refurbished Paganism was not a simple faith welling up spontaneously from below, but an involved and distinctly self-conscious pseudo-mysticism imposed from above. As a consequence, it could not possibly prevail. The eager optimism with which Julian began his labor gave way first to disquiet and then to harsh impatience. He found himself thwarted on every side, despised for his devoutness by his own priests, laughed at by his friends, and loathed by his enemies. When, after two years of frantic and unavailing effort, he fell mortally wounded in battle, his last words are said to have been: *Vicisti, Galilæe!*—"Thou hast conquered, O Galilean!"

In all probability Julian never uttered the cry, but if he did he was as mistaken at the moment of death as he had been throughout his life. Not the Galilean but Kyrios Christos had conquered, not the lovable Son of Man who had preached forgiveness to sinners, but the awful Son of God who dealt out hell to heretics. But how was Julian, the nephew of Constantine and pupil of Ætius, to know the difference?

3

ITH Julian the "Apostate" gone, the Church once more returned to official favor. The new emperor, Jovian, showed himself ready to lend orthodoxy the prestige of his police power, as did most of his successors, and heresy-baiting became incessant once more. The controversy over the Nicene creed was still raging. Indeed, not until 381, at the Second Council of Constantinople, was it finally settled. The conservatives triumphed, and it was agreed once more—at least, so far as the orthodox were concerned—that the Son *was* of the same substance as the Father. Incidentally it was also agreed that the Holy Ghost was likewise of the same substance, thus establishing a balanced trinity in the Christian heaven.

But no sooner was this problem settled than others arose out of the very terms of the settlement. Just how was this Trinity compounded, and just what was the nature of its parts? For instance in the case of the Son: since he had been voted completely divine, did it not follow that he had never been more than incompletely human? Such at least was the argument of a certain Bishop Apollinaris, and it seemed rather logical. But it was nevertheless anathematized, and its author had to go out and found a sect of his own. The orthodox bishops, jealous for Christ's perfection in every sphere, insisted that he was no less completely human than completely divine. It was a position easier to take than to maintain, for how could both divinity and humanity, which were by definition mutually exclusive, be included in one person? The riddle kept the theologians embroiled for centuries, and no sooner did one of them come forward with a fresh solution than the rest howled it down as heretical.

In the fifth century a patriarch of Constantinople named Nestorius took the stand that Christ must have two natures and these so distinct as almost to constitute two separate personalities. For that reason he insisted that the current designation of Mary as *theotokos,* the "Mother of God," was incorrect. She should be called "Mother of Christ," he declared, for it was solely the human element in the Son that came from her womb. But this outraged the plain folk in the Church, among whom Mary had come to fill the place once occupied by Cybele, Astarte, Isis, Venus, and the rest of the Pagan fertility-goddesses. Nestorius refused to yield from his position and succeeded in getting himself banished to the wilderness of Upper Egypt, where he died in great misery.[4]

But his teachings continued to find favor, especially in Syria where Nestorius had been schooled. Finally, at the Council of Chalcedon in the year 451, the majority of his holy brethren solemnly declared in contradiction that, *"even as the Lord Jesus Christ himself taught us,"* the Virgin Mary *was* the "Mother of God," and the two natures residing in Christ, though two, were nevertheless one, being "indivisible and inseparable!"

[4] The Church chroniclers relate with righteous satisfaction that Nestorius's tongue was devoured by worms. Dr. C. MacLaurin, in his fascinating volume of medical biography, *Post Mortems of Mere Mortals* (New York, 1930, p. 70) suggests that the unhappy old heretic died of cancer of the tongue.

But Nestorianism survived even this formal condemnation; nor could forty years of relentless persecution root it out. Driven from Syria, the heretics found refuge in Persia, where they were beyond the reach of the "universal" Church. Thence they spread up into Turkestan and into India and China. Even to-day the missionaries sent by Roman Catholics, Anglicans, and American Presbyterians, despite the expenditure of vast sums and incalculable effort, are unable to teach the descendants of those ancient heretics the error of their Nestorian ways.[5]

As one might have expected, the Council of Chalcedon which had been called to settle the Nestorian controversy succeeded only in engendering still another dispute. Its creed had included the phrase "in two natures," and certain extremists insisted that Christ, despite that he was both completely divine and completely human, had in reality only one nature. This teaching was called Monophysitism, and after much turmoil it was finally declared as deep a heresy as Nestorianism. It proved, however, even more redoubtable an error, and after two centuries it was still a thorn in the side of the orthodox. Persecution proved utterly of no avail against it. The Monophysite books were ordered burned and those caught copying the forbidden literature had their hands cut off. The leaders were tortured and banished and put to death. But still the heresy persisted. Freed for a while from persecution,

[5] For a detailed account of Nestorianism, see J. F. Bethune-Baker, *Nestorius and his Teaching,* and G. P. Badger, *The Nestorians and Their Rituals.*

the Monophysites began to fall out among themselves. Recondite questions, such as whether Christ's body had been subject to decay, set the fanatics at each other's throats. Yet the sect—now divided into many sub-sects —still managed to live on.

By the seventh century these Monophysites, who made up the majority of the population in Egypt, had grown so hostile to the orthodox Church and the government which supported it, that they were welcoming the Saracen infidels then invading the land. The emperor, terrified lest he lose Egypt, which was Europe's granary, tried to conciliate the heretics. He suggested that Christ, though possessed of two natures, functionéd as redeemer by only a single will. The compromise might have worked had it been given a chance; but almost at once the orthodox bishops gathered in council and decided that the doctrine of "one will"—Monotheletism, as they called it—was no less a heresy than downright Monophysitism. And thus the attempt to heal one schism ended by creating a second.

Both persisted. The adherents of Monotheletism later took the name of Maronites, from the monastery of St. Maro on Mount Lebanon which became their center. Their descendants—now nominally reconciled to Catholicism—are still to be found in the Syrian hill country, where they are wild herdsmen, and in the United States, where they are usually rug-dealers. And the Monophysites number almost a million in India, more than half-a-million in Egypt and Abyssinia—where they form the Coptic Church—and some two hundred thousand in Syria and Armenia. To this day one may still hear the Coptic peasant recite at mass:

"I believe that this is the life-giving flesh which Thine only Son took from the . . . Holy Mary. He united it with his Divinity without mingling and without confusion and without alteration. . . . I believe that His Divinity was not separated from His Manhood for one moment or for the twinkling of an eye. . . ."

And the Eucharist wine with which the Copt washes down these words is never mixed with water as in the orthodox churches. It must be wine of a single, not a dual nature—for it is the blood of a Monophysite, not a Diophysite Christ. . . .

Arianism, Nestorianism, Monophysitism, Monothele-tism—these have been mentioned only because they were among the most important of the heresies which rent the Church during the early centuries. There were others of a doctrinal nature which were no less violent: for instance Pelagianism and Semi-Pelagianism which aroused bitter controversy in the West during the fifth century. Pelagius, a British monk, maintained that all men possess freedom of will, and that each individual's conduct, character, and destiny are in his own hands. This teaching greatly offended Augustine, whose profligate youth—he had taken a mistress at the age of seventeen and had lived with her fourteen years!—had convinced him that all men were by inherent nature wicked, sinful, guilty, ruined, and incapable of any good except by the special grace of God. Augustine was a man of indubitable genius, and his influence on Christian theology was second only to that of

Paul. But the extravagance of his belief in the innate wickedness of mankind leads one to suspect that he may have suffered from some psychic maladjustment. Perhaps the root of the trouble lay in his peculiar emotional relationship to his mother, whom he seems to have shunned

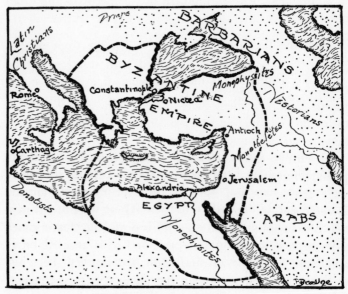

THE EASTERN EMPIRE

and loved with a most disturbing intensity.[6] But though the origin of his dour conviction is obscure, its consequences are plain in Christian thought to this day. He wrote no less than fifteen books to refute Pelagianism, and, due to his impassioned insistence, the Church became

[6] Augustine would make an excellent subject for an enlightened psychological study. His own *Confessions* are full of revealing details which most of his biographers have failed to appreciate.

formally committed to the doctrine of Predestination and the indispensability of Infant Baptism.

But in addition to major "errors" like Arianism and Pelagianism there were scores of minor ones. For instance there was the heresy of Bonosus, a fourth-century bishop, to whom it seemed only gospel truth that Mary, having borne children after Jesus, could hardly be spoken of as the "Perpetual Virgin." Or there was the heresy of Jovinian, who, among other things, insisted that "virgins, widows, and married women are of equal purity once they have been baptized in Christ." At the end of the fourth century a theologian named Philastrius was able to list one hundred and fifty-six individual heresies. And his was an incomplete accounting!

Beneath all these disputes there lay honest even though perhaps misguided convictions; but few if any of them were settled on the basis of those convictions alone. Divergences in theology were used as fronts behind which to fight out quite other differences. The masses took sides because they were miserable and rebellious. Church and State were one in their sight, so they delighted to espouse the heresies, for thus they were able to vent their disaffection with the government. Donatism in North Africa, Nestorianism in Syria, Monophysitism in Egypt— these and countless other heretical agitations were in effect rebel movements induced by hunger rather than meta-physical dissent. If such schisms were able to spread and endure, it was not because a few isolated clerics were stubborn, but because myriads of plain folk were oppressed.

And the ecclesiastics took sides largely because they

were ambitious. The heresies furnished them with righteous excuses for attacking each other and wresting each
others' posts. The Church was growing rich and powerful, and the spoils of ecclesiastical office were well worth
fighting for. As one contemporary declares:

> "If that position [the episcopal throne] is once
> gained, a man enjoys in peace a luxury assured by
> the generosity of the matrons; he can ride abroad in
> a carriage, clothed in magnificent robes, and can give
> banquets which for splendor surpass even those of
> the emperor!" [7]

No wonder, then, that ambitious men were ready to
lie and bribe and murder in order to wrest the bishoprics.
At best the secular clerics were virtually "medicine-men"
to the populace—exalted individuals who by knowledge
and native endowment were equipped to administer the
magic rites. At worst they were predatory gang leaders.
On occasion they did not hesitate even to hire armies and
make open war on each other. For example, in Constantinople in 342 the bishop Macedonius was installed only
after a massacre in which it is said fully three thousand
persons were slain. Or again in 361, in Rome, a cleric
named Damasus actually employed a gang of gladiators
to besiege the church where Ursinus, his rival for the
bishopric, had taken refuge. Battering down the doors,
and storming through the roof, the army of Damasus slew
one hundred and thirty-seven of his rival's supporters.
Nor was the victor ever made to pay for his crime. After

[7] Ammianus Marcellinus, XXVII, 3, 14. Quoted in Duchesne, Vol.
II, p. 364.

a stormy reign Damasus was at length brought to trial at the age of eighty, and the worst charge that could be hatched up against him then was that of adultery!

Almost all these battles, it should be realized, were waged ostensibly over differences in theology. Just what the fine points of doctrinal difference were, the antagonists usually had no notion. Most of the clerics were theologians by pretension alone; in actuality they were rather sacramental politicians. Some of them attained office without ever having been trained for the Church. For example, in 374 at Milan a popular young courtier named Ambrose, who had never been even baptized, was actually elected the bishop of the province. As it happened, in this particular instance the choice was a most fortunate one. Ambrose proved in the course of time a consummate statesman, and was ultimately made a saint. But others who were thus elevated to Church office proved themselves unconscionable rascals. It was no new development in human history. The same sorry thing had already occurred in ancient Egypt, and in India—indeed, wherever else a hierarchy had been able to usurp or been forced to assume to functions of temporal government. When the Western Empire collapsed completely, and all centralized authority ceased in Europe, many of the bishops became local chieftains, carrying on guerrilla wars and pillaging and extorting as ruthlessly as any other of the feudal bandits. It was a far cry from the day when mere peasants gifted with the Spirit were able to head the congregations. The Church was now a mighty institution in the grip of leaders who, if they forgot their duty to the Kingdom of Heaven, could at least lay hold of the earth.

ERHAPS the most impressive evidence of the worldliness that had overcome the Church is to be seen in the rise of the papacy. The Roman congregation had always enjoyed a certain prominence in the cult. Being located in the capital of the empire and boasting possession of the graves and bones of both Peter and Paul, it quite naturally stood out among the churches. When, during the second century, the religion became institutionalized and a vested authority was established, the bishop of Rome came to be looked to with respect not alone by his own congregants but by Christians throughout the West. Officially his power was no greater than that of the prelate of Alexandria or of Antioch in the East. But as the years passed and the power and wealth of the Roman see increased, its ruler began to claim an authority over all Christians. When, at the Second Council of Constantinople in 381, the bishops of the four chief cities in the empire were designated the "patriarchs" of the entire Catholic Church, the prelate in Rome refused the title. To be put on a plane with the bishops of Constantinople, Alexandria, and Antioch, hardly suited the incumbent of the throne which—according to tradition—had once been occupied by a Galilean fisherman named Peter. Instead he took the title of "pope"—which meant the same thing as patriarch but sounded more archaic—and proceeded to speak of himself as the "visible head of the Church."

And circumstances conspired to give legitimacy to this claim. Once the capital was moved a thousand miles away to Constantinople, the Roman see was relatively free of interference on the part of the emperors. Its might could grow without hindrance—and it did grow. The position of the Roman see in Christendom was much like that of the United States to-day in the family of nations. While in the East the patriarchs screamed at each other till all were hoarse, in the West the pope conserved his voice. Interested in organization rather than theology, he usually held aloof from the squabbles of his distant colleagues, interfering only when the others were near exhaustion and then deciding the contest with a word. And thus it came about that by the end of the fourth century Rome was widely regarded as a court of last appeal. By the middle of the fifth century, under Pope Leo the Great, the final rung was surmounted. Rome's primacy, which had been brought about so obviously by geography and politics, was at last claimed to be divine in origin.

There was a tradition in the Gospel of Matthew that Jesus had once blessed his disciple, Simon the son of Jonah, with the words:

> "But I tell you your name is Peter, a rock, and on this rock I will build my church, and the powers of death shall not subdue it. I will give you the keys of the Kingdom of Heaven, and whatever you forbid on earth will be held in heaven to be forbidden, and whatever you permit on earth will be held in heaven to be permitted." [8]

[8] Ch. 16:17-19.

[143]

The whole passage has the appearance of an interpolation, for it does not appear in John, which was the latest of the Gospels, nor in Mark, which was probably based on Peter's own reminiscences, nor in Luke, which is especially devoted to Jesus's sayings. But even if authentic, there is no assurance that the Master's promise bears reference to Rome, for Peter taught in many other cities.[9]

Yet such was the interpretation now insisted upon. At the Council of Ephesus in 449, Pope Leo came forward with the claim that his word must be final, for, as Peter's successor, he alone possessed the authority delegated to the apostle by the Lord Jesus Christ himself. The claim was of course sharply contested by the other bishops, but to no avail. Already four years earlier the emperor, Valentinian III, had recognized the primacy of the Roman see. In a rescript published in 445 he had ordered that

> "no bishop of any province is permitted . . . to do anything without the authority of the venerable Pope of the Eternal City; but on the contrary . . . whatsoever the authority of the Apostolic See has ordained, does ordain, or shall ordain, shall be the law, and if any bishop be summoned to judgment by the Roman pontiff the governor of the province shall see to it that he obeys."

With the police power of the whole empire at the pope's command, rival ecclesiastics were helpless. Thenceforth the supremacy of Rome was firm.

[9] See F. J. Foakes-Jackson, *Peter: Prince of Apostles,* 1927, pp. 65-68. Long before the Protestant theologians began to oppose the orthodox interpretation of this passage, it was questioned by Church Fathers of no less repute than St. Augustine and Cyril of Alexandria.

The development was destined to work incalculable mischief in later times; but in those early centuries it had its value. The Church was too far gone to be governed by parliamentary methods. Synods and councils were a failure, for they made for chaos rather than order. In the fourth century some forty-five councils had to be called merely to settle the Trinitarian controversy, and of these thirteen rendered decisions adverse to the Arians, fifteen favored them, and seventeen voted for the Semi-Arians. Clearly such a method could not be continued.

Yet the attempt on the part of Rome to establish a dictatorship was long contested. Indeed, the East never surrendered. After centuries of dispute there came a final break, the West acknowledging the authority of the pope and the East clinging to its patriarchs. Thenceforth there was one church which called itself "Catholic" and was denominated Roman, and another which called itself "Orthodox" and was named Greek: nor have the two been reunited to this day.

The ostensible reasons for the final break between the two communions were differences as to dogma and ritual. The Eastern Church accused Rome of heresy because it prohibited the singing of the Hallelujah during Lent, enjoined celibacy on the clergy, insisted that the Holy Ghost proceeded from the Son as well as the Father, and, above all, used a wafer instead of a pellet of leavened bread in administering the Lord's Supper.[10]

[10] On all of these points the Eastern Church seems to have clung to the more primitive usage. For instance, it favored leavened bread rather than the wafer because it still preserved the ancient custom of allowing the laity rather than the clergy to provide the elements for the Eucharist. See J. H. Kurtz, *Text-Book of Church History*, Vol. I, p. 230.

But the real differences between the two communions were, of course, of a far profounder nature. As has already been suggested, Rome and Byzantium were opposed in their essential devotions, the one being interested primarily in the problems of organization and the other in the riddles of theology. That they should have differed thus was only natural. In the first place, the West spoke Latin, which did not lend itself to theology. The language was rich in legal terminology, but incapable of expressing those delicate shades of meaning which made Greek so fecund in the production of heresies. In the second place, the patriarchs in the East were given no opportunity to develop as legislators. Functioning within the shadow of the imperial palace, all that was left for them was to wrangle over minutiæ of dogma and ritual. But the pope of Rome, far removed from the center of secular control, had a chance to expend his energies on more mundane and practical concerns. The empire persisted as a power in the East until Constantinople fell to the Turks in 1453; but in the West it was already a shadow when the Goths sacked Rome in 410. And thus it came about that the pope fell heir to half of what was left of the glory that had once been Rome.

It was no great legacy to inherit. The West was now a wilderness, its valleys littered with the wreckage of ancient cities, its roads destroyed, bridges shattered, and farms deserted and in flames. The Barbarians, so long held back at the sagging frontiers, had at last stormed their way in. They had come at first not as nations seeking new dwelling places, but as heterogeneous armed bands looking for booty. But as the pressure of the hordes in the forests behind them became stronger, those in the van began to settle down in the lands they invaded. Vandals, Goths, Franks, Danes, Angles, Saxons, Alemanni, Lombards— they swept down upon the West, laying waste whatever was in their path; and then they stayed to herd their goats amid the ruins. The Ostrogoths became masters of Italy, the Visigoths of Spain, the Vandals of North Africa; and the pope of Rome, deserted by the emperor in far-off Constantinople, had to fend for himself. He had no time to argue over the mysteries of the Beyond; he had to cope with the here and now. He had to find ways and means of converting these invading hordes and of binding them to him with the chains of awe and faith.

He succeeded. He became in effect the emperor of the West, going so far as to assume even the ancient title of the Roman rulers and call himself Pontifex Maximus. He came to regard himself as Christ's viceroy, and sought to replace the military order once exercised by the Empire with a new order governed by Christ's ordinances. Those ordinances were, of course, not literally Christ's; they could not be. The Galilean had taught a perfectionist creed: he had counseled love and forgiveness and an end to acquisitiveness and competition. For the popes to have urged such a teaching in the fifth and sixth and seventh centuries would have been sheer suicide. Jesus had preached to a folk already weary of striving, to an ancient race that had spent itself and could yearn for naught save rest. But the popes of the Dark Ages were surrounded by tribes just emerged from the forest, young tribes full of savage vigor and craving not rest but strife. To have tried to break their spirit all at once would have been so much effort wasted. The Barbarians were, for the present at least, beyond taming, and if they were to be baptized it could only be to a Christianity brought much nearer their own level.

The popes seem to have realized this state of affairs, for they made no effort to demand overmuch of their converts. They salted the Gospel teaching till it was drained of all its blood, and then fed it to the tribesmen well-spiced and garnished. And thus they saved the day. They saved it, one must add, not alone for themselves and their Church, but also for all mankind. The papacy in our day may impress many people as an anachronism, a curious relic, picturesque but in the way. In the Dark Ages, however, it literally salvaged what was left of civilization. When the Western Empire crumpled beneath the hammerings of the Barbarians, and the fairest lands of Europe returned to the wilderness whence they had once been so painfully won; when learning was blotted out and art was destroyed, and every last vestige of order was gone; when it seemed that night had settled on the earth forever and the very memory of the sun had grown dim—in that dreadful hour it was the papacy alone that dared dream of a dawn yet to come.

Nor was it content with dreaming; it worked and strained to make the dream real. Even when fire and violence and disease were making a shambles of the Eternal City itself, the popes were already struggling to rear the "City of God" in its place. They were to that extent in advance of those first believers who sat down in Jerusalem and waited for the Kingdom to overtake them. These popes went out to *create* the Kingdom. They were not like children, closing their eyes and wishing, but grown men who strode forth with eyes wide open and with a will as well as a wish in their hearts. If in the end their labor did more hurt than good to the purpose of the religion and the career of man, the fault lay not with them but with their successors. Those first Vicars of Christ had their idealism, and the best of them were men of great valor and energy. They sought to make the whole world a theocracy, to bring all the nations into one great league which would have Christ for its Heavenly King and the pope for its viceroy. And then—so they hoped—war would be no more, for all men would be brethren; neither would there be oppression, greed, nor violence, for all would be children of the Church. The Kingdom of God would be here at last, and the whole earth would be a paradise!

The dream was first set down in words in a great fifth-century work entitled the *City of God,* written by St. Augustine. In conception it was magnificent, and had there been a succession of popes wise and able enough to carry it out, mankind might be enjoying to-day the civilization it can only hope to attain a thousand years hence. But no such succession arose. After the first flush of enthusiasm, the headlong charge changed to a cautious marking of time. Those who ascended the papal throne ceased to be men of the heroic type; far more frequently they were careerists at whose hands the dream of St. Augustine became no more than an excuse for temporal aggressions and usurpations. The end, the establishment of the "City of God," was forgotten; only the means, the exaltation of papal power, was pursued. When the stir and ferment subsided in Europe, and the Barbarian races settled down and became Christian, the pope of Rome began to claim the suzerainty over their kings. The development was in no sense unique. The chronicles of all organized religions since the ancient days in Egypt and Babylonia are replete with instances of high priests who sought to dominate their kings. To enter into the papal claims and tell of all the frauds and forgeries and intrigues and wars to which they gave rise, would lead us far afield. We are concerned in this book with the history of a religion, not the development of a political institution, and, though it is rarely possible to separate the two, it is important that we try. The main trail of Christianity now is not that which wanders down into the fortified cities and loses itself in the courtyards of prelates, but one which goes elsewhere—into the depths of the desert and high into the mountains. Henceforth for many generations it is the cloister, not the episcopal palace, that shelters what remains of Christian living.

5

THE ways parted very early, though for long none marked their parting. Somewhen in the third century an intense disquiet began to make itself felt in certain Christian circles. It was no organized revolt like that which Montanus had led a century earlier, but rather a sporadic revulsion, leaderless, and for the most part negative in spirit. Isolated individuals began to grow restive in the congregations and murmur against the trend the Church was taking. They recalled the tradition that Jesus had praised those who made themselves "eunuchs for the Kingdom of Heaven's sake," and that he had told the rich young man, "If you would be perfect, go, sell your property and give the money to the poor." And they began to complain because these teachings were no longer being followed in the congregations. At first they complained with hesitancy, for the persecutions were still harrying their brethren. But with the coming of Constantine and the establishment of Christianity as a state institution, these protestants began to grow more clamorous. They could see that the ethical teachings were being forgotten, and only the sacerdotal elements were surviving. And this seemed to them a betrayal of the very essence of Christianity. The Church, they cried, had not been founded as a mere agency for cheap salvation; Christ had intended it to be a communion of saints.

Nor were they content simply to proclaim this doctrine; they sought to carry it out in their own lives. Increasing numbers of Christians began to dedicate themselves to celibacy and willful poverty, striving by their example to lead the entire Church back to its pristine austerity. Such were the consecrated virgins—of both sexes—whom we found taking part in the Arian controversy. Significantly, they were recruited almost entirely from the laity, and though they were interested in theology and not opposed to the sacraments, their chief concern was always with behavior. Many were noble and gentle souls, naïve perhaps in their unworldliness, but admirable and attractive nonetheless. Others, however, seem to have been choleric and contentious creatures, as sure of their own virtue as they were of all other men's sins—strident, vindictive, and unbearably intolerant. But whether gentle or harsh, they were quite impotent to reform their brethren. Even the priests, who should have been the first to emulate the ascetics, refused to put aside their wives or forego their interest in worldly gain. So finally the uncommonly holy gathered up their skirts and withdrew from the congregations. They were revolted—and dreadfully tempted—by the carnality rampant in the haunts of men; so they left their neighbors to their fate and took to the desert.

The first historic character to resort to this measure was an earnest young Christian named Anthony, who took up his abode in the wilderness of southern Egypt toward the end of the third century. It was no new departure in religious experience. There had been Jewish anchorites in Palestine before the time of Jesus, and there had been monasteries in India as early as Buddha's day. In Egypt itself a form of cloistral life had obtained among some of the Pagan philosophers. In all probability, however, Anthony had never heard of these earlier monastics; his flight from the world may have been almost an "instinctive" reflex. But others did hear of him, and soon he was surrounded by a whole throng of imitators. Before a generation had passed an organization sprang up among these anchorites. Led by a certain Pachomius, who had been a soldier in his youth and knew the value of regimentation, a number of hermits gathered together and built themselves a monastery on the Upper Nile. Pachomius became the abbot, the "father," of the company, and he made all the "brethren" shave part of their heads as had the priests of Isis in earlier days, wear uniform clothing, keep regular hours of worship, and labor in the fields a certain portion of each day. This was, of course, a less drastic form of monasticism than that of Anthony, who had lived all by himself and who had devised his own mortifications. It was possible even for women, and before long Pachomius had to found a convent for them not far from the monastery.

Yet the earlier anchoritic form persisted, and by the fourth century there were hermits to be found in the deserts and forests and mountain fastnesses throughout the empire. Some of them must have been stark lunatics, and others were probably neurotic individuals craving a chance for self-expression. They vied with each other in endurance much as poor boys and girls in our day will vie with each other in "marathon dances" and other such absurd contests calculated to attract attention. St. Jerome assures us that he once saw a monk who for thirty years had lived exclusively on crumbs of barley bread and muddy water, and another who stayed continually in a hole, never washing, never changing his tunic till it fell away in pieces, and who starved himself till his skin was "like pumice stone" and his eyes were almost blind. An Alexandrian named Macarius is reported to have slept for six months in a marsh, his body naked to the stings of venomous insects. When he walked by day he was wont to burden himself with a load of iron weighing eighty pounds—a penance in which he was outdone by St. Eusebius, who tottered around beneath a load weighing one hundred and fifty pounds!

The favorite lairs of these sorry masochists were the deserted dens of wild animals, or dry wells, or ruined cemeteries. In Mesopotamia a whole sect of them came to be known as the "Grazers" because they never dwelt under a roof but roamed about half-naked over the mountain sides and lived off the herbage like cattle. In Syria there was another sect, the "Stylites," who in imitation of the notorious Simeon Stylites lived continually on the tops of tall pillars, their bodies tied with ropes to hold them from falling when they slept. Most of the hermits very rarely washed or cut their hair; some refrained altogether. A disciple of Simeon Stylites boasts of his master that "a horrible stench, intolerable to the bystanders, exhaled from his body, and worms dropped from him whenever he moved." We read of a famous virgin named Sylvia who, though already sixty and deathly ill, nevertheless refused to wash any part of her body except her finger tips. St. Mary of Egypt, once a ravishing beauty, spent forty-seven years naked in the desert, and at the end of that time was so black with sunburn and dirt that a hermit who once caught sight of her crawling through the underbrush thought her a demon from Hell! [11]

Such creatures were, of course, exceptional—but only in degree, not in kind. Save for a rare soul like old St. Poemen, who tried to teach his followers that their aim should be to destroy their passions, not their bodies, the ascetics regarded the maddest of their kind as the noblest. If they themselves did not all become St. Simeons and St. Marys, it was solely because they lacked the fortitude. They contented themselves with the less vicious mortifications,

[11] Lecky, *History of European Morals*, 1873, Vol. XI, pp. 108-194, describes the ascetic movement with verve and good documentation. For a more detailed account see Gregory Smith, *Christian Monasticism from the Fourth to the Ninth Century,* and O. Zöckler, *Askese und Mönchthum,* 1897, pp. 149-285.

dwelling not by themselves in caves or on pillars, but in groups in monasteries. Of such monastics there were many thousands by the end of the fourth century. St. Jerome informs us that in his day—he died in the year 420—some fifty thousand monks used to assemble for the Easter festivals; and his contemporary, Rufinus, declares in his *Historia Eremitica* that the monastic population in Egypt was nearly equal to that of the cities. No doubt the evil conditions of the time had much to do with the popularity of asceticism, for, since hunger was already a necessity, it was comforting to make it a virtue. Whatever the reason, however, the flight from the world began to take on the aspect of an epidemic during these sorry centuries. From Egypt the movement spread southward into Ethiopia, eastward to Persia, northward to the Black Sea, and westward to Italy, Gaul, and Britain, and especially Ireland.

The cloister was in the Middle Ages what the laboratory is in our day—the institutional expression of the spirit of its age. The one may seem grotesque to us, and the other palpably natural; but that is only because the intellectual climate has changed in the intervening centuries. In medieval times the monastery was not a mere convenience but a necessity. It was in fact as well as name a "retreat" from a world grown hateful to mankind. A vast empire had collapsed, dragging with it an order of existence; and the race was left in terror. Gone were the old amenities and securities; now there was naught save hate and dread. And the finest of the race, the most sensitive souls, could not endure it. To dream of redeeming the world was no longer possible; things had gone too far for that. Dreaming of any sort was well-nigh impossible; it was a time only for nightmares. For this life was not the only affliction; even worse was the dread of the life to come. Heaven, which had seemed very close to the Christians in the excitement of the missionizing days, had since receded into the distance. Now Hell was the nearer prospect. The world had grown gray with the breath of the theologians, and the dearest wish of men was not so much to reach God as to escape the Devil.

That was why men flocked to the cloisters. They were panic-stricken lest death overtake them while still in sin and plunge them into the eternal fires of Hell. They sought to isolate themselves from this guilt-infested world and live a life of otherworldly virtue. They searched the Scriptures and read of the Way urged by Jesus; and in that Way they tried with all their desperate might to go. The sacraments in which the commonalty of Christians put their trust seemed not enough for the extremists. Indeed, monasticism was at first very largely an unsacerdotal movement. The anchorites who fled into the wilderness cut themselves off from all chance of taking Communion; and even later, when they began to gather in monasteries, their chief concern was still with conduct rather than the sacraments. They went ravening after perfection, forsaking the world and its vaunts, denying the desires of the flesh, laboring at the meanest tasks, wearing the foulest clothes, eating little, sleeping brokenly, and praying hour after hour. They were, to use William James's language, "sick souls"—but the race itself was sick. The world was in ruins, and life was a feeble and wounded thing crawling about amid the wreckage. No wonder then that these, the flower of the race, the noblest and bravest and most learned of the day, could only cry: "We speak as dying men to dying men: repent while there is yet time!"

Had monasticism remained sporadic and unorganized, it might have spent itself before long and disappeared. What saved it—and ultimately destroyed it—was the order which crept into it and changed it from a scattered rout to a steady movement. As early as the beginning of the fifth century the Eastern monasteries began to accept the "Rule of St. Basil" which fixed a routine for their inmates. Western monasticism took longer to regulate, largely because of the greater chaos in the region. Until the middle of the sixth century, each establishment had its own rule which usually was influenced by the local environment. For instance in Ireland, which was inhabited by tribes traditionally addicted to fighting, the monasteries were largely armed camps which terrorized the countryside and sometimes made forays even against each other.

But gradually this anarchy disappeared and the abuses and laxities were suppressed. The man chiefly responsible for the reform was St. Benedict, who about 529 founded a great monastery on Monte Cassino, in Italy. Possessing both Christian piety and a Roman genius for organization, he drew up a "rule" which became in time even more widely accepted in the West than was St. Basil's in the East. Benedict insisted that each monastery should be a permanent, self-contained, and self-supporting garrison of Christ's soldiers. A monk was not free to wander about from one establishment to another. Once he had served his year of trial and was established in a "house," he was bound by vows to remain there till he died. His cloister had to be the whole world to him thenceforth, and its inmates his entire society.

The common life of the brethren was subsumed under three heads: Prayer, Labor, and Self-denial. At least four hours of each day had to be spent in worship, and the periods, seven in number, were fixed with precision. The aim was to fulfill the words of the 119th psalm: "In the midst of the night I will rise up to give thanks unto Thee . . . seven times a day do I praise Thee." Accordingly the monks were commanded to rise up at midnight for Matins and Lauds, which were practically one service. At six in the morning came the second service, Prime, and then at three-hour intervals came Tierce, Sext, and None. The sixth service, Vespers, was chanted shortly after sundown, and the seventh, Compline, came after a short public reading from the *Collationes* of St. Cassian.[12] Each service, as a rule, consisted of three psalms and a little additional matter, and therefore took from twenty minutes to half an hour. But besides these there was to be considerable private prayer.

Even more time, however, was to be given to labor, for, as the wise Benedict declared, "idleness is the enemy of the soul." Usually this work was in the fields and vineyards, since enough food and drink had to be produced by the monastery to provide for the wants of all its inmates. And a portion of each day had to be devoted to reading, for

[12] Later it became customary to anticipate the morning services (perhaps to leave time for an unbroken siesta) so that None fell at about midday—which then came to be called *noon*. And from the later habit of taking a light meal after reading from St. Cassian's pious book, we get our modern use of the word "collation" in the sense of a snack. See Coulton, *Five Centuries of Religion,* Vol. I, p. 213—a great work on the rise and fall of Western monasticism.

ignorance like idleness was frowned upon by Benedict. The monks were to assemble in the cloister, which, though covered in, was open to the weather, and there they were to pore over their scrolls. Those who were skilled with the pen were assigned to copy manuscripts, for each monastery had to have a library. And such as were well versed in letters, and had good voices, might read to those who were near of sight or illiterate. Benedict did not expect the monks to be scholars. He himself was no scholar, as is evident from his colloquial Latin, and from his biographer's comment that he was "knowingly ignorant and wisely unlearned." All he demanded was that the mind as well as the body be occupied.

The self-denial ordained for the brethren was relatively moderate. There were three vows to be taken, Poverty, Obedience, and Chastity, and from at least the last two not even the pope could grant a dispensation. Poverty was to be absolute in the personal sense—though the corporation was allowed to own all it could legitimately lay hold of. But there was to be no private property whatsoever, and the abbot was instructed to make frequent search in the corners, and even in the monks' mattresses, for hidden hoards. If a brother was found guilty of hiding possessions, he might be buried alive in the middle of the convent dunghill! [13]

Obedience, too, was to be absolute. The monk must be utterly subservient to his abbot, who stood in the place of Christ, and must obey implicitly without ever asking why. And the practice of Chastity, the third of the vows, was, of course, taken for granted.

[13] Coulton, *Five Centuries of Religion*, Vol. I, p. 214.

Beside these *tria substantialia*, there were certain minor prescriptions. Food and drink were to be reduced to an endurable minimum, but no further. Only the sick were permitted the meat of animals, but the rest might on occasion eat poultry. Bread, vegetables, and fish—which was counted the least defiling of fleshly foods because it was imagined to be produced without copulation—were the staples of diet. And a daily allowance of a hemina—about half a pint—of wine was permitted to each monk. Silence was to be absolute during most of the day, and there was to be no buffoonery or laughter. Warm baths were a rare concession; cold ones were never taken even as a penance. Finally there was to be frequent resort to corporal punishment even for the slightest infractions.

Such in brief was Benedict's Rule, and its sanity and practicability soon commended it to earnest men throughout the West. It established a mode of life immensely desirable in that age. Europe was still a wasteland swarming with marauding tribes and robber bands. Might was the only law, and he who was not attached to some feudal chieftain was lost. In the monastery, however, a man was safe. Once enrolled as a monk, the round of daily tasks was established beyond change, and all life became ordered and plain. One ceased to be a man among men; one became a sworn soldier of Christ.

By the time of Charlemagne, in the ninth century, the whole of the West was dotted with these garrisons of Christ's soldiers, and through them a new spirit was brought into the life of Christendom. There was never an "order" of Benedictines; each "house" was autonomous and self-contained. Yet all were bound together by a common routine, and the monks formed as it were one cohesive army. They spread out everywhere, setting up religious blockhouses in the midst of the newly conquered lands to hold them fast to what came to be called the Holy Roman Empire. They became the chief instruments in the conversion of the Barbarians, and in the reformation of the Christians themselves.

Most important of all, the monks became the conservers of what little learning still survived in the West. From the time of Cassiodorus, a contemporary of Benedict whom some historians consider of even greater significance, the cowled men labored to save for posterity the divine and human knowledge which the tide of barbarism threatened to obliterate completely. If their success was limited, it was solely because the task was too severe. By the time the monks came to see that it was their duty to save the world's culture as well as their own souls, the process of decay was already too far gone. What "profane" manuscripts the earlier Christians had failed to burn in their campaigns against Paganism, were largely destroyed or mislaid during the Barbarian invasions. Very little save the Holy Writ and the writings of the Church Fathers was left in the West, and even that little was in a tragically garbled form. Greek and Hebrew were hardly known, and even classic Latin was rapidly becoming a forgotten tongue. The populace spoke the jargons of the Barbarian races, or, in Italy itself, a vernacular Latin lacking grammar and literature. Even so great a monarch as Charlemagne could hardly read or write. Most of the lesser priests were able to serve at the altars only because they knew the prayers by rote.

In a world so dark the wonder is not that the monks accomplished little, but that they accomplished anything at

all. For aside from them, and a rare king like Charlemagne or Alfred the Great, there were none who gave a
thought to learning. The monks alone conducted what
few schools were to be found in Europe in the Dark Ages.
They alone preserved the ancient manuscripts and copied
them. They alone wrote commentaries on the Scriptures
and on the surviving fragments of Plato and Aristotle.
They alone kept chronicles, compiled texts, and stared at
earth and sky with inquiring eyes. One pictures the monasteries as so many tiny candle flames glimmering fitfully
in the blackness of the night. Here they were clustered
thickly, and there scattered wide; in Italy, France, and the
British Isles they seemed actually to have flared for a time,
but in the northern forests and on the Eastern steppes
they were barely able to gutter. Yet everywhere they kept
burning—the last embers of a glory that had once
illumined the earth, and the first of a greater glory to come.

6

 UT one must guard against exagger-
ation. In its best days—and these
were numbered—monasticism was
indeed a leaven in Christendom. It
did help keep alive a spark of learning and charity when Europe was
steeped in barbarism. It did purge
the hierarchy to a degree and curb
the laity in a measure. But with all
that it was able to accomplish very
little. The lump was too vast and the dough too sodden to
be lifted. Even after five centuries of Benedictinism, the

religion of the Church was still in a very low state. If anything it sank during that period, largely because of the
missionary gains made among the Barbarians. Christianity
conquered the world—or at least that small promontory
reaching westward from Asia which we occidentals are
wont to think of as the world—but it paid dearly for the
triumph. Even in the earlier centuries, when the gains of
the Church had been achieved gradually and more or less
by moral suasion, there had been a tendency to compromise with the older religions. But in the Dark Ages, when
a missionary like Augustine could baptize ten thousand
Angli on a Christmas Day, or a warrior like Charlemagne
could convert a whole nation of Slavonians in a single
military campaign, or a prince like Vladimir of Kieff
could Christianize all Russia by mere fiat, the tendency
was not to compromise but to surrender.

One aspect of Christianity's surrender is revealed in the
feasts it adopted. We have already noticed how the Church
took over the spring rites of the Pagans and made of them
the sacred festival of Easter. (The very name Easter comes
from Eostre, the ancient Teutonic goddess of fertility and
daybreak.) Later a prolonged period of fasting called
Lent was made the overture to the feast, and this, too, was
a borrowing from Paganism. Originally it had been the
taboo period observed by the primitive husbandmen at
the end of winter to insure the coming of spring, and the
hilarious Shrove Tuesday which preceded Lent was derived from the day of unbridled license with which the
primitive folk had ushered in their fast.

Christmas was even more flagrantly a borrowing. From
time immemorial the Romans had rejoiced at the time of

the winter solstice, opening their festivities with the Saturnalia, which was marked by wild abandonment, continuing through the Sigillaria, on which the children received presents of dolls made of wax (*sigilla*), and concluding with the Brumalia on the twenty-fifth of December, which was called the Birthday of the Sun. Later, with the spread of Mithraism throughout the empire, this Birthday of the Sun became one of the most popular festivals in the Pagan calendar, and when the masses came over to Christianity they brought the holy day with them. The Church, unable to suppress the festival, finally adopted it —though not until the fourth century. The order was reversed, and the festive period began now with the twenty-fifth of December—which was belatedly discovered to be the anniversary of Christ's birth—and concluded seven days later with the Feast of Circumcision, which, though supposed to be an occasion for fasting, rapidly became a Saturnalian New Year's Day. When the northern tribes were converted, Christmas took on new characteristics. The Barbarians had long been wont to celebrate the winter solstice with a noisy fire-festival called Yule—the word is probably onomatopœic in origin, like "ululate"—and from this source came the Christmas tree and its attendant rites.

Such concessions to heathen ceremonialism were made quite openly when the Barbarian tribes were converted. Just as in the seventeenth century Robert de Nobili forged a document in Sanskrit to prove to the Hindus that he and his fellow-Jesuits were descendants of Brahma, and Father Ricci told the Chinese that the ancestors they worshiped were really the saints of the Roman Catholic calendar, so now in the sixth century Pope Gregory the Great instructed his emissaries in Britain to keep the old Saxon temples as churches—"that they [the Barbarians] may the more familiarly resort to the places to which they have been accustomed." Even the sacrificial festivals were to be retained, Gregory directed, though the beasts were to be offered now not to the idols but to the glory of God.

The policy was eminently sensible, for, as the pontiff pointed out, "it is impossible to efface everything at once from obdurate minds." But it was also dangerous, for in the train of these ancient rites came the ancient gods. Some were smuggled into the Christian heaven in the guise of saints, and others were converted into demons. The development was quite inevitable, for, as we have already seen, perversion and conversion follow on each other as night and day. The relegation of the old gods to the status of devils opened the door to the dualism of the early Gnostics, and of their successors, the Manicheans. The universe of Christianity became an arena in which good and evil, Christ and Satan, were seen to be continuously at war. And though Christ was assured of the eventual victory, Satan was from the first the noisier and more obstreperous champion.

Nothing is more striking than the extent to which the dread of the Devil dominated the thought of the people in medieval times. In him was contained the vigor of immemorial centuries of superstition, for he was compounded of elements drawn from any number of ancient cults. He was not merely the fallen angel of Jewish theology; he had a body—indeed, many bodies—and could be seen and smelled and touched. Sometimes he appeared in the form of a black dog, like the classic hell-hound Cerberus. More usually, however, he was a biped with the goatlike body, the horns, and the cloven hoofs of Pan, and the red beard and pitchfork of Thor.[14] A whole host of demons served him, going about up and down the earth and incessantly trapping men into sin. Not alone the plain people, but also the monks and theologians believed in the existence of this infernal host. The skepticism of the Stoics and Epicureans, who had laughed at all demonology, was gone from the world. It had been swept away in the debacle of the empire, and the superstition of the real *paganes,* of the peasants and the backwoods folk, now dominated men's minds. The fear of the Devil was the beginning and end of all wisdom in these, the so-called "Ages of Faith." That was one of the chief reasons why men fled to the monasteries: they imagined that in those retreats they would be immune to demonic infection and could die in a state of grace.

And even as Satan grew ever closer to the consciousness of the Christians, so did Christ recede farther away. Time and the theologians had dealt hard with the Galilean who had once been worshiped as the heaven-sent messenger of comfort. He had been robbed of his lovable human traits and made part of a transcendental and dismayingly impersonal Godhead. The one direct hold which men still had on him was through the ritual, and they tried to exert

[14] See Cox, *Mythology of the Aryan Nations,* Vol. II, p. 358ff., or for a more summary treatment, Fiske, *Myths and Mythmakers,* 1877, p. 123ff.

that hold with a frequency which may have reflected secret misgiving far more than confidence. Spontaneous prayer had been supplanted almost entirely by fixed rites conducted by priests. The various liturgical services, or Masses, were multiplied, and were recited for the dead as well as the living. Too terrified at the thought of immediate consignment to Hell, men had begun to believe that most souls went first to Purgatory, whence they could be redeemed if enough Masses were offered in their name. We read, for example, of a certain Lady Alice West who, before her death in 1395, ordered four thousand four hundred Masses to be recited "in the most haste that it may be do, withynne xiiii nyght next after my deces."

The actual sacrament of the Lord's Supper, which was associated with the principal Mass, had been made increasingly gross in its implications. It had become undisguisedly a sacrificial rite; its celebration was declared to be a miraculous reënactment of the human offering of Christ on the cross. Sacrifices, either human or animal, had been regarded since time immemorial as essential in the worship of the gods; and it was but natural that the idea should persist among the populace even long after its conversion to Christianity. The worshipers began to believe that the Lamb himself lay on the altar during the Eucharist. Indeed, in Gaul it actually became the custom to fashion the consecrated bread in the form of a man, and to dismember it on the altar and distribute the parts among the worshipers, one receiving an eye, another an arm, a third the nose![15]

[15] *Encyc. Britannica,* 11th ed., Art., "Eucharist."

UT though the Masses were multiplied and the Eucharist was made so crudely thaumaturgic, men still remained afraid. They felt the need for some added means of preserving themselves in this world and of saving themselves from torment in the next. The theologians had made Christ too remote and terrifying for the people to hope to move him themselves with direct appeals. Men felt they must secure intermediaries to plead for them with the Son of God, and therefore took to invoking the aid of the holy ones of the past. Transcendence in a deity is impressive, but not comforting. Just as the worshipers in the first centuries had sought to reach God through Christ, so in medieval times they sought to reach Christ through the saints. The first saints were the martyrs who died in the persecutions, and we find them already venerated as early as the middle of the second century. By the close of the fourth century this veneration had changed to virtual worship. The "athletes of Christ" were thought to have influence in heaven, and men began to turn to them for aid and healing and protection. The graves of the martyrs grew to be holy shrines, and their bones, or at any rate bones which might well have been theirs, became miracle-working relics.

This development, like almost every other in Christian history, was not unique. The Solomonic dictum that there is nothing new under the sun is nowhere truer than in the field of religion. Like exigencies have everywhere and always driven men to like beliefs. Thus we find that wherever a god has fallen into the hands of theologians and been exalted overmuch, there the people have been prone to resort to saints. Centuries before the very emergence of Christianity, the Buddhists had already learnt to venerate their *boddhisatvas,* the Chinese their *seng jen,* the Jainists their *tirthankaras,* the Hindus their *siddhs,* and the Zoroastrians their *ashavans.* And when circumstances forced such a development to occur in Christianity, the clergy, far from frowning on it, gave it active encouragement.

There were, indeed, occasional leaders like Jovinian and Vigilantius in the fourth century who tried to halt these reversions to Paganism; but they were invariably cast out of the Church as heretics. The majority of the clerics saw only good in the growing veneration of saints and relics. They began to draw up a calendar of the days sacred to the various saints, and arranged a ritual for their celebration. And they began to unearth or to manufacture a seemingly inexhaustible supply of relics. They discovered Noah's beard, the stone on which Jacob slept at Bethel, the branch from which Absalom hung, milk from Mary's breasts, Christ's coat, the tears he shed at the grave of Lazarus, the table on which he ate the Last Supper, even his foreskin! The authenticity of the last-mentioned of these relics was challenged by men like Guibert of Nogent, but, significantly enough, only on the ground that when Christ rose from the dead he was in possession of all the parts of his body! More obvious objections seem not to have occurred even to the most advanced minds in that credulous age. The most preposterous objects were accepted as relics, even metaphors like the "horns" of Moses and Paul's "stake in the flesh!" [16] At the Seventh General Council in 787 it was decreed: "If any bishop from this time forward is found consecrating a church without holy relics, he shall be deposed as a transgressor of the ecclesiastical traditions."

The obvious explanation of this whole development is that it was a reversion to the old polytheism. The saints were the Christian counterparts of those heathen deities in whom the masses had put their trust in earlier days; and the holy relics were the Christian substitutes for the old heathen fetishes. One sees this plainly when one examines the calendar of the saints. Many of the names are quite obviously those of mythical characters belonging to pre-Christian folklore. Thus the Egyptian god Osiris, whom the Copts called Onufri, is known as St. Onuphrius; the Greek gods Dionysis and Zeus Eleutherios are called St. Dionysis and St. Eleutherius; and the Hindu god Boddhisatva is named St. Josephat. The translation of these gods into saints may have been accomplished unconsciously in most instances. The memory of the populace is long but unstable, and it was not difficult for the local heroes of heathen mythology to become Christian martyrs to a later generation. And at times the clergy deliberately facilitated the transfer. For instance, in Antioch in the fourth century the Christian authorities moved the remains of St. Babylus, the martyred bishop, to the local shrine of Daphne, their express purpose being to divert to the Church the devotion

---

[16] The examples here given are from the partial list in Schaff, *History of the Christian Church,* Vol. 5, pt. 1, p. 846. For a detailed discussion see E. A. Stückelberg, *Reliquien und Reliquiare.*

and offerings which until then had gone to the goddess! [17]

At first there was no attempt made to weigh the claims to sainthood. The people decided the matter for themselves, and each city and region and trade and nation somehow hit upon its own particular patron saint. The most that the clergy could do was strive to keep these saints from actually crowding out the Godhead. They tried to make the people realize that the saints could do nothing of themselves. They were only intermediaries between man and the Trinity, and at most deserved to be venerated, not worshiped. The proper formula when invoking their aid was *ora pro nobis*, "Pray for us."

But there was one sacred personage who was conceded even by the clergy to be deserving of more than simple veneration. This was Mary, the mother of Jesus—the "Blessed Virgin Mary" as she came to be called. Her popularity arose very early in the history of the Church, and could not but have been stimulated by the widespread popularity of certain goddesses among the Pagans. Astarte, Ashtoreth, Ishtar, Ma, Isis, Venus, Aphrodite, Cybele— these and countless other female deities had long been revered in the Mediterranean world. In the north too, there were such goddesses—for instance, Brigit in Ireland and Eostre in the Teutonic lands. And baptism could no more remove them from the minds of the converts than it

[17] Duchesne, *Early History of the Church*, Vol. II, p. 251. For a discussion of the whole subject of Christian hagiolatry, see H. R. Percival, *The Invocation of Saints*, and especially P. Saintyves, *Les Saints, successeurs des Dieux*.

could eradicate the lusts from their hearts. Throughout untold ages the natives had prayed to those deities to fructify the soil, and the wombs of their cattle and wives; and now they feared that all the world would become sterile if their prayers ceased.

It was apparently out of this habit and fear that there first arose the devotion to Mary. In the beginning she was merely one of the saints, but by the fourth century she became preëminent among them, and by the thirteenth she seemed to eclipse even Christ. Not alone was she proclaimed the "Mother of God"—Cybele, it should be noted, had been known to the Romans as the "Great Mother of the Gods"—and called the "Perpetual Virgin"—many of the Pagan goddesses were reputedly virgins—but, in addition, she was declared to have been "immaculately conceived," and to have quitted this earth not in death but through an "assumption" into Heaven. Unlike all other mortals since Eve, she had come into life without the taint of Original Sin, and had never known temptation or death.[18]

It is significant that just as the priests of Cybele and Astarte and many of the other fertility goddesses had been the self-emasculated *corybantes* and *galli,* so the most intense devotees of the Virgin were the monks and nuns. And just as those deities had been the patronesses of sacred

[18] The doctrine of the "Immaculate Conception," though not pronounced a dogma until 1854, is at least as old as the 13th century. It is not to be confused with the doctrine of the "Virgin Birth," which refers to the origin of Jesus. The rabidest atheist can accept the former, for, unpersuaded that there is any Original Sin, he has no reason to deny that Mary—like all other mortals—was immaculately conceived. But only the orthodox can believe that Jesus was born of a virgin. The rise of the veneration of Mary is well outlined in S. B. Pusey's *Eirenicon.*

harlotry, so did Mary become the special protector of wanton monks and frail nuns. The medieval chronicles are filled with tales of Mary's indulgence to such sinners. For instance, Pelbart in his *Pomerium Sermonum de Beata Virgine,* recounts five of her best known miracles, among them that of saving from damnation "a cleric given up to lechery, in whom, however, there was this one good thing, that he was wont to say the Hours of the Blessed Virgin with devotion." [19] It came to be the fixed belief in medieval times that even a perfunctory reverence for her name was enough to redeem the most heinous vices. Razzi, in his famous collection of Mary-legends, the *Miracoli della Gloriosa Virgine Maria,* tells of "a knight of infamous life, whose castle stood by a high road, a man devoid of all respect or compassion, who was wont to rob and despoil all wayfarers," yet who was saved from the Devil because "by God's high providence it was his custom to salute the Virgin daily." Another of the saved was "a woman of sin, who never did any virtuous thing in the whole space of her life, except that she visited the Virgin Mary daily and saluted her with an *Ave,* and one single Saturday she caused a Mass to be sung in praise and glory of the said blessed Virgin.". . .

The introduction of such a character into the grim heaven of medieval Christianity was no doubt a blessing to the race; but it was not nearly so extensive a blessing as some writers have tried to make out. The common notion that it raised the status of woman is not at all established by history. The fact that Mary was a woman

[19] Quoted in Coulton, *Five Centuries of Religion,* Vol. I, p. 146. Much that follows is taken from this most erudite work.

made the Church no more respectful toward her sex than the fact that Jesus had been an Israelite made the Christians kindly to the Jews. Actually Mary was not at all a woman in the minds of the believers; rather she was a goddess. She was deemed superior to Christ himself by many in that age. The good monk Gautier de Coincy declares:

"She is more truly Lady in earth and heaven, by one degree, than God Himself. He loveth her so, and hath such faith in her, that she can neither do nor say aught that He will disavow or gainsay. . . . If she were to say that the magpie is black, or that muddy water is as clear as crystal, then would He make answer: 'My Mother saith sooth!' " [20]

Little wonder, then, that in the thirteenth century the great Vincent de Beauvais could cry: "O Lady, Lady, if thou fail thy servants, who will succor them?"; or that in the fifteenth century some poor layman making his will could bequeath his soul to "his mooste blessed moder, Saint Mary Virgyn Quene of heven Lady of the Worlde and Emporesse of Helle." Little wonder that to this day the Sicilian marks his spade handle with a magic sign consisting of four strokes, in honor of the Holy Quaternity— Father, Son, Holy Ghost, and "Maria Santissima"!

And thus, through the veneration of the saints and the Virgin, did the masses avenge themselves for what had

[20] Quoted in Henry Adams, *Mont St-Michel and Chartres,* 1913, p. 274—a beautiful and stimulating book, but not altogether convincing in its tenor. It is usually prudent to secrete a rich enzyme of skepticism when digesting American books on medieval times.

been done to their Jesus. The theologians had removed him from the earth and had made him Christ the Judge; and the populace was not content with such a deity. If they could find mercy even on earth, they had to find it also in Heaven. And they did find it there. A monastic document of the period casts a most illuminating sidelight on popular thinking in that feudal age. It declares:

> "We ought to imitate the man who has incurred the king's anger. What does he do? He goes secretly to the queen and promises a present, then to the earls and barons and does the same; then to the free men of the household, and lastly to the footmen. So when we have offended Christ, we should first go to the Queen of Heaven and offer her a gift of prayers, fasting, vigils, and alms; then she, like a mother, will come between thee and Christ, the father who wishes to beat us, and she will throw the cloak of mercy between the rod of punishment and us, and soften the king's anger against us. Afterwards we should go to the earls and barons, *i.e.,* the apostles, and ask them to intercede for us; then to the knights and esquires, *i.e.,* martyrs and confessors; then to the ladies of the Queen's Chambers, *i.e.,* the woman saints; and lastly to the footmen, *i.e.,* to the poor." [21]

As has already been remarked, some few of the clerics did attempt to protest against this virtual polytheism that had arisen in Christianity; but their efforts were of no avail. Even open idolatry could not be kept out of the

[21] The *Fasciculus Morum,* quoted in A. G. Little, *Studies in English Franciscan History,* 1917, p. 149.

Church. In the first centuries the Christians had abhorred the very thought of images. That was why the Pagans had accused them of atheism. But as time passed and the religion spread, this antipathy began to wane. As early as 305 we discover the Synod of Elvira unable to say more than that "pictures ought not to be placed in churches." The common people evidently could not be content without representations of the beings they venerated and worshiped, and gradually such representations began to make their appearance on the tombs of martyrs, on the walls of the churches, over the doors of private dwellings, on the furniture, even on clothes.[22]

The clergy, unable to halt the development, excused it on the ground that these images served the illiterate as the words of the Holy Writ served the learned. The walls of the churches, daubed from end to end with crude representations of the saints and the Virgin and Christ, and even God and the Holy Ghost, came to be called the "Poor Man's Bible"; and, since these representations were at first only painted, not carved, they did not seem to transgress the Mosaic commandment against graven images. What the clergy did try to impress upon the people was the fact that the pictures were only symbols, and therefore were never to be worshiped. But even in this they were powerless to succeed, for the visible symbol was much more impressive than the invisible reality which was said to be behind it. Certain of the pictures came to be regarded as potent fetishes, and all manner of legends were told re-

[22] The development of iconolatry and the history of the Iconoclastic Controversy is well recounted in Neander, *General History of the Christian Religion and Church*, 1856, Vol. III, pp. 194-243.

garding them. At Edessa there was a portrait of Jesus which it was said he himself had presented to the king of the land. In many places there were paintings which were reputed to have been made "without human hands."

Pagan influence was marked in these images, for the Christ they depicted was strikingly like Apollo, and the Virgin with the Christ-child was almost a precise replica of the old Egyptian representations of Isis holding the infant Horus in her arms. And, just as the Pagans had believed that the statues of Minerva could brandish spears and those of Venus could weep, so did the Christians now say that certain images of Christ could bleed, and others of Mary could wink. And not all the sermons in a year of Lenten days could keep the people from bowing to these icons and kissing them adoringly.

By the eighth century this image-worship had become so rife that the Jews—who were to be found scattered everywhere—and the Moslems—who were now an aggressive power in the East—were wont to taunt the Christians with being rank idolators. The taunt provoked the emperor than ruling in Constantinople, a man of rare ability named Leo the Isaurian, who cherished ambitions of converting these Jews and Moslems. Conceding the justice of the complaint, he issued an edict in the year 726 prohibiting prostration before the images, and directing that they be put so high that none could kiss them. This was in effect an attempt at compromise, for it did not order the destruction of the images but only a cessation of their worship. Yet it aroused such furious opposition on the part of the clergy as well as the populace, that Leo soon found himself an excommunicant. His son, Constantine Capronymus, continued the struggle, and for some thirty years waged incessant war on the icons and those who favored them. All public officials, and all ecclesiastics and monks, were peremptorily commanded to abjure image-worship; those who refused were ruthlessly slaughtered. Unhappily for him, Rome was beyond his reach, and he had to confine his iconoclastic outrages to the East. There his armies almost exterminated the monks because they would not obey his commands, and by the time he died there was hardly a picture left undefaced in any church within his realm.

Five years later, however, a woman, the empress Irene, came into power, and, although she was capable of seizing her own son and gouging out his eyes in the very chamber in which she had borne him, she was far too devout to favor iconoclasm. In 787 the Seventh General Council— the last ever to be held by a united "universal" church— decreed that pictures, the cross, and the Gospels "should be given due salutation and honorable reverence. . . . For the honor which is paid to the image passes on to that which the image represents.". . .

Even then, however, the controversy did not cease. Succeeding emperors, anxious to assert their authority over the hierarchy and the monks, renewed the iconoclastic movement, and for some two generations there was inter-mittent persecution. But finally when another woman, the empress Theodora, came into power, the clerics were able to have their way once more. The images were again allowed in the churches, and those who opposed them were crushed without mercy. These images were still only paintings on flat surfaces; but they did not remain so for long. Gradually it became the fashion to leave the hands and face painted flat, but to raise and carve the clothes on the body of the icon. Finally—but only in the Roman, not in the Greek Church—real statues began to make their appearance. And therewith the reversion to the externalities of Paganism was complete.

BOOK FOUR

𝕿𝖍𝖊 𝕳𝖆𝖑𝖈𝖞𝖔𝖓 𝖄𝖊𝖆𝖗𝖘
𝕬. 𝕯. 800=1415

THE HALCYON YEARS: 800-1415 A.D.

1: The Papacy and the World and the Flesh. 2: Corruption of the Church. 3: The Cluniac Reform —Hildebrand. 4: On to the Holy Land! 5: The Crusades. 6: More Crusades. 7: The Shattering of Papal Power. 8: The Faith Wanes. 9: The Spread of Heresy. 10: The Franciscan and Dominican Revivals. 11: Wyclif and Huss.

HERE were three fundamental elements in the faith of the early Church: an apocalyptic hope that Christ would soon return, a conviction that the practice of Christ's ethical teachings would hasten the return, and a belief that the observance of certain sacraments assured one of salvation in the hour of that return. Of these, only the third remained conspicuous in the medieval Church. The first, the apocalyptic hope, was betrayed by time: though it never died out completely, it was never able to thrive save fitfully. And the second, the striving for perfection, was betrayed by man: though it managed to survive in a distorted form in the monasteries, it could never command the life of more than a minority. Only the sacramental element was able to flourish throughout the Church, and, as a consequence, that alone dominated the medieval faith. There were saints left in Christendom, men and women who saw visions and tasted ecstasy and lived in and for the love of Christ. But they were the rare, rare exceptions. To the vast majority, whether in orders or of the laity, Christianity had become a religion of routine and observance—a filling draught for their incessant thirst, but one that was flat, very flat.

There were powerful economic forces working for this triumph of sacramentalism. In the very beginning Christianity was a religion of the proletariat, and therefore could well afford to be adventist in its faith and communist in its practice. But after the third century it became the religion of folk who had much to lose if the world came to an end, and nothing to gain in any sharing of wealth. As a result Christianity had to slough off its pristine radicalism. It had to preach stability rather than destruction, and conservation rather than change. And no force is so favorable to stability, none is so prejudicial to change, as ceremonialism. A people devoted to rites is bound hand and foot, and those who are the masters of the rites are the absolute masters of all. And that may have been one of the underlying reasons why the sacraments became central in Christian belief and practice. They surrendered all power into the hands of the priests, and thus into the hands of the lords who were able for a long time to control the priests.

That is why we must now leave the field of faith for a while, and concern ourselves largely with politics. The history of medieval Christianity is primarily the history of the struggles of the priests to dominate even the lords. The Greek establishment, in which there was little of such struggling, plays a minor rôle after the early centuries. Inherently given to theology and a dark kind of mysticism, and suffering always from the immanence of the imperial throne, the Eastern patriarchs were allowed no chance to reach out and assert themselves. Indeed, had it not been for the conversion of Russia, their Orthodox Church might have become in time a mere minor communion like that of the Copts.

But the Roman Church was subject to conditions quite different from those obtaining in the East, and had a totally different career. The campaign of Leo the Isaurian to abolish image-worship gave the papacy its long-sought excuse for a break with the Byzantine palace. Rome no longer needed Constantinople; it could profit more by an alliance with some secular power in the West. Such a power existed in the Franks, whose "mayor," Charles Martel, had just halted the Saracens and had saved Europe for Christianity. The Franks formed a cohesive and virile nation, and, though their kings belonged to a defunct and impotent line, their dictators, the "mayors of the palace," were successively men of marked ability. Accordingly the popes began to negotiate with these dictators and finally aided one of them, Pepin the Short, to usurp the throne. In the year 754, Pope Stephen II journeyed north to St. Denis, near Paris, and there anointed Pepin as King of the Franks and "Patrician of the Romans." In return, Pepin marched south with an army, defeated the barbarous Lombards who had been threatening Rome, and turned over a portion of northern Italy to the papacy. Thus at a single stroke Pope Stephen became the anointer of kings and possessor of a temporal realm.

His successor accomplished even more. The Roman See was still nominally subject to the emperor at Constantinople, as was also the Frankish crown. Now, however, this subjection was definitely ended, and in a manner worth recounting. Pepin the Short was succeeded in the year 771 by his son Charles—later called Charlemagne—who was destined to prove one of the great rulers of history. He was both a devout Christian and a good soldier, and, by combining these qualities, he was able to wage a series of religious wars against the still unconverted Saxons and Slavonians in northern and central Europe, which finally made his realm at least as extensive as that of the old Western Empire. The pope of the day, Leo III, soon had reason to be grateful that he had such a monarch for an ally. Leo III was unpopular in Rome, and one day, during a religious procession, he was set upon in the streets, severely bruised, and forced to flee. He took refuge in Germany with Charlemagne, but the following year (800) he returned under the escort of that mighty king, and was reinstated as pope.

Then it was Leo's turn to do something for the partnership, and he did more than had been bargained for. Charlemagne stayed to spend Christmas in Rome, and, good Christian that he was, he went to St. Peter's for the holy-day service. But there a shock awaited him. As he was rising from prayer at the feet of the pope, the king suddenly felt a crown being clapped on his head and heard himself loudly proclaimed Cæsar and Augustus of the empire! The coup infuriated Charlemagne. He had long cherished the ambition of becoming emperor, but he had thought to achieve it by marrying the empress Irene, who was then reigning in Constantinople. That scheme, however, was spoiled now. The crafty Leo had stolen a march on him, and had forced him to accept the imperial title as a gift from the papacy. Charlemagne's friend and biographer, Eginhard, assures us that had the king suspected what was awaiting him that day, "he would never have entered the church, great festival though it was." But he had known nothing, and, after the pope had sprung his surprise and the populace had hailed him emperor, it was already too late.

And thus was adumbrated the "Holy Roman Empire," which, as has so often been remarked, was neither holy nor Roman nor an empire.[1] Brought into actuality through deception, it bred contention and strife so long as it endured. The kings never became reconciled to the overlordship of the popes, and generation after generation they struggled to put an end to the exasperating situation. But the popes, prolific in the forging of new documents to substantiate their claim, and armed with the power of excommunication against such as had no respect for documents, managed to hold on.

It cost them their souls, but, all things considered, the price was small. For the pontiffs during this and succeeding centuries were for the most part sullied creatures. They could be called men of God only in irony; in sober fact the best of them were astute statesmen and the worst were low-lived courtiers. Many were able to reign no more than a few months, toppling from the throne, even as they had attained it, through intrigue and violence. Sometimes there were two, three, even four rival popes ruling simultaneously. Usually they were the tools of one or other of the contending political parties in Italy, and in at least two instances they were elected to Christ's vicarage only because they were the paramours of rich Roman matrons.

[1] See Bryce, *Holy Roman Empire*, the outstanding work on the subject.

That was the case with Pope Sergius III, who marched on Rome in 904 with a force of mercenaries, deposed Pope Christopher—who himself had just deposed Pope Leo V, who in turn had reigned less than two months—and with the help of a courtesan named Marozia, whose cunning was not confined to the bedchamber, managed to hold onto St. Peter's throne for some six years. Then came the turn of Marozia's mother, Theodora, who, although the wife of a Roman senator and mistress of a Tuscan nobleman, was in love also with a cleric. Inconveniently the man resided in Ravenna, where he was archbishop, and Theodora found it hard to gratify her passion at such a distance. Once her daughter's lover was dead, however, and the papacy was vacant, Theodora knew what to do. She had *her* lover called to Rome to be the pope, and he managed to retain that office some fourteen years. When he finally fell it was solely because of the jealousy of the daughter. Resenting the loss of power she had once wielded in Rome, Marozia arranged for the murder of her stepfather-in-sin, and, after a short interregnum, elevated her own son to the throne.

The young man who now became Pope John XI was not yet twenty-one, and his only claim to sanctity was the doubtful one that he may have been the bastard son of Pope Sergius III. He was succeeded by a grandson of that same Marozia, a depraved youth, barely eighteen years of age, who took the name of John XII. The lout, after eight years of unbridled debauchery, was finally ordered to appear before the Roman synod and refute the charges that he had made a ten-year-old boy a bishop, had drunk to the health of the Devil, had committed murder, had violated virgins and widows and wives high and low, and had failed to attend matins and vespers regularly! When the summons reached him, however, he sent back word that he had "gone out hunting," failing to add that he had carried off with him all that was portable of the papal treasury. He was condemned and deposed, but in a short while he was back again and then actually got reinstated as pope. Soon after, however, an enraged husband caught him in the act of adultery and strangled him to death. *"Qualis artifex pereo!"* he might have cried as had an earlier ruler in Rome: "How artistically I die!" [2]

There was a measure of improvement in the character of the popes during the ensuing century; but then the pontificate fell into the hands of Benedict IX, a twelve-year-old boy, and thereupon even the career of John XII was outdone for rascality. At first the puppet and then the leader of a gang of Roman politicians, the boy was able to hold on to the papal throne until he was twenty-four. He ruled like a captain of banditti, committing murders and adulteries in open daylight, robbing pilgrims at the graves of martyrs, and turning all Rome into a den of thieves. Finally, in 1045, after emptying the treasury, he put up the Apostolic See at auction and sold it to a presbyter for a thousand pounds of silver! One wonders whether it was a bargain even at so small a price. . . .

[2] This infamous period beginning with Sergius III in 904 and continuing through John XII to 963 is often spoken of even by Catholic historians as the Papal Pornocracy. Distorted recollections of the activities of Marozia and her mother may be the source of the curious legend that one of the popes was a woman in disguise. According to the story, this imposter took the name of John and reigned two and a half years before she betrayed herself by falling in the midst of a religious procession and giving sudden birth to a child. See Schaff, *History of the Christian Church*, Vol. IV, p. 265.

THE befouling of the papacy was not an isolated phenomenon but rather one symptom of a blight that had struck the entire Church. There were, of course, many clerics in the tenth and eleventh centuries who were men of probity, and true servants of the Lord. But this saving remnant was as yet so scattered and lacking in influence as to be lost among the rest. Christianity, it must be remembered, was no longer a shout of courage uttered in a world whimpering with despair. Its purpose now was not so much to arouse men as to cow them into docility. The Church had become the bulwark of the State, for its teaching constituted a defense of the contemporary social order. In essence Catholicism now was but a doctrinal sanction for feudalism. The Catholic Church, with its papal overlord and descending ranks of clergy, was itself a feudal institution. Even Heaven had been made a feudal court with its Lord and Blessed Lady and graded classes of angels, saints, and scholars. In such a time-serving religion it was only to be expected that the majority of the clerics should be mere job-holders. What had happened centuries earlier in Brahmanism had now come to pass in Christianity: the poison of caste had eaten into the faith and made it rank.

No single man, even no class of men, was to blame for this debacle. There had never been any conspiracy on the part of the priests to prey upon the laity, nor on the part of the bishops to exploit the priests. Very few of the clerics could have had wit enough, let alone the will, to make themselves oppressors. They were as much the victims of circumstances as the people off whom they lived. It may well have been a malicious sense of irony which prompted the iconoclastic emperor, Constantine Capronymus, to reinstate his patriarch after having gouged out the holy man's eyes. With or without their eyes, the majority of the ecclesiastics were blind men. The ordinary parish priests were barely able to read, and in the Catholic Church, where the ritual was in Latin, most of them did not understand even the commonest prayers. One must remember that there were as yet no established seminaries where a candidate for orders could prepare himself for his vocation. The least ignorant of the clergy came from the cloisters or were reared in the houses of old priests; the majority, however, were men who by hook or crook had been able to persuade some bishop to grant them ordination.

Such individuals were usually quite incompetent to give true Christian instruction to their flocks. They were content merely to perform the customary rites like so many medicine-men working magic. They were quite as superstitious as the serfs who brought them offerings and confessed to them their sins. They, too, believed in the miraculous powers of the Virgin and the saints and the relics and the Mass. One medieval chronicler assures us that even the popes were commanded to turn toward the congregation at the time of the Communion, because it was feared that otherwise they might slip the bread out of their mouths and save it for black magical purposes. The priests were wont to dispense the rinsings of the chalice as an eye-wash for the blind, or as a magic extinguisher in case of a fire. Nor did they do these things as charlatans seeking to delude the masses; they were themselves deluded. Nothing is clearer than that the vast majority, at least of the lower clerics, were not knaves but honest simpletons.[3]

Their conception of God was what one might expect it to be in these circumstances. When in the tenth century the comparatively enlightened Ratherius of Verona tried to preach the doctrine that God was a spirit, certain of his clergy were dismayed and cried: "But God is nothing at all if he has not a head."[4] And their conduct was as crude as their theology. They observed what might be termed a middle morality, neither aspiring to the asceticism of the devout monks nor confessing the carnality of honest peasants. A contemporary assures us that in the year 1040 "it would have been very difficult to find a single priest who was not illiterate, who had not purchased his office, and who did not have a concubine." Hildebrand declares that when he began his reforms he found within St. Peter's sixty married laymen who made their living by dressing in the vestments of cardinals and reading Masses for the money-laden pilgrims. Another adds concerning the priests of Milan that "they vied with each other as to who should have the most sumptuous dresses, the most abundant tables, and the most beautiful mistresses."[5]

Many of the priests had no churches, and wandered about from village to village, earning their bread by blessing relics and celebrating Masses. Probably these were rather like the lower-grade itinerant evangelists of our own

[3] See Coulton, *Five Centuries of Religion*, Appendix XII.
[4] Quoted in Fisher, *History of the Christian Church*, p. 176.
[5] All three quotations are given in Workman, *The Church of the West in the Middle Ages*, 1912, Vol. I, p. 55.

day: mountebanks of a seedy and ignoble order. But even
the priests who did have churches were not much better as
a lot. They may have been rather more honest, according
to their own lights; but the holy office was a "living" to
most of them, not a life.

Nor was the situation better in the higher ranks of the
clergy. The bishops usually purchased their offices from
the kings or the ducal princes, and they conducted themselves quite like the temporal nobles. The best were
provident landlords or astute statesmen; but most of them
were ordinary feudal barons. If they were *sans peur et
sans reproche,* it was solely because they were too brazen to
be afraid and too powerful to be reproached. As St. Peter
Damiani cried in despair: "It is easier even to convert a
Jew than reform a prelate."

But the secular clerics had never been conspicuous for
saintliness, and if they were now in bondage to the flesh
and the Devil it was because they had always been inden-
tured to the world. What was far more alarming was the
corruption that had set in among the monks, for these were
men who in the beginning had been clean. They, too, had
succumbed, however, and the worldliness they had once
sought to flee was now intrenched in their very cloisters.
The wave of frenetic idealism that had swept men into the
monasteries in St. Benedict's day had long since spent
itself. Baser motives were now impelling men to put on
the cowl. The cloister had come to be a convenient refuge
for those too indolent or too weak for that iron age. Peasants weary of struggling with a reluctant soil, artisans tired
of toiling day and night in fetid towns, maidens sick of
their parents' homes, sons too frail to bear the heavy
armor, wives revolted by their brutal mates, and penniless

[193]

widows, stranded harlots, and runaway debtors and thieves —to all such hapless creatures the monastery was almost a heaven on earth. Once enrolled as monks or nuns, or at least as lay helpers, they were safe from the terrors that had obsessed them in the world.

Worse still, the cloister had degenerated into a sort of dump heap for those who were unwanted in the world. Upper-class children who were in the way, especially illegitimate sons and younger daughters—for a man had to be exceedingly rich to afford dowries for more than one daughter—were quite frequently delivered to the monks or nuns with an "oblation" for their lifelong keep. And these oblate children made sorry saints. They had never willingly renounced the world; it had renounced *them.* As a consequence, they brought into the cloisters a spirit of resentment and rebelliousness which very swiftly demoralized those institutions.

Worst of all, the cloister had come to be used at times as a boarding house for women and the sick. Lords going off to war were wont to deposit their wives and daughters with the nuns for safekeeping.[6] Idiots, epileptics, and other such unfortunates were similarly quartered on the monastics. And rich folk when critically ill would often resort to the cloisters of their own will, believing that the holy garb might stave off death, or, failing that, could save their souls from hell.[7] And the continual coming and going of these transient guests could not but destroy the morale in the institutions.

Each of these elements alone would have been enough

[6] Eileen Power, *Medieval People,* 1924, p. 74. The whole chapter entitled "Madame Eglentyne" is worth reading in this connection.

[7] Coulton, *Five Centuries of Religion,* Vol. I, pp. 90ff, 476ff. Chapter 14 in this work discusses in detail the subject of "oblate children."

to disturb monastic discipline; all of them together simply shattered it. From the end of the ninth century onward we hear increasing complaint because of conditions in the cloisters. The monks had grown lazy; they left it for the many serfs and slaves attached to the monasteries to cultivate the fields. They themselves, being in their own language "God's fishes swimming in God's stewpond," felt manual toil to be beneath them. The great Abelard confesses concerning his own abbey, St. Gildas de Ruys in Brittany:

> "Every lean fellow, when he reaches this stewpond of the cloister, soon waxes so fat, that seeing him again after a brief while, you can scarce recognize him. You will find more fat and sleek folk, more heated with wine, and more bald heads in any small company of monks than among a thousand layfolk."

Even in the best monasteries of the old Benedictine type there was no longer any strict observance of the Rule. The monastic estates were now far flung, and it was necessary for the monks to travel long distances to attend to their management. This made for a relaxing of discipline which soon had its effect on all the other Benedictine restrictions. The monks began to eat meat; they even stayed out all night ostensibly to hunt for it. The hemina of wine permitted in the Rule became a hogshead. To evade the prohibition of speech, the monks used a sign language which in time became so widespread that directories were compiled for the instruction of novitiates. In some of the stricter houses, where the manual signs were forbidden—"because," says Cardinal Jacques de Vitry, "they were wont by such signs to tell vain and curious things to their fellows"—the monks even learned to converse with their toes! [8]

Not alone the lesser rules but even the *tria substantialia* were transgressed. The monasteries had acquired enormous wealth and vast lands, and the only poverty connected with them was that which ground their serfs. St. Germaine-des-Prés possessed some forty thousand tenants and dependants, and its annual income around 800 A.D. has been estimated by Guerard to have been in excess of a quarter of a million dollars. [9] When in the thirteenth century the monks began to take the title of *Dominus*—abbreviated usually to *Dom*—meaning "my lord," few voices were raised in protest. By that time the monks had already been lords in effect if not in name for hundreds of years.

Where wealth accumulates, men decay. Idleness and overeating left the monks easy prey to other temptations. We have it on the authority of Abelard that in his abbey in Brittany the monks lived with their concubines quite openly, and kept their sons and daughters in the monastery itself. That was an exceptional case; it was more common for the brethren to try to conceal their unchastity. But even then it was usually discovered, and a whole host of ribald tales arose about the monastery on one hill, the nunnery

[8] Coulton, *Five Centuries of Religion,* Vol. I, p. 87, Appendix I, p. 473ff., gives excerpts from a sign directory dating from about the year 1000. For instance: "For the sign of fish in general, imitate with your hand the commotion of a fish's tail in the water. . . . For a pike, put your right hand over your nostrils, with the tips of your fingers sticking upwards. . . . For an eel, clench both hands, as if you were thus holding an eel tightly. . . . For kissing, lay your forefinger on your lips. . . ." The signs for twelve different liquors are given in this particular lexicon!

[9] Coulton, *op. cit.,* Vol. II, p. 35.

on the next, and the orphanage in the valley between. The records of the episcopal inspectors are replete with scandals. We read, for instance, in the *Register* of Archbishop Rigaud:

"We visited the priory of Villa Arcelli. Thirty-three nuns are there and three lay sisters. They confess and take communion six times a year. . . . Johanna of Aularlari once went out and lived with some one, returning with a child . . . she is also suspected with a man named Gaillard. The stewardess is suspected with Thomas the teamster; Idonia with Crispinatus; and the Prior of Gisorcium is always coming for this Idonia. Philippa of Rouen is suspected with a priest of Suentre; Agnes de Fontenai with a priest of Guerreville. . . . Jacqueline came back pregnant after visiting a certain chaplain. . . . Agnes de Mousec was suspected with the same. . . . The prioress is drunk almost every night. . . ."

The attitude of the inspectors toward such derelictions can be gathered from the reports which state the official recommendations. For instance:

"We were again at Ouville. We found that the prior wanders about; he is not in his cloister one day in five. *Item,* he is a drunkard, and of such vileness that he sometimes lies out in the fields because of it. *Item,* he frequents feasts and drinking bouts with laymen. *Item,* he is incontinent, and is accused with respect to a certain woman of Grainville, and also with the wife of Robertot, and also with a woman of Rouen named Agnes. *Item,* brother Geoffrey was publicly accused with respect to the wife of Walter of Esquaquelon, who recently had a child from him. *Item,* they do not keep proper accounts of the revenues. [Recommendation:] We ordered that they keep proper accounts." [10]

With poverty gone and chastity thus transgressed, obedience was of course not to be expected. The monks knew too much about their abbots and priors to stand in awe of them, and insubordination became the rule rather than the exception. If a zealous abbot arose here or there and tried to tame his monks, he was either forced out by intrigue or murdered. The world had triumphed. Most of the "stewponds of God" had become cloacas of the Devil.

3

ET the degradation was by no means complete. There were still men left in the Church who were devoted to Christ and loyal to their vows. We can tell this from the literature of the period, for had there been no regenerate men in that day, there would have been no complaint against the waywardness of the majority. That is a point that needs to be stressed, for the critical eye is inclined to see only the sores, and be blind to the healthy flesh still left on

[10] Both excerpts are from the *Regestrum visitationum archiepiscopi Rothomagensis,* and are quoted in Taylor, *The Medieval Mind,* 1927, Vol. I, pp. 493, 495.

the body of the Church. Even in this hour, there was still rich and unpolluted blood coursing in the veins of Christendom; and in time that blood was able to send a new glow to the surface of the entire body. The process of recuperation had already set in early in the ninth century, during the reign of Charlemagne; but it had receded then almost at once. A hundred years later, however, it was once more under way, and that time it was not so easily halted. The movement had its origin then in a new monastery founded at Cluny, in eastern France, and culminated a century and a half later in the election of a Cluniac monk named Hildebrand to the papacy.

In the beginning the aim was to reform no more than the monasteries. The first abbots of Cluny set out to show their colleagues how a garrison of *true* soldiers of Christ should be conducted; and their example of strict discipline and fast piety was so impressive that before long they had many imitators. Even the mother Benedictine cloister, at Monte Cassino in Italy, reformed itself on Cluny lines. The next step was the founding of a "congregation" of reformed monasteries, each governed by priors appointed by, and responsible to, the abbot of Cluny. This was something new in Western monasticism, for it made Cluny practically an order, and lent it all the strength and influence implicit in such a "chain" organization. With this growth came an enlargement of the aims of the movement. It reached out from the monasteries and began to agitate for the reform of all clerical life. Cluny began to get its best members elected to the important presbyteries and bishoprics—for by now most of the monks were ordained priests, not laymen any more—and through them the leaven was brought to work in the whole Church.

The main aims of the reform party were the suppression of "simony"—that is, the buying and selling of clerical offices—and the enforcement of celibacy among the clergy. Before the first of these aims could be accomplished, however, it was absolutely essential to free the local benefices of lay control. Originally the bishops and presbyters had been elected by the congregations, but that had been before Constantine made theology the bedfellow of politics. Since then the kings and dukes had assumed control of the benefices, distributing them among their courtiers and relatives as they might any of the other feudal spoils. Religion had become an apparently inexhaustible source of revenue, and the higher clerical positions were very handsome plums to give or sell. Religious zeal, or learning, or probity, were only exceptionally considered as qualifications for episcopal office. Investiture was a rich investment, and to obtain it one needed either influence with the local ruler or ability to pay the highest price. And this condition of affairs had gone on for so long that by now it seemed divinely sanctioned. In seeking to wrest from the kings and princes their right to make ecclesiastical appointments, the Cluny movement was confronted with the task of changing the entire structure of medieval government.

To reform the lay rulers was out of the question. One abbot of Cluny had tried hard to popularize the "Truce of God," an institution which aimed to make Wednesday evening to Monday morning of each week a closed season for fighting; but very little had come of his effort. Obviously there was nothing to be looked for from the iron men of that age. War and wastefulness were in their blood, and they could never be expected to forego the chance of profiting by their control of the ecclesiastical offices. If the Church was to be saved, it *had* to be taken out of lay politics.

And thus began the long and bitter contest over "lay investiture"—the right of the temporal ruler to give to an elected bishop the ring and staff which were the tokens of his office. In effect it was a contest between the pope and the emperor—for the Cluny movement aimed to reform Church government not by reinvesting it in the hands of the worshipers, but by surrendering it entirely to the Apostolic See. The ideal of the reformers was the establishment of a complete autocracy in religion, and it was actually realized—for a while, at least—by one of the ablest and noblest and severest autocrats in medieval history. He was a man of humble origin and unimpressive appearance named Hildebrand. Educated in a Cluniac monastery, he had very early been fired with a passion for reform, and, what with his genius for administration and his indefatigable energy, he soon became the dominant influence in papal affairs. During twenty-four years, under six successive popes, the small, tight-lipped monk named Hildebrand was the power behind the throne; and finally, in the year 1073, he himself was raised to the see as Gregory VII.[11]

Open conflict became unavoidable then, for Hildebrand had no kidney for temporizing. The first time the reigning emperor, Henry IV, himself a man of determination, tried

[11] For the details see M. R. Vincent, *The Age of Hildebrand.*

to exercise the right to fill an ecclesiastical office in his realm, Hildebrand called him to severe account. Henry retorted by repudiating the pope's authority and ordering him to abdicate. That brought matters to an issue. There was no possible chance of compromise, for Hildebrand had already declared his attitude in a famous document, the *Dictatus Papæ,* which he himself may not have written, but which almost certainly expressed his views. He took his stand with St. Augustine, whose *City of God* had inspired the first great popes to claim a divinely appointed sovereignty over the whole universe. He insisted that the Roman pontiff was the Rock of the Church, the Universal Bishop, entrusted with the care of all Christendom (including the Greek Church, which had never acknowledged him); that he could be judged by no earthly tribunal, but was responsible only to God; that he alone could depose or reinstate bishops, and that his representatives, the legates, took precedence of all other ecclesiastics; that he was the supreme arbiter of right and wrong in the whole Christian world; and, finally, that he was above all earthly sovereigns, could absolve their subjects of allegiance to them if they were unworthy, and could even depose them at will!

Hildebrand was no vainglorious despot. He took so extreme a stand not out of personal arrogance but because he genuinely believed that whoever sat on the throne of Peter was guided by none other than God. But the emperor was in no position to appreciate the pope's sincerity. Calling a council of his nobles and bishops, he officially deposed Hildebrand on the ground of treason, witchcraft, covenant with the Devil, and impurity, and transmitted the decree in a vituperative letter which read in part:

"Henry, King not by usurpation, but by God's holy ordinance, to Hildebrand, not pope, but a false monk. How dare you stretch forth your hand against the Lord's anointed, despising the precept of the true pope, St. Peter: 'Fear God, honor thy King'? . . . Therefore I, Henry, King by the grace of God, with all my bishops, say to you, come down, come down, and be damned throughout all eternity!"

Hildebrand did not stop to argue. Calling a synod at Rome, he peremptorily excommunicated the king, forbade him authority over the empire, and released all his subjects from their oaths of allegiance.

"I bind him in the bands of anathema," read the papal sentence, "that all nations of the earth may know that upon this rock the Son of the living God hath built His Church, and the gates of hell shall not prevail against it."

It was a stroke of imperious daring. The heir of all the Cæsars was declared an outlaw by the successor of a Galilean fisherman! Yet it worked. The emperor was helpless, for the pope had called out against him the invincible force of medieval superstition. In a later day the sentence of anathema specified the curses entailed. One formula read:

"Let him [the excommunicant] be damned in his going out and coming in! The Lord strike him with madness and blindness and idiocy! May the heavens empty upon him their thunderbolts, and the wrath of the Almighty burn itself into him in the present and the future world! May the universe fight against him and the earth open to swallow him up alive! [12]

But though no such execrations were uttered in the condemnation of Henry, they were all implicit in the sentence. He was cut off from the living and rendered "untouchable." His realm began to fall apart. His own nobles and prelates turned against him, threatening to depose him.

Yet he would not give in. For two dreadful months he stayed shut up in his castle, deserted by all save his wife and a few servants. But finally he was simply forced to capitulate. It was winter—the coldest and longest winter within the memory of that generation. The Rhine had been a mass of solid ice since November, and the Alpine passes were almost impenetrable. Yet there was nothing left for the monarch but to make the long journey across the mountains and prostrate himself at the feet of the pope. He set out a few days before Christmas, accompanied only by his wife, their six-year-old son, and a faithful servant. The roads were filled with snow, and the horses that bore them fell dead in their tracks because of the bitter cold and the cruel going. When they reached the mountains, the queen and her child had to be carried up and lowered down the icy slopes in rough sledges of

[12] Used by Clement VI against Louis the Bavarian in 1346. Quoted in Hastings, *Encyc. of Religion and Ethics,* Vol. IV, p. 717.

oxhide. At last, after four weeks of travel, they reached the village of Canossa in northern Italy, where Hildebrand was resting on his way to a council. Henry sent word that he was ready to submit if released from the interdict; but the pope would not listen. Only the abdication of the throne and the surrender forever of all royal dignity would satisfy the iron-willed pope. Henry became desperate. He pleaded with Hildebrand's friends to intercede for him; he raged and begged. Finally he assumed the severest penance the Church could require of a sinner. Clad in a coarse woolen shirt, barefoot and with no covering on his head, he walked through the snow to the castle gate and implored to be admitted. But the old pope, hard as a rock and cold as the snow, was still unmoved. For three whole days he kept the king shivering outside the gate before he at last relented. The gate opened and the king was allowed to enter. He was a tall man in the prime of life, and even in rags, half frozen with cold, he was still somehow regally impressive. Before him sat a little peasant-born old priest, gray-haired, bowed, and emaciated. Yet of the two it was the king who had to fall on his knees. Bursting into tears, he cried from the ground: "Spare me, holy father, spare me!" The onlookers, even those of Hildebrand's court, were overcome; but the stern little pontiff barely winced. Reaching out his hand, he absolved the monarch of his sin, gave him the apostolic blessing, and then led him to the chapel where a Mass was performed.

And thus, in the year 1077, the papacy reached its apogee. The greatest monarch on earth had been made to come begging for a pope's mercy, and the triumph of priestcraft seemed complete.[13]

But the triumph was overcomplete. Hildebrand might have gained more had he exacted less, for his victory brought a reaction in its train. Enemies began to spring up on every side, and before long it was the pope's turn to fight for his throne. As soon as Henry was back in Germany, he began to plot vengeance; nor was it hard for him to find abettors then. Even within the Church he discovered widespread hostility to Hildebrand, largely because of the pope's unremitting campaign to enforce celibacy on the clergy. Ever since Paul's day there had been a horror of sex in the more devout Christian circles, and from the outset the priests had been expected to set an example of intemperate virtue. So far as they were concerned, all sexual intercourse was "fornication"—a term derived from the Latin *fornices,* meaning the "arches" beneath which the prostitutes of ancient Rome had carried on their sordid trade. But the pious expectation was only rarely fulfilled, and the majority of the priests, especially in the rural sections, married and begat children quite openly. Nor was anyone greatly exercised that principle and practice should be so divergent; the two rarely tallied in any department of life during the Middle Ages. Not until the rise of the Cluny party was there great agitation because the priesthood paid so little heed to the command of celibacy, and even then little was done at first save pass resolutions.

[13] The account here given of the dramatic episode at Canossa is taken very largely from Schaff, *History of the Christian Church,* 1926, Vol. V, pt. I, p. 47ff., a monumental work in seven volumes which deserves the highest praise.

But when Hildebrand ascended the papal throne he set out to enforce those resolutions. He was steeped in the unhappy conviction that sex was essentially "unclean" and fit only for laymen. In addition he realized the hurt to the Church which resulted from clerical marriage. Priests entangled in domesticity could not give themselves completely to their priestly work. Besides, if they had offspring they were tempted to favor them and make them heirs to their altars. Worst of all, the thought of a priest abed with his wife hardly made for that aura of sanctity which was indispensable if the clergy was to retain its hold on the people. For all these reasons Hildebrand believed that celibacy simply had to be enforced among the clergy. Accordingly he not alone passed decrees prohibiting sacerdotal marriage, but also ordered that all married priests must immediately put away their wives. To insure obedience, he forbade the laity to attend the services of such as persisted in their guilt, and even urged that violence be used against them.

These drastic measures aroused a storm of opposition. Many clerics denounced Hildebrand as a madman and a heretic, crying that he wanted men to live like angels, and reminding him that even Paul had declared: "It is better to marry than to burn." Some said they would far rather give up their calling than their wives, and tauntingly asked the pope to seek out angels to fill their places. Hildebrand, however, would not be shaken. Unable to procure the coöperation of the bishops in his campaign, he tried to incite the lay rulers. He called on the dukes and barons to use their swords if the immoral priests could not otherwise be prevented from officiating at the altars. And many of the lay rulers, glad of the chance to harry the ecclesiastics, rushed to the pope's support. A contemporary priest gives a frightful picture of the immediate results of the campaign.

"Friend informed against friend, faith and truth were violated, the offices of religion were neglected, society was almost dissolved. The peccant priests were exposed to the scorn and contempt of the laity, reduced to extreme poverty, or even mutilated by the populace. . . . Their wives who had been legally married with ring and religious rites, were insulted as harlots, and their children branded as bastards. Many of these unfortunate women died from hunger or grief, or committed suicide in despair, and were buried in unconsecrated earth. Peasants burned their tithes on the field lest they should fall into the hands of disobedient priests, trampled the Host underfoot, and baptized their own children." [14]

But Hildebrand did not count the cost. He was utterly determined to rid the Catholic Church of clerical concubinage, and he did at least drive it underground. Sacerdotal marriage continued to be legal in the Greek Orthodox Church. Celibacy was required there only of the higher ecclesiastics; no stigma was attached to marriage and paternity for the ordinary priests. But among all the clerics in the Catholic Church, as among all the angels in Heaven, there was nevermore to be any marriage or giving

[14] Summarized in Schaff, *History of the Christian Church*, Vol V, pt. i, p. 42. The whole subject is treated in detail in Lea, *Historical Sketch of Sacerdotal Celibacy in the Christian Church.*

in marriage. There were other things, however—or so
at least it soon became rumored. There was still clandes-
tine concubinage, and a great deal of avuncular affection
for "nephews" and "nieces." But of frank, honorable,
life-completing marriage there was soon not even a
memory.

4

ILDEBRAND had his way: he
humiliated the emperor and curbed
the clergy. But he paid bitterly for
the victories. During his last years
he met with one reverse after another, until finally, deposed from
the papacy and hounded from
Rome, he died in wretched exile.

The man he named as his successor refused at first to accept the
dubious honor. The papal palace in Rome was in the
hands of an anti-pope set up by the emperor, and there
seemed to be no chance for a Hildebrandian to regain
control of things. But a decade later, in 1095, there came
a sudden and dramatic change in the situation. It was
brought about by Urban II, who had been named pope by
the defeated reform party. He was a lesser man than
Hildebrand both in character and ability; but he did
possess one precious gift which the iron genius had
lacked—an orator's flare for the sensational and the
appealing. When he was proclaimed pope he was a
fugitive from Rome, and for seven long and bitter years

he was hardly able to better his position. Then suddenly
he hit upon a scheme which almost overnight exalted him
to a place of unchallenged supremacy in Christendom.[15]

The Eastern emperor, Elexius I, had appealed to Urban
for help. The Moslems were advancing once more. They
had been hurled back from Europe almost four hundred
years earlier, and since then had been too busy warring
among themselves to trouble Europe. But now they were
on the march again. A new strain, that of the Seljuk Turks
from the wasteland north of Persia, was responsible for
this latest thrust. These Seljuks, a savage and vigorous
race, had but recently burst in upon the crumbling Moslem Empire and made it their own. Now, intoxicated
with their success and eager for more worlds to conquer,
they were pressing on toward Constantinople. They had
already overrun Asia Minor, and were actually in possession of Nicea, just across the narrow water from the
Christian capital. The Byzantine Empire, its strength
already drained by recurrent wars with tribes of Normans
on the west, piratical Slavs on the east, and savage Petsche-
negs on the north, was helpless at the approach of this
new horde from the south. So in despair its ruler had
sent a letter to the pope, imploring him to move the
Catholic princes to rescue their fellow Christians in the
East.

Urban leaped at the opportunity. He realized that if
he could once turn the rapacity and contentiousness of his
lay rulers in the direction of the Turks, he would be safe
at last. He would become the hunter instead of the

---

[15] The one full-length biography is Paulot's *Un Pape français: Urbain
II*, but it is written with a distinct Catholic bias.

hunted, and, once Constantinople was rescued, his primacy would become unchallengeable throughout Christendom. But he realized also that a call to arms in behalf of the Byzantine Empire would receive very little response. He had to find some more stirring cause, one that could arouse the deepest emotions of the race—its credulity and cupidity and inexhaustible spleen.

And such a cause he did discover before long. A certain wild-eyed monk named Peter the Hermit had turned up in Rome with the most harrowing reports of what the Turks were doing to Catholic pilgrims in Palestine. Urban gave him an audience—the man had already aroused the whole city with his tales—and saw at once that here was what he had been seeking.[16] Keeping his motive secret, he journeyed across the mountains to France, where a council of the Church was being held in the town of Clermont, and there he arose and preached a sermon which literally brought a new epoch into being.

Most of Urban's hearers were Frenchmen like himself —the German clerics were still supporting the anti-pope— and he spoke to them in their own Provençal tongue, not in Latin. There were not alone Churchmen in the audience—fourteen archbishops, two hundred and fifty bishops, four hundred abbots, and no one knows how many priests—but also thousands of laymen. Jugglers, fortune-tellers, vendors, and thieves; knights in heavy iron armor, yeomen with bows in their hands, serfs wearing leathern jerkins all black and hard with dried sweat, and

[16] The importance of Peter the Hermit—indeed, his very existence— has been called into question by many modern historians. But Schaff's argument (*op. cit.,* Vol. V, pt. I, pp. 241-245) seems to the present writer most convincing.

burghers clad in fine broadcloth; great ladies reeking of perfume put on to kill the odor of their unwashed bodies, harlots bedizened with paint, peasant women with sagging bellies, and ragged, rickety, sore-eyed children—they were all there in that open field when Urban uttered his call. They crowded toward the platform, their ears straining to catch the words of the huge, golden-haired pontiff who stood before them.

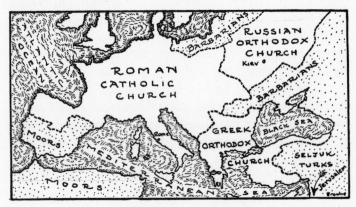

ON THE EVE OF THE CRUSADES

"O ye men of the Franks!" they heard him cry: "know that a grievous cause has brought us hither. From the borders of Jerusalem and the city of Constantinople ominous tidings have gone forth. An accursed race has invaded the lands of the Christians in the East, depopulating them by fire and steel and ravage. They have torn down the churches of God and have befouled the altars with the filth of their bodies. . . ."

Thus did the pope begin, and his listeners stood cold with horror. They heard him tell of the sufferings of the Christian pilgrims, how they were robbed and disemboweled and buried alive. ". . . And these are your blood-brothers," the speaker reminded them, "children of the same Christ and sons of the same Church. . . ."

He reminded them of more than that, much more. He pointed to Spain just across the border, where the infidels were even now slaying and ravishing the Christians. What assurance was there that the fiends would stay there? Was it not more likely that they would become drunk with their unbroken power and invade even France itself? "Remember!" the pope thundered, "the time may yet come when you too will see your wives violated and your children taken away as slaves!" . . .

Thus did Urban play on the terror of the mob, and finally, having so moved them that even strong men covered their faces and wept, he cried:

"On whom shall fall the task of vengeance save on you who have won glory in arms? You have the courage and fitness . . . so come to the defense of Christ. O ye who have been thieves, become soldiers. Fight a just war. . . . Go forth on the journey when winter is ended——"

He could not continue. A mad roar suddenly arose from the multitude. *"Dieu lo vult!* God wills it!" they roared. Women shrieked hysterically; men brandished their weapons or their naked fists. And again and again the cry resounded: "God wills it! God wills it!"

[213]

"Aye," the pope plunged on, "let that be your battle-cry! When you go forth against the enemy, shout out—'God wills it!' And let whoever goes upon this journey wear the sign of the cross on his head or breast. . . . Onward to the holy Sepulcher! Let no possession detain you, nor the love you bear children or parents or homes. . . . Your own land is shut in on all sides by sea and mountains, and is too thickly populated. There is not much wealth here— the soil scarcely yields enough to support you—and that is why you kill and devour each other in civil war. . . . Go then to the Holy Land, that land which, as the Scripture says, is flowing with milk and honey. . . . Go, wrest it from the vile race and keep it for yourselves! . . . Fear not. Your possessions will be safeguarded, and you will despoil the enemy of greater treasures. . . . If any should lose their lives, by land or sea, or in fighting against the heathen, in that hour their sins shall be forgiven them. I grant this to all who go, by the power vested in me by God. . . . The way is short, the reward everlasting. Take up your arms, valiant sons and go! . . ." [17]

And they did go. That sermon burst a dam, and of a sudden all Europe seemed to be flooding toward Jerusalem. It was almost as it had been in the fourth and fifth cen-

[17] There are several contemporary versions of this sermon, all considerably discrepant. Munro, *American Hist. Rev.*, 1906, pp. 231-243, offers a reconstruction of the whole address. So also does Harold Lamb in his deservedly popular work entitled, *The Crusades*, 1930, pp. 39-42.

turies, save that then the migration had been westward, and now it was returning to the East, and that then it had been prompted primarily by hunger, and now primarily by religious faith. The response to Urban's call reveals what the Church had accomplished in Europe. It had welded the tribes into a vast brotherhood of the spirit. They were still envious and suspicious of each other, warring among themselves incessantly; but at least in one thing, in their awe of Christ and fear of Hell, they were united. Despite all the wasteful men who had occupied the Church offices, despite all the indolent monks and venal priests and grasping bishops and popes, Christianity had accomplished a miracle. It had taken the fragments of one order that had been shattered and of another that had not yet been formed, and had made of them an integrated unit. It is true that the religion of Islam had already accomplished a similar miracle in Arabia and North Africa, and in a much shorter space of time. It is true also that the unity of Europe was not effected until Christianity resorted to a Moslem device and proclaimed a holy war. But these considerations, valid as they are, do not lessen the proportions of the miracle. When Urban cried, "Take up your arms, valiant sons!" he was answered not by a single clan but by half a continent.

The time set by the Council of Clermont for the beginning of the Crusade was the fifteenth of August, 1096, but the people refused to wait until then. Frenzied exhorters, chief among them Peter the Hermit, had spread Urban's message far and wide, and as early as March there were already vast throngs of peasants clamoring to be led at once against the infidel. The urge to wrest the holy places from the hated Turk had become an obsession with the people. Parents forced their sons to take the cross, and wives their husbands. Cæsarius of Heisterbach tells us of a woman suffering with dreadful pains in childbirth who was delivered with ease the moment she consented to her husband's departure on the Crusade![18] And there was more than superstition at the bottom of this sudden desire to go East. Misery, disaffection, restlessness, boredom—these elements, too, may have had something to do with it. Life was hard for the plain folk in feudal Europe. Herded in foul huts with the kine and the pigs, they were not much above those beasts. Bound as serfs to their lords, the women knew surcease from labor only when they lay abed in childbirth, and the men only when they fell ill and died. Rains rotted the grain in the fields, or else there was drought or incendiary fire. Plagues swept through the land, felling young and old. No wonder the masses craved to go on the Crusade. They wanted to escape their intolerable serfdom, to run away and be free. And the way was open to them now. They could go with a blessing, assured of absolution if they died on the road, and of glory and booty if they survived.

So they went. The peasants set their wives and children on ox-drawn carts and started forth in happy blindness. The monk forsook his cell, the cobbler his last, the harlot her noisome lair. And off they all went to wrest the native place of the Savior. They had no faintest notion where that place was. When they got as far as Hungary, where the people were darker of hue and spoke an incomprehensible tongue, the wanderers felt sure they had

[18] *Dial,* X, 22.

reached their destination. When they drew near the Danube many of them shouted for joy, thinking the river to be the Jordan. "Is that Jerusalem? Is that Jerusalem?" they asked each time they sighted a city.

They moved in unwieldy, undisciplined, leaderless hordes, sustaining themselves by begging or looting as they went. One band started out by robbing and massacring the Jews in the Rhine country, committing atrocities far worse even than those imputed to the Turks.[19] Another hastened on, pillaging and burning its way through Hungary, and coming to a disastrous end in the forests of Bulgaria. It was followed by a larger swarm led by Peter the Hermit and containing several knights and ecclesiastics; but this too suffered a terrible fate. Of some forty thousand who started out, only seven thousand reached Constantinople, and they in a most pitiable condition. The Emperor Elexius, afraid to let them remain in his capital—for they had become a murderous and ungovernable mob—hurried them across the channel to Asia Minor and told them to wait there for reënforcements. But they preferred to rove about and plunder the rich provinces, and finally they were trapped by the Turks and massacred. Still another swarm started out for the East, this one numbering two hundred thousand souls it is said; but it was cut to pieces by the now exasperated Hungarians. Several smaller bands tried to get through, but they were slaughtered or dispersed in the Danube region.

[19] A poignant description of these excesses against the Jews is to be found in Ludwig Lewissohn's novel, *The Island Within*, N. Y., 1928, pp. 327-339.

UT then the real Crusaders, the lords with their trained archers and horsemen, got under way. As in the case of the hordes that had gone on in advance, this army was motivated by more than pure love of Christ. There were some among its leaders, for instance the renowned Tancred, who were exemplary characters in that brutal age—devoted, brave, and generous. But the majority were typical knights; coarse and vicious warriors, untamed, unlettered, and unwashed. They had joined up largely because they were spoiling for a fight. Trained for naught save war, and with the barbarian blood lust still strong in their veins, they were elated to have an enemy to rend. The local feuds which had absorbed them in the past had fallen from favor, for the scarcity of booty had made them unprofitable, and the recurrent opposition of the Church had made them difficult. It was a joy, therefore, to have this chance of waging a war that not alone promised plunder but also carried with it a blessing.

It is estimated that over three hundred thousand soldiers were in this army that now marched on the East, and their fate was unlike that of the peasant hordes that had preceded them. Led by able and hard-fighting generals—Godfrey of Bouillon, one of the greatest of them, is said to have hacked a horseman clean through from head to saddle with a single blow of his enormous sword—and well equipped with arms, they seemed invincible.

But even this army was not able to prevail at once, largely because of the treachery of the Emperor Elexius and the jealousies of the leaders. Nicea was taken in 1097, but it required another two years before the host could make its way thence to Jerusalem. The privations of the soldiers were indescribable. They were forced to eat camels, dogs, and rats; they went mad for lack of water. Only their inexhaustible faith and their desperate plight gave them the strength to go on with the struggle. Finally, in June, 1097, a host of some twenty thousand fighting men managed to come within sight of the Holy City. It was a most dramatic moment. A lowly Jewish peasant had once been put to death in that city for preaching the doctrine of Peace; and now, more than a thousand years later, twenty thousand men of war were come to wrest his sepulcher with the sword.

The siege of Jerusalem lasted several weeks and entailed dreadful sufferings. The Turks tried to hold the Crusaders at bay by pouring boiling pitch and oil, and hurling showers of rocks, from the wall tops. The valleys and hills roundabout were strewn with dead horses and men whose putrefying carcasses made life in the camp almost unendurable. In vain did the Crusaders, led by the priests in full vestments and bearing holy relics in their hands, march barefoot round and round the walls: the miracle that had occurred to Joshua's army at Jericho was not repeated.

Finally help came by way of the sea. The city of Genoa, which was vitally interested in the capture of Palestine because of its need for an open trade route to the Orient, sent a fleet of ships laden with food and arms and workmen. Strengthened by these reënforcements, a final assault was made on the beleaguered city. It was on a Friday, the day of the crucifixion, and the first man to scale the walls got over just at three o'clock, the traditional hour of the Savior's death. And then a scene was enacted which for savage irony is perhaps without its equal in human history.

The Crusaders swept into the city and began to slaughter all in sight. The Jews, who had taken refuge in their synagogues during the assault, were burnt with the sanctuaries; the Moslems were butchered in the streets. Neither the tears of women, nor the cries of children, nor the protests of gentler men like Tancred, availed to soften the ferocity of the conquerors. "They cut down with the sword everyone whom they found in Jerusalem," writes William, Archbishop of Tyre. "The victors were spattered with blood from head to foot." The worst carnage was in the Temple inclosure, the very place where, according to tradition, Jesus had once stood and taught: "Thou shalt love thy neighbor as thyself." There, if we are to believe the gloating report of Raymond of Agiles, who was an eyewitness, the blood of the massacred reached *usque ad genua et usque ad frenos equorum,* "to the very knees and bridles of the horses." All through that torrid summer day the Crusaders continued their butchery. They threw back the visors of their helmets because of the sweat blinding their eyes; their voices cracked from shouting, "God wills it!" And finally, as the sun went down and night crept over the city, the gory carnage ceased. Letting the swords fall from their weary hands, the victors formed ranks and, "sobbing for excess of joy," proceeded to the Church of the Holy Sepulcher. "It was a most affecting sight," the Archbishop of Tyre assures us ecstatically; "it filled the heart with holy joy to see the soldiers tread the holy places in the fervor of an excellent devotion." Gathered in the sanctuary, the warriors folded their blood-stained hands and knelt in prayer before the "true" cross. "This is the day which the Lord hath made," their voices intoned with hoarse fervor: "Let us rejoice and be glad in it!" . . .

And thus was the Holy City redeemed.

A week later the Kingdom of Jerusalem was established. Palestine and Syria were divided and organized in feudal fashion, and the Frankish knights who had led the First Crusade began to rule in true feudal style. The Emperor Elexius, who had invited their help, now groaned to be rid of them. Like the Hindu peasant of whom Gibbon tells, "he had prayed for water and the Ganges was turned into his grounds." The Greeks, resentful of the encroachments of the Catholic conquerors, began to betray them into the hands of the Moslems. And the Catholics began to fall out among themselves. In the year 1147 it became necessary to rush a second army of Crusaders to rescue the tottering Kingdom of Jerusalem. It was a far statelier host than the first, being led by the emperor of Germany and the king of France—the latter accompanied by his beautiful queen, whom he afterwards divorced because of her indiscretions while en route. Such an expedition, encumbered with court ladies and haltered with etiquette, was of course doomed from the start. Bit by bit the Moslems won back their old possessions until finally, in a new "holy war" led by a romantic adventurer named Saladin, they recaptured Jerusalem itself.

A third Crusade was then launched, but this like the second was too stately to succeed. It was led by the three most powerful rulers in western Europe, the Emperor Frederick Barbarossa, Philip Augustus of France, and Richard the Lionhearted of England; and its adventures, handsomely elaborated by the medieval minstrels, became part of the stock-in-trade of subsequent romantic literature. As a military expedition, however, it was a total failure. A fourth Crusade was organized in 1202, but the bulk of this army never even reached the Holy Land. It got diverted and stopped to wrest the port of Zara from Hungary, and then to besiege and capture Constantinople from the Greeks.

The religious zeal had died out of the Crusades. More than a century had elapsed since the first great army marched off to Jerusalem, and the knights were sick of crusading. Their ranks had been decimated, and those who survived preferred to remain at home. The middle-class had gained by the Crusades, for the absence of the lords, the insolvency of their estates, and the growth of trade, had all conspired to lift the merchants to a status they had never before enjoyed; but this class, too, had grown weary of the expeditions. As Mr. H. G. Wells puts it with his characteristic vigor: "In the eleventh century, the idea of the Crusade must have been like a strange and wonderful light in the sky; in the thirteenth one can imagine honest burghers saying in tones of protest, 'What! *another* crusade!' "

6

CHARACTERISTICALLY, however, the crusading obsession lived on among the peasantry. Gathered around their peat fires after dark, or in their taverns on Sunday, they still talked excitedly of the wickedness of the Turks and of the need to tear the Holy City from their grasp. Hundreds of thousands of their fellows had already taken the cross and ventured beyond the eastern horizon; but few had returned, and fewer still had dared to tell of the things they had seen there.

In actuality the Moslems were far superior to the Christians of that day. They had resurrected the science of the ancient Greeks, borrowed from the wisdom of the Hindus, and profited by the world-awareness of the Jews. Universities had sprung up at Basra, Bagdad, Cairo, and Cordova, and throughout the Moslem world there had long been a ferment of thinking and experimentation. In Europe the Church was still expecting all cures to be effected by religious rites, but among the Arabs the science of medicine had reached a state beyond which there has been small advance to this day. Their surgeons understood the use of anæsthetics and were performing the most difficult operations. They studied physiology and hygiene, and their *materia medica* was much what ours is to-day. Their chemists had discovered alcohol, potash, nitrate of silver, sulphuric acid, and numerous other substances. Their mathematicians had learned the use of numbers from the Hindus, had improved on the geometry of the Greeks, and had created algebra—the very word is Arabic —and the decimal system. Their physicists had invented the pendulum and had written works on optics; their astronomers had built observatories and had calculated the procession of the equinoxes; their craftsmen worked in all the metals, knew the secrets of dyeing, wove the finest fabrics, and—most important of all in view of what was to come to pass—knew how to manufacture paper. Their farmers had discovered the value of fertilizers, and had built great irrigation systems. Their horticulturists, having learned how to graft, were producing varieties of fruit and flowers unimagined in the West.

Life in all its aspects was relatively civilized among the Moslems. They were fanatical in their faith and furious in war; but they could also be kindly, generous, and honorable. Saladin, that Kurdish adventurer who preached the "holy war" against the Crusaders, was a man of such chivalry, culture, and magnanimity that even the Christians sang his praises. When he recaptured Jerusalem in 1187 there were no such scenes of savage butchery as had followed the entry of the Franks ninety years earlier. The Christians were given their liberty, and permitted to depart unmolested. Saladin even allowed a station of two Latin priests to remain and offer Masses in the churches at Jerusalem, Nazareth, and Bethlehem. A century later, in the very midst of the Fifth Crusade, St. Francis of Assisi was courteously received and permitted to expound his faith in the presence of the sultan himself! Compared to a people who could show such tolerance, the Christians were no more than barbarians.

But the serfs dwelling in the dark hamlets of Europe

knew nothing of these things. To them the Moslems were accursed infidels whose very existence on earth seemed a blasphemy. Again and again, in one locality after another, small bands of peasants gathered together and attempted to launch new crusades.

Finally the obsession took hold of the children, and in the year 1212 three armies of youngsters started out to drive the Turk from the Holy Land. One army gathered in France around the person of an hysterical twelve-year-old shepherd boy named Stephen, who claimed that Christ had appeared to him in a vision and had appealed to him to rescue Jerusalem. Children from all over the land flocked to the lad's banner, and, despite the efforts of the king and the saner adults to halt the movement, some thirty thousand boys and girls marched off to the sea. Asked where they were going, their only reply was: "We go to God, and seek for the holy cross beyond the sea." Asked how they would cross the water, their leader gave answer that the sea would part for them even as it had for the Israelites of old.

But when they reached Marseilles the sea did not part. The children stood and wept with vexation, for they were half mad by now with frenzy and weariness. Finally two slave-dealers appeared and offered "for the sake of God and without price" to convey them across the Mediterranean. The innocents accepted with alacrity, crowding aboard seven vessels which set sail at once for Africa. Two were shipwrecked off Sardinia, going down with all they carried. The other five ships got safely across, but there the hapless little passengers were taken captive by the dealers and sold into slavery.

A similar fate awaited the other armies. A host of some

twenty thousand German children gathered around a ten-year-old lad named Nicholas, and started forth from Cologne, singing songs as they went. No one knows just what became of them. Thousands died by the wayside, and the remnant that finally reached Italy became dispersed and disappeared there. Another army started out from Germany at about the same time under the leadership of a boy whose name has been lost. Straggling across the Alps, it got to the port of Brindisi in Italy and there set sail never to be heard from again. And thus ended the Children's Crusades, at once the most horrifying episode in medieval history and the most devastating commentary on medieval faith.

In later centuries the legend arose of a Pied Piper who had led away an army of children to be swallowed up behind a mountain, and it may well have been a distorted reminiscence of these tragic incidents. The Children's Crusades must have had a shocking effect on the generation which witnessed them. Thenceforth the crusading mania dwindled swiftly, and not all the threatenings of the popes or the harangues of the monks could fan it to vigor again. A Fifth Crusade was launched under protest by Henry II of Germany, and terminated quite absurdly in a friendly treaty between him and the sultan he had been sent to destroy. The Sixth Crusade was largely a private expedition led by the very devout Louis IX— Saint Louis—of France, and the Seventh, led by that same king, was never carried out. Smitten with the plague while still a thousand miles from his destination, the poor old zealot kept tossing on his couch and crying: "Jerusalem! Jerusalem! We will go!" But he was crying in delirium.

No one went; neither he nor any other warrior after him. Thenceforth the armies of Christendom left the Moslems alone.

7

THE Crusades were a failure. The Holy Land was not taken from the Moslems for another seven hundred years; the Turkish advance, far from being checked, swept on later to the very walls of Vienna; and the Greek and Latin churches were left more hostile to each other than ever before. Yet the Crusades did serve at least one immediate purpose: they lifted the papacy to a position of absolute supremacy in Christendom. It was only natural that this should happen, for, as we have already seen, the papacy was primarily responsible for the Crusades. The popes instigated them, encouraged them, blessed them, helped pay for them—indeed, did everything except fight and die in them. So long as those holy wars remained the major interest of the believers, so long was the pope necessarily the leading figure in Christendom. At the very height of the crusading movement, when Innocent III wore the tiara, even the Greek Church was subject to him. Constantinople had been sacked by the Crusaders in 1204, and, though Innocent had condemned the outrage, he had not scrupled to take advantage of it. He had allowed the relics looted in Constantinople to be placed in the churches of Italy,

[227]

France, and Germany, and had made one of his Latin clerics the patriarch over the Greeks.[20]

Within his own immediate realm, Innocent III lorded it as had none of his predecessors. He called himself the vicar not merely of Christ, but of God. If he did not lay claim to infallibility, it was because he seems to have taken that for granted. He extended the Papal States, dictated the imperial succession in Germany, compelled King Philip II of France to take back the wife he had illegally divorced, drove King Alfonso IX of Leon to put away the wife he had illegally married, forced King Peter of Aragon to receive his realm as a fief from the papacy, and made King John of England pay him a feudal tax. He called and controlled the Fourth Lateran Council (1215) which instituted the Inquisition, fixed the dogma of Transubstantiation, and ordained that all worshipers should make confession to the priests at least once a year.[21] He organized crusades against the heretics within the Church and the infidels without, excommunicated kings, and interdicted lands. Whether he possessed the keys to heaven may have remained a question; but that he held the keys to the earth was sure

It did not last, however. When the crusading hysteria

---

[20] Among these relics stolen from Constantinople were the bronze horses which stand to this day before the Church of St. Mark in Venice. Of quite another and more valued order were, for instance, the relics which Abbot Martin obtained for his monastery in Alsace: a spot of the blood of the Savior, a piece of the true cross, an arm of the Apostle James, part of the skeleton of John the Baptist, and a flask containing milk from the breast of the Mother of God!

[21] For the history of this institution see Lea, *History of Auricular Confession and Indulgences in the Latin Church*. The only English biography of Innocent III is by C. H. C. Pirie-Gordon, and is inadequate. The account in Gregorovius' great work, *Rome in the Middle Ages* (Eng. tr. Vol. V, pp. 5-110), is preferable.

died down, papal dictatorship went with it. The popes continued to clamor and plead for new assaults on the Turk, but Christendom turned a deafened ear. Enough was enough: two hundred years of furious, costly, and utterly futile crusading had exhausted Europe. Besides, the successors of Innocent had to pay for one grave miscalculation which he had made. He had forced himself to the top by letting the kings of France batter down the German emperor. But he had forgotten to raise up some other secular ruler to batter down the king of France—and the oversight cost the papacy all that Innocent had gained for it, and a great deal more. Had there been a succession of popes like Innocent, the disaster might have been averted; but there was not. The men who came after him, though quite as ambitious for the papacy, were far less astute and vigorous. Like almost all their predecessors, they were raised to the papal throne when they were already aged men—Innocent's election at the age of thirty-eight was a most exceptional occurrence—and their gouty hands could not possibly hold on to the reins.

The crisis came in the opening years of the fourteenth century, when Philip IV of France, with the consent of his parliament, flatly defied the papacy to interfere in temporal affairs. The pope, Boniface VIII, repeated the old warning that "it is altogether necessary to salvation for every human being to be subject to the Roman pontiff," and threatened to excommunicate the rebel. But Philip only laughed. The world had moved in the two centuries since Canossa. The Crusades, by decimating the nobility, had greatly strengthened the position of the kings; and this in turn had given rise to a spirit of nationalism which was inherently hostile to an international papacy. The French

parliament, the University of Paris, and even a section of
the French clergy, all came to the support of the king. In a
vituperative document the pope was accused of graft, sorcery, immoral relations with his niece, having a demon in
his chambers, and murder. And when Boniface was about
to carry out his threat of excommunication, a force of
mercenaries marched down on his palace, looted it of its
treasures—upsetting incidentally a vase (another one!)
containing milk from the breasts of the Blessed Virgin—
and took the pope prisoner. A month later the old pontiff
died insane.

That was the beginning of the end. Two years later a
Frenchman was made pope, and his residence was moved
from Rome to Avignon in southern France. Thereafter
for some seventy years the popes, all tools of the French
kings, continued to reside in France. And the blow dealt
to papal prestige by this "Babylonish Captivity" was one
from which it was never able to recover. Finally, in 1378,
the Roman populace rebelled and insisted that the papal
residence be brought back to their city. The cardinals,
most of them Frenchmen, were gathered in the Vatican to
choose a new pope, and the mob outside was violent. It
had broken into the papal wine-cellars and was now roar-
ing with drunken zeal: "We want a Roman! We want an
Italian!" The cardinals were terrified. "Better elect the
devil than die," one whispered to another. So they elected
an Italian to the papacy.[22]

But a few months later these same cardinals, having
escaped from Rome, repented of their choice and elected a

[22] The details of this episode are given by the papal secretary,
Theodorich of Nieheim, and other contemporaries. Good modern accounts
of the whole period are to be found in Locke, *Age of the Great Western
Schism,* and Bruce, *The Age of Schism.*

Frenchman in the other's stead. The Italian refused to surrender his office, and Europe was then scandalized by the spectacle of two popes ruling side by side, neither of whom could be branded a usurper, since both had been properly elected by the same proper body of cardinals. The duel continued from 1378 to 1409, and then, in an attempt to end it, both popes were declared deposed and a third was elected. But that only complicated matters, for now the fight became three-cornered. And three-cornered it remained for some nine years until at the Council of Constance all the rivals were effectively put away and a fourth man was raised to the throne.

The "Babylonish Captivity," followed as it was by the even more scandalous "Great Schism," so reduced the papacy that the old claim to sovereignty in temporal matters was never again asserted with success. Even the quite orthodox Dante was moved to insist that State and Church were both derived directly from God and were therefore independent of each other. More daring men went much further. A new class of scholars had just arisen in Europe, a class of laymen trained in the universities rather than the monasteries. Drawn from theology by their affection for philosophy, freed from awe of the Church canons by their reverence for Roman law, they dared to write and teach doctrines which made the popes fume and groan. Some, for instance the authors of a great treatise entitled *Defensor Pacis* (1324), went so far as to say that the New Testament, which was in their eyes the only final authority in the Church, did not grant the bishop any spiritual authority over the priests, nor the pope any power over the bishops. They even challenged the doctrine of the Petrine succession, pointing out that the New Testament contains no evidence whatsoever that Peter ever appeared in Rome! The authors, both professors at the University of Paris, were denounced by the reigning pope as "sons of perdition, sons of Belial, pestiferous wretches, beasts from the abyss," and were summarily excommunicated. But they remained unperturbed. Excommunications had been flung about far too indiscriminately in the past century to retain any of their old terror. Enjoying the protection of a powerful lay ruler, the authors knew they were safe from the pope while on earth; and, possessing sound knowledge of the Scriptures, they felt themselves even safer from him in Heaven.

This insurrection on the part of learned men was something novel and highly significant. Until the fourteenth century the scholars had all been undividedly loyal to the hierarchy. Trained in the Church, it had never occurred to them to use their minds save for the greater glory of the institution. What they accomplished may not be very impressive to us of a different age. There were keen minds among them, but, buried beneath a mountain of tradition and authority, they were helpless to do more than drill in the dark. The best of those scholars were men of the profoundest insight, and, in the fields still unillumined by modern research, their wisdom is still unsurpassed. But the majority of those medieval schoolmen were mere casuists. They spent their time on arid dialectics, debating with the most elaborate and ingenious dexterity the fundamentally undebatable dogmas of the faith. They argued, for example, whether a mouse that nibbles the consecrated wafer really eats the Lord's body, or—this is the proverbial instance—how many angels can dance on the point of a needle.

In and of themselves, such problems were not without their validity. They were, so to speak, the sounding-leads with which men sought to chart the ocean bed of reason, and in new terms many of them form the basic problems of theoretical science to this day. For instance, the scholastic dispute as to the continuity or discontinuity of the process by which the wafer and wine became the flesh and blood of Christ is, when stripped of its alchemical implications, very much the modern dispute involving Dedekind's Axiom. Of course, the medieval argument was always corrupted by the irrationality of its premises. The scholastics took ideas which pertain to the process of knowing and regarded them as of the nature of knowledge. But even so their disputation had its value. Though it sank at times to the absurdest casuistry, it was nevertheless an improvement over the willful credulity, the perverse "crucifying of the mind," which marked the centuries when Christianity was still in part a revulsion against Paganism. Even though reason was employed only to prove what was already believed, at least *it was employed*. Beginning with men like Alcuin and John Scotus the Erin-Born (Erigena) in the ninth century, waning for a while, waxing again with Anselm, Roscellinus and Abelard in the eleventh and twelfth centuries, and flowering fully with Thomas Aquinas, John Duns Scotus, Albertus Magnus, and William Occam in the thirteenth century, Scholasticism was an incalculably valuable discipline.

But finally it had to come to an end. In the very beginning this rationalizing movement showed signs of genuine daring. For example, John Scotus Erigena dared to write in the ninth century: "Authority proceeds from true reason, but true reason by no means proceeds from authority. All

[233]

authority that is not approved by true reason seems to be false." But in later years such insurgency died down almost completely. Abelard in the twelfth century did venture a treatise called "Yes and No" (*Sic et Non*), which arrayed the authorities against each other, and thus inferentially proved the worthlessness of authority; but his position in the Schools was decidedly peccable. The pride of Scholasticism was Duns Scotus, the "Subtle Doctor," who insisted that "nothing is to be held as of the substance of the truth, except what can be expressly or indirectly derived from Scripture, or has been expressly or tacitly determined by the Church." In a later age the followers of Duns Scotus were derisively dubbed the "dunces"; but in the heydey of medievalism the teaching of the "Subtle Doctor" was counted unchallengeable. Scholasticism immured itself in authority, seeking truth not by going out and away, but by circling round and round as in a cavern. Not until the fourteenth century did the learned men think to do otherwise.

8

UT by the time a revolution could occur among the intellectuals, it was already well advanced among the common folk. That is why so little heed has been paid in this book to the activity of the Scholastics. The theological wranglings of the early Church Fathers did at least create heretical schisms and lead to popular uprisings and wars. But the discussions of their medieval successors caused very little disturbance outside the Schools. The keenest, most en-

lightened, and best educated men in the later Middle Ages
—for instance Dante and Thomas Aquinas—were largely
content with orthodoxy, and it was left for the unlearned
men, the popular exhorters, to sow the seeds of heresy.
Most of these agitators were, of course, clerics, but it is
significant that they were never men who belonged in high
office. Perhaps that was partly the reason for their insurgency: some of them may have been disappointed careerists
venting their spite. But that is a hazardous accusation, for
it might be leveled as justly against Jeremiah, Zoroaster,
Mohammed, and any number of other great reformers
who are recorded to have come of minor priestly families.

Certainly there was reason enough for an impersonal
resentment against ecclesiastical conditions in the Middle
Ages. As in every other organized religion, the leaven of
ethics had been smothered beneath a mountain of rites.
The clergy, despite recurrent abortive attempts at reform,
was steeped in corruption. As St. Bernard himself complained: "We can no longer say with Isaiah that 'the
priest is as the people,' for the priests of our day are
worse than the people." The monasteries, far from being
communities of saints, were pleasant clubs for club-
able men of "gentle" breeding. "Almshouses for the
nobility," they were dubbed. Their lands extended everywhere, and they treated their hordes of serfs no less un-
feelingly than did the lay lords. And the secular clerics
were even worse than the monastics, for they did not make
even pretensions to poverty. The parish priests mulcted
the poor folk—it was their right, for instance, to take a
dead man's bedding as the "mortuary fee" for the funeral,
no matter how poor the widow and orphans—and the
higher clerics mulcted the priests. On top of the heap sat

the pope, and his extortions were the worst of all. As Vicar of Christ he demanded the first year's revenue collected by each new appointee to a bishopric, auctioned off "expectancies" to lucrative offices, sold "indulgences" for sins, and begged for "Peter's Pence." During the seventy years at Avignon he learnt to be quite brazen in his venality, hoarding wealth and lending it out like a pawnbroker.

And all the while the poor people, out of whose toil this wealth was drawn, had to live on in hunger and pain. They had been far worse off in the Dark Ages, but so far worse off then as to be incapable of complaining. By the twelfth century, however, the common folk had gained enough to be eager for more. (Revolutions almost always occur not when conditions are at their worst but when they are getting better.) And the Church, far from siding with the common folk in their demands, gave its support to the landlords. How could it do otherwise, seeing that it was itself the greatest landlord of all? St. Thomas Aquinas, perhaps the foremost theologian of the Middle Ages, voiced the characteristic attitude of the clergy when he wrote that the ideal state is one in which the toilers are all strong of arm, dull of intellect, and divided among themselves by mutual distrust, so as to give less trouble to their masters.[23]

It was only natural, therefore, that the peasantry should begin to drift from the Church. What happened in Russia in the twentieth century, happened in western Europe toward the end of the Middle Ages: the common folk discovered the religious establishment to be their enemy. Though it lived off the serfs, it gave itself to the masters.

[23] See Coulton, *The Medieval Village*, ch. 18, in which ample evidence is given that this was the usual point of view of the Church.

Postulants who came empty-handed to the monasteries were either turned away or relegated to the class of lay-brethren. Only exceptionally was a peasant's son able to rise to high office in the Church. Even Heaven seemed to be closed to the poor folk, for almost all the new saints in the calendar were men and women who on earth had belonged to the aristocracy.

Nor was this the worst. The poor folk were inured to social abasement. Having been taught for centuries to know their place and respect their betters, it occurred only to isolated individuals to resent discrimination in the matter of clerical appointments. But what did affect the masses was the growing callousness of the clergy to their spiritual needs. The Church had become swollen and lame with a sort of spiritual dropsy. Europe had changed in these last generations. New towns had sprung up and old ones had grown; the population had shifted, settling certain regions thickly, and leaving others deserted. Yet the Church still clung to its ancient distribution of bishoprics and parishes, seeking to serve an increasingly urban world with a machinery that was still almost entirely rural. Only in its afferent functions had the Church kept abreast of the times; in its efferent ones it was dismayingly antiquated. A great city like Antwerp, for instance, was served as late as 1115 by but a single church and priest. London, Paris, and other swollen centers of population, though surrounded by monasteries, were little better off so far as pastoral service was concerned. Except for the few devoted brethren who belonged to certain reformed orders like the Premonstratensians, the monks kept to themselves behind their high walls and wide moats, rarely going down into the towns save to collect their rents and other revenues.

Such conditions could not but lead to a falling away from the Church, especially among the lower classes. Here and there, as we shall soon see, groups of artisans and peasants dared to set up religious circles of their own— vigorous and usually frenetic evangelical sects which were openly hostile to the feudalized Church. But the majority, too apathetic to rebel, yet too little satisfied to be staunchly loyal, simply became indifferent in the matter of religion. The so-called Ages of Faith were, as Professor Coulton has well observed, really the Ages of Acquiescence. The ordinary peasant or slum dweller merely plodded along with lowered head, looking neither in front nor behind. He did not become a skeptic: his mind was incapable of such daring. He was as superstitious as he had ever been, be- lieving in all the phantasms of demonology and all the non-sequiturs of magic. Paradoxically enough, though he had long ceased to be devout, he was still very credulous. In time of crisis he knew no other place to turn but to the Church, clamoring for a priest whenever death seemed near, or some other disaster threatened. He begged that the church bells be rung in time of flood, or that holy water be sprinkled on the ground in time of drought. He believed that caterpillars and other pests could be de- stroyed by priestly "excommunication," and that wounds could be healed and diseases cured by the mere laying-on of priestly hands. Above all he believed that souls could be saved from Purgatory by repeated Masses.

But, save for such exigencies, the common man learnt to get along without benefit of the clergy. His was a harshly simple life; six days in the week he toiled like a beast of burden, and on the seventh he got drunk. That is no ex- aggeration: it is attested by any number of medieval writers. The Church festivals were so marked by drunken-ness, license, and crime, that we find the clergy repeatedly pleading for a reduction in the number of saints' days. For the clergy, it should be remembered, was not at all pleased with this disorderliness of the plain folk. The medieval Church, despite all that modern sentimentalists may say of it, was as puritanical in theory as the dourest of our Protestant denominations. It was not, however, a volun-tary puritanism instituted by free men for the good of their own souls; rather it was a chafing tyranny thrust upon the populace by a despotic ruling caste. Its strictness was moti-vated only in part by religious scruples; apparently of far greater influence was the ulterior consideration that it was wise to keep a tight rein on the subject classes. There were laws restricting amusements on week days, and forbidding them absolutely on Sunday and the holy days. Not alone dancing on the village green, but even football and wrestling were regarded with disapproval by the authorities. The disapproval was ineffective, of course; the people continued to dance and play their rough games. And the tirades of the clerics, anxious to enforce the laws, simply served to intensify the growing indifference of the masses. St. Antonio of Florence seems to have indulged in no hyperbole when he declared:

"On holy days they [the peasants] spend little time in divine service, or in hearing the whole Mass, but in games, or in taverns, or in contentions at the church-doors." [24]

[24] Coulton, in his *Five Centuries of Religion*, Vol. II, pp. 71-75, has considerable to say on the Sabbatarianism of the clergy and its effect on the populace.

NDIFFERENCE, however, was not
the only consequence of ecclesiasti-
cal corruption and tyranny; in scattered places the result was open
revolt. The Dark Ages were passed;
the fitful gleams of light let in by
the more scholarly monks, and by
the soldiers and merchants returned
from Moslem lands, had begun to
spread in the Western world. The
race slowly awoke from its long stupor and began to stare
around it amazed. "Where are we?" men asked in bewilderment. And, in order to find out, they began to
search about in the writings left from the ages before they
fell asleep. The learned began to read the Pagan classics
rediscovered by the Arabs and translated by the Jews; and
the common folk began to read the Bible. How the
scholars were affected has already been mentioned; what
happened to the masses deserves more careful consideration.

It must be realized that until now the Bible had been
practically a closed book to all save the most learned
clerics. It had never been retranslated out of Latin for the
good reason that the book was not deemed safe reading
for the common folk in feudal Europe. When the missionary Ulfilus in the fourth century translated the Bible into
Gothic, he left out the books of Kings, lest in reading them
his converts be encouraged in their warlike ways. It was
not so easy for the medieval pastors to expunge from the
Bible all that *they* considered harmful for their sheep, so

they improved on Ulfilus and virtually suppressed the whole work by letting it remain in a language the people did not understand.

By the twelfth century, however, translations did begin to appear in the vernaculars, and then startling things occurred. They were crude and incomplete translations, fugitive efforts made by men of great earnestness but little learning—that was the ostensible reason why the Church opposed such versions—but nonetheless they seared the dark which had so long enveloped Catholic Christendom. Of a sudden the inconsistency between Gospel teaching and Church practice began to become common knowledge, and there was a ferment and disquiet. Men began to regard the Church with new eyes. Was this the Church which Christ had ordained? . . . Where was the righteousness which he had commanded? Where the voluntary poverty, the boundless charity, the meekness, the virtue, the love? . . . More and more people learnt to ask such questions, and, receiving no good reply from the churchmen, they began to answer them for themselves.

From Hungary to Spain, from Milan to Bremen, violent anticlerical movements suddenly burst into flame. There were the Albigenses, the Petrobrusians, and the Waldenses in southern France, the Patarenes in Milan, the Arnoldists and the Humiliati throughout northern Italy, the Ortlibenses in Strassburg, the Beghards along the lower Rhine, the Apostolicals in Belgium, the followers of Eudo de Stella in Brittany, of Tanchelm in the Netherlands, and the Amauricians, the Passagii, the Josephini, the Circumcisi, and the Luciferans, in other localities. Salimbene, a contemporary chronicler, speaks of one hundred and thirty heretical sects existing within the confines of Catholic Christendom at this period.

Significantly, these sects were particularly rife in the most civilized regions of Europe—in southern France, northern Italy, and the Rhineland. Significantly, too, their following was made up—to use St. Bernard's language—of "ignorant peasant women . . . a vile and rustic crew, unlettered and altogether unwarlike." No one of these sects was intellectual, and few made any articulate protest against the theological extravagances that had crept into Christian belief. At bottom they were chiefly exercised over the flagrant moral and ritual abuses, the crude paganization and the devitalizing formalism, that had come with worldly success. They cried for a return to the simplicity of the pristine faith, and required their followers to live even as had the first believers. Nothing is more revelatory of the character of their morality than the defense which a man suspected of sectarianism offered an inquisitorial court in 1233. "Hear me," the hapless man is quoted to have cried: "Hear me, my lords! I am no heretic, for I have a wife and lie with her, and have children; and I eat meat *and lie and swear and am a faithful Christian!*" [25]

Necessarily, therefore, though the movements varied

[25] Pelisso's *Chronicon;* ed. Moliner, p. 17; quoted in Coulton's admirable little essay, *The Inquisition,* p. 28. The student should also read Coulton's Eng. tr. of *Salimbene,* and for further details concerning these sects, Lea, *History of the Inquisition,* 1888, Vol. I, pp. 57-208. Also Newman, "Recent Researches concerning Medieval Sects," in *Proceedings Am. Soc. of Church Hist.,* 1892, IV, 167-221, and the summary in the same author's comprehensive *Manual of Church History,* 1901, Vol. I, pp. 541-621.

widely in their outward characteristics, they were all vehemently anticlerical. In the language of the Fourth Lateral Council, they were like Samson's foxes: their faces were different, but their tails were all bound together for one and the same fell purpose.

It is impossible to go into detail here concerning these sects. Some were Messianic cults led by men and women who were clearly psychopaths. For instance, Tanchelm in the Netherlands is reported to have given himself out as the Son of God, and to have gone through the public ceremony of marrying the Virgin Mary with her portrait before him. We are told that his credulous followers fought with each other to drink the very water in which he had bathed. It is similarly reported that Gulielma of Milan claimed to be the incarnation of the Holy Spirit, and around her was created a church which had a woman for a pope. Such reports may well have been false, for they come to us from hostile ecclesiastical sources; but that some of the cult leaders may have been madmen, and that many of their followers may have been simpletons, is hardly to be doubted.

Certain of the sects, however, were of a far higher character. For instance the Amauricians, the Beghards, the Brethren of the Free Spirit, and the Ortlibenses, arose out of the teachings of mystics and were pantheistic in their nature. They held—somewhat as does Christian Science to-day—that God is in everything, and that Hell is no more than the consciousness of sin.

Still others, for instance the Arnoldists, were insurrectionary movements intent chiefly on destroying the wealth and temporal power of the clergy.

Still others, for instance the Petrobrusians, were anti-sacerdotal as well as anticlerical, declaring that sanctuaries were unnecessary, and that the veneration of crosses was rank superstition. God hears prayers as well in a tavern as in a church, they argued; and if all crosses are holy, why not also all mangers? Peter de Bruys, the most noted of these evangelicals, went up and down southern France making bonfires of crucifixes, and finally was himself burnt to death on one of the pyres.

Still other cults, for instance the Waldenses, the Beghards, the Humiliati, and the like, arose out of the conviction that only the renunciation of private property and the practice of otherworldly love—in other words, the perfectionism of the first believers—could make one truly a Christian.

And finally, certain sects like the Cathari were essentially anti-Christian.

Only two of these many heresies were widespread and of enduring strength, the Waldenses and the Cathari. The former, a group founded in 1177 by a French merchant named Peter Waldo, were believers in an apostolic Christianity reft of all sacramentalism. Refusing to disband despite repeated commands of the ecclesiastical authorities, they suffered persecution for centuries.[26]

The Catharist movement, unlike the Waldensian, was

[26] The Waldenses exist to the present day in Italy, and in scattered colonies in South America. They are said to number about 26,000. For their history, see Melia, *Origin, Persecutions, and Doctrines of the Waldensians.*

rooted out after a time, and as a consequence almost no accurate knowledge exists today concerning it. According to the Inquisitorial records—unhappily almost our sole source on the subject—Catharism was in essence an attempt to revive the ancient religion of Manicheism, which had been Christianity's formidable rival during the early centuries, and which had never completely died out. Itself in part a survival of the even more ancient Gnostic heresies, Manicheism, which had remained underground in Christendom for some eight hundred years, now of a sudden came out into the open once more. In the twelfth and thirteenth centuries it broke out like a veritable plague, spotting Flanders, Germany, England, and Lorraine with half-hidden centers of agitation, and inflaming the whole of northern Italy and southern France. Its devotees went by different names in different places. They were called the Patarenes in Milan (from Pataria, the "junk-dealers" quarter where most of the local Catharists dwelt), the Albigenses in southern France (from the town of Albi, one of the centers of their strength), and the Bogomiles in Bulgaria. In some places they were known also as the Textores, probably because of their prevalence among the weavers. They believed in celibacy, pacifism, vegetarianism, and communism, and their austerity and fanaticism appalled the orthodox. Rather than utter an oath or slay a living thing, the Cathari would submit to torture and death. Often they would voluntarily starve themselves to death to escape defection from their furiously moral code. It was a harshly puritanical religion —the Cathari derived their name from the Greek *katharos,* meaning pure—and the popularity of the heresy can be explained only as due to a revulsion against the apathy and formalism which had taken hold of the Church. It called the Catholic Church the "Synagogue of Satan," and spat at the priests dressed out in their vestments. And this hostility seems to have attracted the populace. The old awe of the hierarchy and of the whole sacerdotal system had waned. There was mutiny in the air.

10

BUT the Church was not nearly so far gone in corruption as these heretics imagined. The sap of prophetic zeal was not yet dry in the old tree whose roots stood in soil enriched by the blood of so many martyrs. Even while exasperated souls turned on the Church and declared it withered beyond hope, others set out to prune away the deadwood and restore the Church to the vigor it had once known. The greatest of these reformers was a certain Italian named Francis, one of the noblest men in all of history.[27] He was born at Assisi in the year 1182, the son of a well-to-do manufacturer. Spoiled from childhood, he would not devote himself to study and never learnt even to write with ease. Throughout his early youth he was a typical small-town blade, frivolous, extravagant, and the despair of his ambitious father. But then, seemingly of a sudden, a

[27] The best biography of St. Francis of Assisi is by Sabatier, a great work worthy of its great subject. Renan's essay translated in his *New Studies* is also well worth reading.

change came over him. At the age of twenty-one, after a severe illness, he arose and went on a pilgrimage to Rome. It was not the pleasant sight-seeing tour which too frequently went by the name of pilgrimage in that day, but a journey undertaken in genuine disquiet of heart. When Francis got to the Eternal City it was not the great churches that impressed him so much as the mendicants seated on the steps. All at once the impulse came to him, as it had centuries earlier to Buddha, to become himself a beggar. Exchanging clothes with one of the poor men, he spent the day with outstretched palm; and the joy he felt in thus humbling himself left a memory which he never forgot.

Returning to Assisi, the changed demeanor of the youth soon made him the laughingstock of the neighbors. Francis no longer drank and gamed with the other young noblemen of the district; instead he went about among the lepers and the homeless, or else hid himself in a cave and meditated all day long. Finally his father caught him taking merchandise from the warehouse and giving it away to a poor priest; whereupon he turned the young man out of his house.

Francis was elated. Henceforth he had but one father, he declared, and that was his Father in Heaven. He continued to wander around Assisi, a beggar clad in rags, and still devoted himself to the lepers and the poor. And in time the conviction took hold of him that such was the office to which God had called him. Naked he would follow the naked Christ, teaching his fellow-men by precept and example to love poverty and humility. Soon a number of like-minded young men joined him, and in the year 1210 Francis journeyed to Rome and appealed to Pope

Innocent III for permission to found a new society. Thirty years earlier a similar appeal had been made by the merchant of Lyons named Waldo; but then it had been refused. The hierarchy had been loath to recognize an order made up of untutored laymen, and the result had been the creation of the Waldensian sect, which had since grown to be a sharp thorn in the side of the Church. Innocent, profiting by the earlier mistake, bestowed his blessing on the work of Francis; and thus was founded the Order of the Minor (that is, the humbler) Brethren, more commonly called the Friars, or the Mendicants.

Francis was in no sense a conscious radical. He did love birds and flowers, and he did respond with a quite modern sensitiveness to the beauties of nature on this earth; but in his respect for authority he was still completely a medieval. From first to last he showed himself completely submissive to the Church. But his purpose was as opposed to the prevalent spirit in the establishment as was that of most of the heretics. His one desire was to free the Church of its worldliness, and make it once more the "communion of saints" which it had been in the days of the apostles. And in the beginning it looked as though his teaching might prevail. Before long there were friars wandering about and preaching and giving comfort in every corner of Europe. They worked wherever they could find employment, but never demanded pay. "Let the brethren who know no trade, learn one," Francis commanded. If they received food and shelter in return for their labor, they were satisfied; if they did not, they simply moved on without a murmur and begged next door. They were no grim lot with long faces; on the contrary they always sought to be cheerful, playing their lutes to the careworn toilers, and singing psalms and even secular songs. They bathed the sores of the lepers, kept fellowship with the outcasts, and aided the oppressed and downtrodden. True disciples of the Galilean they were in the first years of the movement.

But these conditions did not last. Francis went away to carry the good tidings to the Moslems, feeling sure that his doctrine of love could accomplish far more than the swords of the Crusaders. He failed, of course, though not ignominiously. Such was the power of the man's saintliness that even the Moslems, who were being invaded by a new horde of Crusaders just then, refrained from doing him hurt, and the very sultan asked to hear him preach. But when Francis returned to Europe he found that the work he had started among his own brethren was ruined. His free society of good men doing the work of the loving Christ had been made over into another monastic order. It had become organized and had acquired officers, a uniform, irrevocable vows, and a precise discipline.

Always deferential to Church authority, Francis uttered no word of protest. He merely turned to his brethren and said: "From henceforth I am dead to you"; and then he began to withdraw more and more from their company. He died at the age of forty-four, sick at heart and broken in body. No sooner had he passed away, however, than the citizens of Assisi—the very ones who had mocked Francis only a few years earlier—seized hold of his corpse and made its tomb a shrine. The next day the vicar of the order hastened to broadcast the announcement that the holy man's hands and feet and side had borne the *stigmata,* the very wounds inflicted on the crucified Christ. Two years later, on July 26, 1228, the man who had fled all honors was canonized a saint. The following day the pope himself laid the corner stone of a cathedral to his memory. Soon the order began to accept endowments and acquire buildings. The brethren ceased to learn trades and work side by side with the peasants and artisans; they did nothing but beg. Less than a century after the saint's death, four of the friars were burnt at the stake for daring to claim that St. Francis had believed in absolute poverty!

The story of Franciscanism, like the story of every other idealistic movement since time began, is an epic of frustration. It was paralleled in its own day in the career of Dominicanism, which likewise set out to reform the Church and which failed no less pathetically. St. Dominic was a Spanish monk born some twelve years before St. Francis.[28] A man of keen zeal for the faith, he was alarmed to see how swiftly heresy was spreading in Christendom, and how poorly the orthodox were equipped to combat it. But, unlike the "little brother" of Assisi, Dominic believed that what the Church needed most in that hour was not love, but learning. The Cathari in southern France, he discovered, were far better trained in the Scriptures than the orthodox priests who had been sent to convert them. So Dominic threw himself into the labor of creating an order

[28] Dominic's life still awaits its Sabatier. The least inadequate biography in the English language at present is probably Drane's *History of St. Dominic,* a work marred by special pleading.

of preaching friars. Like the Franciscans, they were to rove at will and beg when there was need; but they were commanded to study rather than work, and preach to the heretics rather than comfort the lowly.

The ideal was a noble one. For centuries already the Church had known no better way of missionizing save with sword and fire. It was thus that the Crusaders had gone out against the Jews in the Rhineland and the Moslems in Palestine. But Dominic urged a better way. He wanted men to go out as had the early apostles and save souls by means of suasion. But, significantly, the suasion was to be of a new order: not exhortation so much as argument. Christianity had long ceased to be a simple faith whose final validity lay in the immediacy of its appeal to the emotions. It had become complicated and intellectual, and the distinctions between orthodoxy and heterodoxy were of the stuff of logic, not intuition. That was why Dominic laid such emphasis on learning.

Dominic's first efforts were carried on among the Albigenses in southern France, but no sooner had he begun his campaign than the pope—that same great Innocent III who made himself master of Europe—declared a holy war against the heretics in that region. Political expediency may have had something to do with the pontiff's act, for his ally, the king of France, was most eager to deal a blow to the independent nobles reigning in the southern provinces. But whatever the cause, the result was unspeakable. The fairest corner of Europe was overrun by hordes of plunderers wearing the cross on their shields, and when they finally retreated after some thirty years of looting and carnage, southern France was left a wilderness. The savagery of those crusaders can be judged by their conduct when they captured Béziers in 1208. The sanctified ruffians had been commanded by the papal legate not to pause to find out which of the inhabitants were heretics and which orthodox, but to cut down all in sight, leaving it to the Lord to save the innocent. The command was obeyed. Even the thousands of women and children who took refuge in the church were put to the sword. It was, as the legate blissfully reported to the pope, "a very rich slaughter. . . . The vengeance of God raged wonderfully over the city!"

Dominic did not retreat when those crusaders befell the land. He remained in southern France, wandering about barefoot and penniless and preaching wherever he found heretics hiding from the sword. His success was slight. Just as Italy became more and more a land of usurers despite the example of the good St. Francis, so Provence became more and more heretical, despite the preaching of St. Dominic. Not until the region was depopulated, and its cities and vineyards and fat plowlands were left charred and smoking, was Albigensianism exterminated.

But Dominic's failure in southern France, far from discouraging him, spurred him on to greater activity. He began to send his followers abroad, directing them especially to the great universities which had recently come into existence. They quickly attracted attention, and their number multiplied. By the time of his death in 1221, Dominic was the "master-general" of more than five hundred brethren settled in sixty friaries stretching from Spain to Germany and England. Forbidden by their vows to go seeking wealth or carnal love, and left free to devote themselves whole-heartedly to learning and preaching, they rapidly became a dominant element in the intellectual life of Christendom. But, like the Franciscans, they were soon deflected from the course which their founder had laid out for them. Some Dominicans continued to be missionaries, going off into Asia and Africa to carry the Gospel to the heathen. But the majority remained within Christendom and found service not as apostles but inquisitors.

Dominic's dream of converting the heretics by argument was not shared by those who came after him. Becoming convinced that reasoning was wasted and tolerance was a crime, they resorted to the rack and the stake. The Church established the "holy office" of the Inquisition, a judicial body with branches scattered everywhere, whose purpose it was to ferret out the heretics, try them, and turn them over to the lay authorities for punishment. And, because the learned Dominicans knew as did few others just what was heresy and what was not, they were made to serve on this body. Their cruelty became a byword; they did not hesitate to employ the most fearful tortures in order to extort confessions from their victims, nor to prescribe the most heinous punishments for those whom they found guilty. Rack and thumbscrew, flaying, burning, drawing, quartering—these were penalties which they meted out daily. And by such means did the followers of Dominic seek to carry out his dream of saving souls by the might of truth.

11

UTINY continued to spread, however. Neither sporadic crusades nor
sustained inquisitions were of avail,
and the established order in Western Christendom seemed doomed.
The papacy with its claims to universal overlordship had become an
anachronism. Europe was no longer
a chaotic jumble of feudal fiefs and
manors. The rival gang leaders
called lords or barons had long ceased to be the rulers;
many of them had been killed off, and the rest had been
made completely subservient to certain mightier ones
among them called kings. Nationalism had begun to loom
up as the integrating force in the various lands of Europe,
and the old manorial loyalties were fast passing away. But
the Roman hierarchy refused to accommodate itself to the
change. It had come into power in a feudal society, and it
wanted to stay in power even though that society had
largely disappeared. The pope, having lorded it over clans
and chieftains, could see no reason why he should not lord
it also over nations and kings.

And not alone the papacy, but the whole sacerdotal system had lost caste in the eyes of the laity. More and more
people were laying hold of the Bible and discovering the
origins of Christian faith and order. The Church tried to
restrain them, forbidding the laymen to possess any vernacular translations of the Scriptures—for fear, of course, that
the versions be inaccurate!—and advising against the reading even of the Latin text. But all efforts were fruitless.

Despite threats and fulminations of individuals prelates and regional synods, the people continued to study the Bible at first hand. And the more they did so, the more intense became their dissatisfaction with the Church.

In England the storm broke in the latter half of the fourteenth century, and was brought on by a certain scholar named Wyclif. England was ready for a storm at that time. It had just reached its adolescence as a nation, and the sudden rush of self-consciousness had made it peculiarly cocksure and proud of itself. It had more or less subjugated Scotland and had annexed a good portion of France. At home, despite repeated epidemics of bubonic plague, it had grown enormously in wealth and culture. Chaucer was singing his *Canterbury Tales* not in Latin or French, but in the tongue of the nation. The first of the "public schools" had been founded, and as many as thirty thousand students thronged the halls and colleges of Oxford. Patriotism, that new spirit destined to work such good and such hurt to mankind, was coming into its own in the land, and the English were growing to be suspicious of all that was foreign.

These changes could not but affect the attitude of the English toward the Church. The pope, it was now realized, was nothing but a foreigner, as had been all his predecessors, with one half-forgotten exception. His claim to suzerainty over their king therefore seemed an insult to England's new-found dignity. Especially insulting—because also costly—were his insistent demands for the annual tribute which the English king was supposed to pay as the pope's vassal. When Wyclif, a learned theologian teaching at Oxford, prepared a brief which gave

sound reasons for refusing those demands and for repudiating all papal claims to temporal overlordship, he became
the king's favorite cleric and the hero of the populace.[29]

But Wyclif, once he had begun to question Church
authority, had to do more than assail the position of the
papacy. He was a religious man as well as a patriot, and
he could not blind himself to the fact that the entire
ecclesiastical system had become corrupt with wealth and
luxury. Bequests made by pious landlords fearful for the
future of their souls, coupled with extortions made by the
clerics themselves, had made the Church master of half
the real property in England. The prelates, most of them
foreigners appointed by the pope, had a combined revenue
greatly exceeding that of the king. Even the mendicant
friars, whose vows bound them to live the life of the
Savior, had become a bane in the land. Many among them
were no more than sacramental tramps who wandered
through the countryside and robbed the peasants of their
hard-earned farthings. They recited Masses, heard Confessions, gave absolution, all for a price. They carried
around either for sale or exhibition the most outrageously
spurious relics—arms and legs of the apostles, tears from
the eyes of the Blessed Virgin, fragments of the true cross.
And the monks who remained within their cloisters,
though a less ruffianly lot, were hardly less guilty of what
Wyclif in indignation called "depraved apostasy." As he
read the Scriptures, Christ had ordained only two orders
of ministry—presbyters and deacons—and all other orders
seemed to him the handiwork of the Devil.

[29] By far the most comprehensive biography of Wyclif is by G. V.
Lechler, and has been translated into English. Workman's biography is
also recommended.

Nor did Wyclif halt with his attack on the clergy; he had to go farther and assail the abuses in dogma which gave the clergy its power. He scorned the worship of saints declaring: "It is a folly to leave the Fountain and seek to drink in a distant trickle." The very sacraments, in their multiplication, seemed to him an abomination. Baptism and the Lord's Supper he accepted in full faith, for these he saw ordained in the Holy Writ. But Confirmation, Ordination, Penance, Matrimony, and Extreme Unction, which had been added by the Church Fathers and which increased the subjection of the laity to the priesthood, seemed to him without justification. Even the Lord's Supper, in so far as the dogma of Transubstantiation made it a magical rite, was profaned by the priests, he insisted. Only that which was ordained in Scripture was incumbent on true believers; all else was false and abominable. As he himself put it:

> "If there were one hundred popes, and all the friars were made cardinals, their opinion should carry no weight in matters of faith except it be based on Scripture!"

It was more daring a stand than had ever before been taken in England; yet at first nothing was done to Wyclif. The pope in Italy fulminated "bulls" against him, and the clerics and friars in England cursed and raged. But the king continued to protect the heretic, and the plain folk sang his praise. He lectured and wrote almost incessantly, using both Latin and English. He prepared innumerable tracts, and finally translated the Bible. And, equipping them with this literature, he sent out an army of devout laymen to carry the true teaching to the masses. He called

these emissaries the "poor priests," for in his belief it was
zeal for the faith, not formal ordination, that rendered a
man worthy to be called a priest. They went about barefoot, preaching, expounding, and singing psalms to the
toilers in the fields and towns. The mendicant friars, for-
getting their own origin, tried to make sport of these evangelists, nicknaming them the "Lollards" because they were
forever mumbling and singing. The masses, however,
looked with love on the "poor priests," flocking to hear
them preach and taking their fiery words to heart.

But this success of the "poor priests" with the commoners undermined Wyclif's position among the nobles.
It became plain that the Bible was a dangerous book to put
in the hands of the populace. It bred sedition not alone
against the Church but also against the State. The people
who listened to the Lollards began to turn on the landlords as well as the priests, for they saw that Jesus had
inveighed against all oppressors. The toilers in England
were no longer the cowed brutes they had been during so
many centuries. The "Black Death" had just swept away
full half of the population, and the survivors, realizing
their enhanced value in the depleted labor market, began
to demand more rights and better wages. Like Wyclif—
though in this regard much against his approval—they
took their stand on the Bible, crying:

> "When Adam delved and Eve span,
> Who was then the gentleman?"

Finally, under the leadership of a priest named John
Ball and an artisan named Wat Tyler, the peasantry broke
out in open revolt. Marching on London, they captured
the city and burnt the palace of the duke of Lancaster,

who, as it happened, had been one of Wyclif's most ardent supporters. That turned the tide against the reformer.

Until then the Lords had favored his agitation, for they had long coveted the wealth in the hands of the Church. But now they saw that they and the clerics were in the same boat, and would be drowned together if the sea on which they sailed was disturbed. So the lay lords joined hands with their rivals, whom they now recognized as their partners in privilege, and set out to crush Lollardy. They were afraid to put Wyclif to death, but they did condemn his doctrines and deprived him of the right to teach in Oxford. They were unrestrained, however, in their persecution of his "poor priests," throwing them into dungeons, and beheading or burning their leaders. The rulers had learnt their lesson. When, in the year 1408, the archbishop of Canterbury made the reading of Wyclif's Bible a penal crime, the lords temporal were all approval.

12

YCLIF'S influence did not die, however. A spark from the fire he started was carried to Bohemia, and there it was fanned into a new and greater blaze. Bohemia, like England, was well prepared for heresy. In no other country of Europe was the Church so extensive a landowner, or the clergy so largely foreign. At the same time, in no other country had the spirit of nationalism taken a firmer hold on the people. An anticlerical revolt was therefore inevitable, and, as in England, it found its leader in a man who was motivated by patriotic fervor as well as religious zeal. He was a Czech named John Huss, a peasant by birth who had managed to acquire such learning that he was appointed "rector" of the University of Prague before he was thirty years of age. Though an ordained priest, he never held a regular "living." Instead, largely under the influence of Wyclif's ideas, he had become a lay preacher, holding forth in the Bohemian tongue in a chapel near the university. His fiery sermons quickly won him a large audience, especially among the Czech students, who saw in his teachings, as well as in the language he spoke, an affront to the Germans who occupied most of the clerical offices in Bohemia. There was bad blood then—as there has been ever since—between the Czechs and the Germans: and, because the latter had been largely responsible for the original Romanizing of Bohemia, and still held the richest benefices in the lands, any attack on the Church seemed a covert expression of Czechish patriotism.

Huss's ideas were very largely those of Wyclif; indeed, his writings are full of excerpts from the Englishman.[30] He denounced the clerics unsparingly, calling them usurpers and tyrants. The whole hierarchical system, Huss cried, was as riddled with heathenish superstition as it was empty of Christian warrant. Like Wyclif, he took his stand on the Holy Writ—which had already been translated into the Bohemian language—and by it sought to prove his every point. But on certain matters he was less

---

[30] See Loserth, *Wiclif and Hus,* pp. 181ff. For a brief account of the Hussite movement see Creighton, *History of the Papacy,* Vol. I, pp. 314-361. For a good biography of the leader see Schaff's *John Huss.*

radical than his predecessor. For example, Huss did not deny the dogma of Transubstantiation, and never declared, as did Wyclif, that the bread and wine remained bread and wine no matter how many prayers were recited over them.

Nevertheless, Huss was made to suffer as Wyclif had never been. That was in part just because Huss, despite all he said against the clerics, still imagined them capable of honor. Having been summoned to appear before them at the Council of Constance and defend his teachings, he obeyed. Protected by an imperial safe-conduct, he undertook the long journey—it required eighteen days—and presented himself at Constance. But instead of receiving a hearing he was flung into a dungeon of the Dominican monastery. It was a flagrant breach of faith, but the men of God insisted that it would be wrong to keep faith with a heretic. And when Huss cried in despair that they had not yet tried him and therefore could not know if he was a heretic, they would not listen. For seven months they held him captive in that dungeon, dragging him out again and again only to thunder at him that he must recant. But how could he honestly recant, he asked, if he was not shown the error of his teachings? To which the clerics replied that their word must be enough, and that if they told him he had erred, then he had erred. "Recant!" they cried: "recant!" But Huss could not be moved. There was an authority greater than theirs, he insisted, and that was the gospel of Christ Jesus. By it he had lived, and for it he would die if need be!

And finally he did die for it. On the sixth of July, 1415, he was taken from his prison and marched to the great hall

where sat the assembled council. The emperor of the Holy
Roman Empire was there—he who had given Huss his
safe-conduct—and around him sat the princes in state
attire. Thirty cardinals, twenty archbishops, one hundred
and fifty bishops, and thousands of monks and priests were
present. And before them all stood this lone man who
had dared to challenge their pretensions. He was not yet
fifty years of age; but those months of fettered confinement
had bent his body double. Yet his spirit was unbroken.
When the process was read and the sentence of death was
pronounced, he simply fell to his knees and cried: "Lord
Jesus! Forgive my enemies!" Nor did he alter his tone
from then on. They lifted him to his feet, and made him
go through the farce of formal unfrocking. First they
dressed him in all the priestly vestments, and then stripped
them from him one by one. Next they thrust the sacramental chalice into his hand, and then snatched it away
again. Finally they came to the problem of his tonsure;
but there they were at a loss to know what to do. His head
being already shaven, how could they *unshave* it again?
There was consternation among the masters of the ceremony, long and vehement dispute carried on in whispers
and gesticulations. In the end it was agreed to cover his
head with a cap painted with devils and inscribed "Arch
heretic." And when that was done, the bishops cried:
"Now we give your soul over to the Devil"—and straightway delivered the prisoner to the lay authorities.

One final chance was given him to go free. At the very
last moment, when Huss was already placed on the
faggots, his neck chained to the stake, the marshal of the
empire rode up and called upon him to recant. But

the man's only reply was: "What shall I recant when I have spoken naught save truth? . . . I sought but to teach men repentance and forgiveness according to the gospel of Jesus Christ. . . . I am not afraid to die!"

So they lighted the faggots. Huss began to chant. Loudly he raised his voice and chanted, "Jesus, Son of the living God, have mercy upon me!" Twice he repeated the refrain; but the third time his voice failed. The wind was driving the smoke and flames in his face, and he was stifled. But his lips continued to move.

And thus did John Huss die. His body was consumed by the flames, and his ashes were cast into the Rhine that naught might remain of him to pollute this holy earth. But his spirit—?

BOOK FIVE

The Breakdown
A.D. 1415-1648

THE BREAKDOWN: 1415-1648 A.D.

1: The Economic Causes of the Reformation. 2: The Cultural Awakening in Europe. 3: The Nationalist Awakening in France and Spain. 4: The Ducal Reformation: Lutheranism. 5: The Royal Reformation: Anglicanism. 6: The Peasants' Reformation: Anabaptism. 7: The Burghers' Reformation: Calvinism. 8: The Dynamics of Puritanism. 9: The Catholic Revival. 10: The Thirty Years War.

CHRISTIANITY in the beginning was like a warming glance that strove to light up the gray face of a spent civilization. It seemed a fugitive and very tenuous thing; for generations it was little more than a trembling hope. Yet it endured. When the old Roman empire passed away, the gleam remained, evoking a face of its own, the Roman Catholic Church, across which to play. It was at first an eager, youthful face, uplifted and mobile. For many years it shone like the morning sun struggling to break through a lowered sky. But then the face began to harden. The fire died down in the narrowing eyes, and the smile became a frozen grimace. By the twelfth century the Church had turned into a mask, a rigid and aged mask made the more hideous by the paint with which it was daubed. The blood of life had retreated from the flesh, leaving it pouched and sallow with tradition. The features stood out in grotesque distortion, the mouth very wide from shrieking anathemas, the nose long and sharp to detect heresies; and the skin was covered with the scabs of corruption.

And when men at last dared to examine that face—for
• until then they had been afraid, thinking that to presume
to look at it would be a damning sin—they recoiled in
horror. Not all of them. Some, for instance the saintly
Francis of Assisi, and Dominic the wandering preacher,
had been moved to sorrow, but not to despair. The Church
had grown corrupt, they admitted, but it was not yet beyond redemption. The blood of fervor could still be made
to course through its veins; the gleam of faith could yet
be restored to its eyes. But the majority, especially when
they saw how vain were the efforts of the orthodox reformers, simply rebelled. It could be to no avail, they felt,
to attempt to galvanize that repellent mask. It must first
be smashed if it was ever to be refashioned—and the
blows, few and ineffective in the twelfth and thirteenth
centuries, grew more numerous in the fourteenth, fiercer
in the fifteenth, and in the sixteenth century at last accomplished their purpose.*

The clamor against the Church came from three sources,
the kings, the peasants, and the townsfolk; and it seems to
have been intensified in each of these groups by definite
social and economic influences. Europe during this whole
period was experiencing what was virtually a change of
life, and the social organism was reacting somewhat as
does the individual when its metabolism is profoundly disturbed. Feudalism, as has already been remarked, was
giving way to nationalism, and that change helped bring
on the revolt of the kings. Serfdom was slowly being supplanted by what was curiously termed "free labor," and
that release, because it was only partial, added vehemence

* See Alexander C. Flick, *The Decline of the Medieval Church*, 2· vols.

to the anticlericalism of the peasants. Finally, the basis of economy was beginning to shift in certain regions from agriculture to commerce, and that turn was responsible for the insurgency of the middle-class. Had all three movements been united in their interests, the Church might have been swept away in a generation. But they were not united, and as a consequence the Church survived.

The rulers were motivated undisguisedly by self-interest. Having vanquished the nobility to a greater or less degree, they were now eager to make themselves completely dominant by vanquishing also the hierarchy. Strong now within their own realms, the monarchs could no longer abide the overlord pretensions of the pope, and the divided loyalty of the clerics. In addition, the lay rulers, hard-pressed for money to defray their mounting expenses, were eager to lay hold of the vast estates and steady revenues of the priories and prelacies in their lands. The kings did not mind that the ecclesiastics were so frequently lecherous and lacking devoutness. They turned upon the hierarchical Church not because they felt morally outraged by its corruption, but because they were covetous of its wealth and power.

The peasants, too, were moved in part by a desire to better their own lot, but in their case the motive was so defensible and so unconscious that it was in effect truly religious. The common folk rebelled against the pope not because he was the spiritual head of the world, but because he was not; they objected to the ecclesiastics not because they were too influential, but because they were influential in the wrong direction. Some among them, having learnt to read, had found out what was written in the

Bible; and the rest had listened. And what they demanded now was a return to the teachings of the Nazarene. They had blunt wits and could not appreciate the ingenious rationalizations and subtle sophistries wherewith the Church Doctors had explained away the Parables and the Sermon on the Mount. Poor men-of-the-earth that they were, they could see only that Christ had died to save them and that the clerics were cheating them of their due. So they revolted. They sought to destroy the Church because they hungered to revive Christianity.

The grievance of the townsfolk was more complicated. With them, too, one of the motives for rebellion was self-interest, but it was not viciously barefaced as in the case of the kings, nor dramatically appealing as in the case of the laborers. The underlying cause of complaint lay in the failure of the Catholic system to accommodate itself to the rise of this new class. From the time the Crusades broke Europe's shell and opened the trade routes to the Orient, the cities had been steadily growing in size and wealth; and now, more than three hundred years later, they were impatient to assert themselves. The Church, lumbering along in its own clumsy, clanking, myopic way, had not yet become conscious of the emergence of the burgher class. Despite that commerce was rapidly becoming the basis of Europe's economy, the Church with its inherent conservatism was still committed to a feudal and landowning order. It went on multiplying holy days and encouraging beggary, paying no heed to the new "busy-ness" which was to become the very name for the townsman's pursuit in life; it still told men who wanted more to eat that they must spend more time in prayer. Having emerged in a time of anarchy and terror, when man's life had indeed seemed full of wind and fury, Catholicism had never sloughed off its initial disdain for this world. Even now in the fifteenth and sixteenth centuries it still continued to praise poverty and despise the man who sought after lucre. All money-making was called avarice, just as all money-lending was branded usury. And this attitude aroused the ire of the burghers, for they wanted to believe that they were doing God's will as well as their own pleasure in following the pursuit of wealth.

Nor was it merely the spirit of the Church that they resented; even more it was the letter. There were certain Church laws regulating money-lending which were like so many knives in the side of the middle-class. On the strength of certain Biblical and classical condemnations of usury—and perhaps with a memory of those early centuries when the chaos in society had made money-lending un-necessary because robbery had been so easy—the hierarchy continued to condemn all taking of interest. And this con-demnation struck at the very heart of capitalism, for the credit system was the organ pumping the lifeblood into the arteries of trade. Doctors of Canon Law had discovered ways of circumventing the restrictions, and men with influ-ence at Rome had been able to carry on widespread financial enterprises with little hindrance. Indeed, on occa-sion even princes of the Church and monastic orders had found excuses for engaging in usury.[1] But the situation

---

[1] Ashley, *Introduction to English Economic History and Theory,* Vol. II, p. 450, tells how the Franciscan order resorted in the 15th century to taking interest on loans made to the poor. The whole subject is dealt with in detail in Cunningham, *Christian Opinion on Usury,* and also in O'Brien, *Medieval Economic Teaching.*

was only aggravated by these forced or purchased immuni-
ties. The fact remained that on the statute-books and in
the canons all money-lending was still declared criminal.
And that may well have been one of the reasons why the
middle-class was drawn to heresy. The Church stood
immobile, refusing obdurately to rescind this legislation;
and the merchants were left with no alternative but
revolt.

2

IT must not be imagined that these
economic considerations were plain
to those who were moved by them.
Even the kings, who were the least
confused as to their motives, had
no conception of the profound
ground swell which swept them into
the churning eddies of heresy. But
even without an understanding of
how different were the reasons
prompting the three classes to anticlericalism, those
classes knew well that they had little in common. And
it was this disharmony that saved the Catholic Church
from being emptied out there and then. The rulers were
afraid to abet the populace in any religious insubordination. They were afraid—and with reason—that once the
commoners overthrew the lords spiritual they might go
on and do the same to the lords temporal.

We have already seen how the English rulers in the
fourteenth century would have no more to do with Wyclif

once they found that his Lollard movement had stimulated an uprising against the landlords. The Bohemian rulers followed precisely the same course in the fifteenth century. The execution of John Huss infuriated his countrymen, and gave rise to a violent dissenting movement which threatened to end papal rule in Bohemia forever. At first the nobles joined heartily in the insurrection, and the Hussites were able to fight off five armies sent against them by the pope and the emperor. But then the rebels fell out among themselves. One faction demanded no more than that the wine as well as the bread be given the laity at Communion, for, characteristically enough, that detail, Communion "in both kinds," had become a paramount issue in the Hussite revolt.[2] But the other faction made up largely of the peasantry, demanded no less than a clean sweep of the entire priestly system. They insisted that tithes and other clerical exactions, as well as the worship of saints, prayers for the dead, ordination, the Latin ritual, and like clerical accretions, he abolished completely. They went even further, rejecting vows, prohibiting dancing—but not drinking!—and, gravest of all, demanding a return to the simple communism described in the Gospels. The nobles and other wealthy folk sided of course with the moderate party, and, after compelling the Church to treat with them and grant them the right to Communion "in both kinds," they turned on the radi-

[2] The insistence on the part of the Church authorities that only the bread, not the wine, be given the laity, was made law by that same Council of Constance which put Huss to death. The reason for the ruling was the danger of spilling the consecrated wine when offering it to the celebrants kneeling at the rail. See Fortesque, *The Mass,* 1917, pp. 376-381, an excellent history of the rite from the Catholic point of view.

cals and exterminated them. When the murder and wailing ceased, religious conditions in Bohemia were practically what they had been before the days of Huss. Even Communion "in two kinds" was abolished after a while. And for this tragic failure the nobles alone were to blame. They had not dared to go through with the reform.

But though such battles were lost, the war went on. It *had* to go on, for, although the greed of the princes, the ambition of the merchants, and the distress of the toilers mounted day by day, the papal institution still refused to yield or mend. There had been a hope in many quarters that the Great Schism, following on the heels of the Avignon "captivity," had destroyed forever the absolute power of the papacy and had paved the way for Church government by general councils. The Council of Constance, which ended the intolerable scandal of the Great Schism by deposing the three rival popes and electing a fourth, tried to take advantage of its moment of authority by decreeing that henceforth there must be a general council of the Church every eight years. But the next gathering, that at Siena in 1423, accomplished nothing; and the third, at Basle, was opposed by the now reinvigorated papacy, and was dispersed by force. In 1459 the reigning pope published a decree that thereafter anyone appealing from his authority to that of a council would be excommunicated. And that was the end of the conciliar movement. Thenceforth the more outspoken no longer talked of reform but of revolution.

The popes of the fifteenth century seem to have had nothing but cynical contempt for the feelings of the devout in the Church.³ The bitter lessons of their predecessors were apparently quite lost on them. They went on living lives of corruption and self-seeking as though their office had never known the degradation of the Avignon interlude and the Great Schism. No one expected them to be mighty prophets; but they were not even decent priests. Most of them were simply ambitious princes scrambling quite shamelessly for power and glory. Their chief concerns were to enlarge the Papal States and rebuild Rome. While the rulers of Austria, France, and Spain struggled with each other for control of a dismembered and helpless Italy, the popes picked their way between the contenders and snatched up what they could. One of these Vicars of Christ, Julius II, organized an army of Swiss mercenaries—the Vatican has had its Swiss Guard ever since—and himself led the troops into battle. But most of the other popes during this period relied rather on intrigue to attain their ends, making and breaking "holy alliances," cheating, bribing, and dealing treacherously on every side. As was inevitable, in the end they emerged with nothing. When two of the great lay powers contending in Italy became merged under a single ruler, the papacy lost out altogether. Charles V, emperor of the Holy Roman Empire and king of Spain in one, sacked Rome in 1527 and made the pope once more the puppet he had been in the Avignon days.

But though the popes failed to extend their temporal

³ For the details see Creighton, *History of the Papacy during the Period of the Reformation* (a rather lenient treatment), Gregorovius, *History of the City of Rome,* Vols. VII and VIII (a brilliant work), and Pastor, *History of the Popes during the Renaissance,* 8 vols. (a Catholic treatment, but unsparing in discussing the vices of the popes).

possessions, they did succeed in beautifying their capital. It was during this period that they built the Vatican, the Sistine Chapel, St. Peter's, and the innumerable other Renaissance structures which adorn Rome to this day. The pontiffs became the most lavish patrons of the great art that had just burgeoned in Italy, and it was largely in their service that Leonardo da Vinci, Raphael, Michelangelo, and the other titans of that age were able to create their most magnificent works. There seems to have been no finickiness as to the sources of the money which was spent on these art projects. One pope, Nicholas V, is reported to have laid the foundations of his new Vatican palace with funds raised in Europe for the rescue of Constantinople from the Turks!

Never before had popes dared to be so corrupt in their personal lives. During this period they seem not to have made even a pretense to virtue, and some actually flaunted their immorality. Innocent VIII, despite his adopted name, had seven illegitimate children whom he openly acknowledged and enriched. But he was almost a saint compared with his successor, Alexander VI, who purchased the papal throne in the year 1492. Alexander, a tall, handsome, gifted man, was the acknowledged father of five children by one lady, two by another, one by a third, and one by a fourth. During his years on the throne he lived quite openly with a famous beauty of the town, appeasing her husband with the gift of castles and her brother with a cardinal's hat. His daughters, among them the notorious Lucrezia Borgia, were married from the Vatican, and his sons, among them the even more notorious Cæsar Borgia, were showered with all sorts of spoils.

The marriages, divorces, crimes, and escapades of those children make the most sensational reading. Cæsar Borgia, who was made a cardinal at the age of sixteen, murdered one of his brothers, seduced one of his sisters-in-law, and committed any number of other outrages. When Lucrezia was married for the first time—she had been betrothed twice and married twice by the time she was twenty-one—the festivities in the Vatican included dancing and obscene comedies, and lasted until five in the morning.[4] And that one, we are assured by the papal master of ceremonies, was one of the more sedate parties in the papal palace.[5]

Such things had gone on before in the papal palaces, especially during the tenth and eleventh centuries. But few people outside of the papal household had known of them in those earlier days, since Europe then was still a dark wilderness and there had been no way for news to travel. In the fifteenth century, however, there were roads in every direction, and the swarms of vendors, pilgrims, minstrels, and other wayfarers had made all of Europe a household.[6] In addition, a new spirit of insubordination made people prick up their ears eagerly when they heard tales of the goings-on at Rome. In former times such tales would not have been believed even had they been told. The populace would probably have done violence then to anyone daring to speak ill of the Holy Father. But now the more scandalous the rumors, the more they were relished.

[4] See Gregorovius, *Lucrezia Borgia.*
[5] See Burchard, *Diarium,* ed. Paris, 1883, Vol. III, p. 167.
[6] See Jusserand's *English Wayfaring Life in the Middle Ages* for a most lucid and vivacious account of this significant element in Europe's renascence.

It would be difficult to exaggerate the change that had come over Europe. The mind of the race had begun to stir and assert itself, sloughing off the gloom that had once made it think of naught save death and the life hereafter. Among the learned the change led to a rebirth of interest in the writings of the ancient Pagans, in whom this-worldliness had been the whole of religion. In Italy men like Petrarch began to devote themselves to the Latin classics, and men like Boccaccio to the Greek. A Platonic Academy was founded in Florence under the patronage of Lorenzo Medici, a great banker whose family coat-of-arms, three gold balls hung in a triangle, has come down to our day as a sardonic proof of his interest in life here on earth. During the Middle Ages there had been almost a moratorium on profane learning; but after the Crusades there started a steady influx into Europe of Latin translations of Arabic versions of the ancient classics, and in 1453, when the Turks captured Constantinople, the Greek manuscripts themselves were carried westward. Thereupon a new era opened. Men began to regard the centuries that had passed as the *Medium Ævium,* the "Middle Ages," intervening between the brightness of the ancient past and the renewed brightness of the present.

Not alone literature, but also the plastic and graphic arts began to flower as never before in Christian history. Until the Renaissance all art had been for God's sake rather than its own. The monks who had illuminated manuscripts and decorated altars and church walls, being ashamed of the flesh, had drawn their figures with only the vaguest knowledge of anatomy. But now the flesh had come into its own once more, and artists no longer flinched from gazing at naked bodies. They still labored largely for the Church; indeed, their finest products were cathedrals and religious images and paintings. Though they drank deep at the fountains of Paganism, they still came to the altars of the Church for bread. But that was only because there was little bread anywhere else—and even artists cannot live on drink alone. Save for pluto-crats like the Medici, the most generous patrons of the new art were the popes and prelates; so the painters and sculptors and architects and scholars had of necessity to go to them for support. But they went in no spirit of Christian piety. Botticelli, Ghirlandajo, Leonardo da Vinci, Michelangelo, Donatello, Brunnelleschi—though these made use of the wealth held in the name of Christ, they were at heart all devotees of Apollo.

Many were devotees of Venus as well as Apollo. The reaction against the restraints of the Middle Ages made men run wild during the Renaissance. Probably they did more boasting of sin than real sinning, for in periods of reaction men are rarely so violent as they like to make themselves seem. Many of the leading figures in the "Revival of Learning" lived lives quite as virtuous as had been those of their grandfathers. Indeed, a whole host of scholars turned to Humanism—which was the literary phase of the Renaissance movement—solely out of interest in the divine; they delved in the classics to uncover the roots of the Scriptures. Men like Pico della Mirandola, John Colet, Erasmus, and Reuchlin mastered Greek and Hebrew primarily in order to be able to read the Bible in the original.

But, as was inevitable, the New Learning played havoc with the old beliefs even of these more conservative scholars. They discovered what errors and frauds had become imbedded in the religion of the Church, and they began to waver in their orthodoxy. It is a revelatory detail, for instance, that England's greatest humanist, John Colet, left absolutely no provisions in his will for Masses to be recited for his soul! Remembering that Colet was dean of St. Paul's, and therefore one of the leaders in the English hierarchy, one realizes the significance of that omission. The ancient bonds of credulity could not stand the strain put upon them by the new discoveries. And, as rumors of these discoveries seeped down to the masses, the bonds began to part everywhere. By the sixteenth century half the populace of Europe had begun to burn with the fever of heresy.

3

IT was the appearance of printed books that contributed most to the spread of the fever. That dominant order of things which many people to-day think of as "Christian civilization" might never have come into being had it not been for the invention of printing on paper—and, ironically enough, the invention was made and transmitted by two races which are now commonly regarded as inherently "backward." [7] Paper seems to have originated in

[7] The history of paper is told fascinatingly in David Hunter's *Papermaking Through Eighteen Centuries*, New York, 1930. The *Encyclopedia Britannica* contains a splendid article on the history of "Typography."

China in about the second century B.C., but its manufacture did not reach Europe until the Moslems set up paper mills in Spain. These mills were later captured by the Christians, but then the product deteriorated sadly. Not until near the end of the fourteenth century was good paper manufactured in Christendom in sufficient abundance and at low enough a cost to make book manufacturing a profitable industry. Printing from blocks had been known in China as early as the sixth century A.D., and, probably again through the agency of the Moslems, the art was later carried to Europe. There, either in Holland by Coster, or in Germany by Gutenberg, movable type was invented before the middle of the fifteenth century; and then printing presses began to spring up all over Europe.

The first consequence was a flood of printed Bibles. By the year 1500 there were translations in print in German, Italian, French, Danish, Slavonic, Dutch, Bohemian, Russian, and Spanish, and more than eighty editions of the Latin version.[8] The effect on the minds of the people can hardly be exaggerated. Until then they had known the Scriptures only orally. With parchment so costly and copying by hand so laborious and slow, manuscripts had always been rare and confined largely to the churches. As a result, the laymen had known the Bible only with their ears. But now that there were printed copies in profusion, they were able to know the Scriptures also with their eyes. That made a profound difference, especially since the Scriptures were printed in the national vernaculars as well as in Latin. Staring at those huge black letters, spell-

[8] See H. W. Hoare, *Evolution of the English Bible,* 1901, p. 106.

ing out the words with joyous pain, the Bible became more real to the people than it had ever been before. Even those who remained illiterate—and they were still in the vast majority—were able to experience this thrill of immediacy, for they could at least peer over the shoulders of the men who did read. And, like Job in the presence of God, they might have cried:

"I had heard of thee by the hearing of the ear,
But now mine eye seeth thee:
Wherefore I abhor myself."

Only they abhorred the ecclesiastics, not themselves. In the glare of that black type the people could not help but see how gross was the disparity between Gospel teaching and Church practice. And then revolt could be staved off no longer. The hierarchy was quick to sense the menace presented by this promiscuous reading of the Bible; but not quick enough. By the time they could proclaim their prohibitions and establish a system of censorship, it was already too late. Having once taken the bit in their mouths, there was no curbing the people any more. They bolted.

But in most places they were not allowed to bolt far, for the kings were at hand to catch the reins even before they could fall from the grasp of the clerics. Nor did those kings return the reins. For example, in 1438 the king of France, taking advantage of the popular resentment against papal abuses, gathered his nobles and clergy at Bourges and adopted what was called the "Pragmatic Sanction." By it he peremptorily relieved his people of the most burdensome taxes exacted by Rome, and asserted his right to have a high hand in Church affairs in France. Succeeding kings improved on this victory, and by the sixteenth century France, though still nominally bound to the pope, had what was practcially a state church.

A like development occurred in Spain during this period. The Christians there were more orthodox than anywhere else in Europe, largely because their history during seven hundred years was one of continual struggle to expel the Moslems. But once the Spanish Christians succeeded in reconquering their land, their joint sovereigns, Ferdinand and Isabella, began to reckon with the pope. They, like their subjects, had no quarrel with Catholic doctrine; but they resented papal interference and abhorred the corruption of the clergy. So they forced Rome to agree to a concordat (1482) which granted them the right to nominate all the higher ecclesiastics in their realm.[9] Having gained that much, the energetic rulers soon asked for more. They began to insist on their right to tax the clergy for the benefit of the state, to supervise the Church courts which tried the clergy, and to censor any decree the pope might proclaim.

They went even further. The reconquest of Spain by the Christians had been marked by the forcible baptism of hundreds of thousand of Moslems and Jews; and these newcomers formed a most dangerous element in the population. It was suspected that they were not firm in their new faith; that though they had been baptized—fre-

[9] See Prescott, *The Reign of Ferdinand and Isabella,* 1902, Vol. I, p. 316.

quently at the point of the sword—they had never become truly converted. In a nation which had fought its way to victory by waging "holy wars," and which was integrated almost entirely by its religion, defection from the Church partook of the nature of treason to the State. In consequence of this, Ferdinand and Isabella determined to make the prosecution of heresy a royal rather than a papal concern. They established an inquisition of their own, appointing the judges—usually Dominican friars of unimpeachable remorselessness—and empowering them to ferret out and try suspects. The pope protested vehemently, saying that this was a trespass on his own rights; but the rulers paid no heed. They felt that the situation in their realm was one which needed far more forceful a hand than any which the dropsical papal arm could lay upon it. Accordingly they went on with their project, and, under the leadership of a sadistic friar named Thomas Torquemada, their inquisition became perhaps the most heinous governmental institution in the history of mankind. It did more than merely suppress heresy; incidentally—or could that have been its main object?—it vastly enriched the royal treasury. Controlled by the throne, it preyed on the rich merchants, and on the less submissive nobles, torturing them until they made false confessions of necromancy or skepticism, and then putting them to death and confiscating their wealth.[10]

And thus Spain too attained for itself what was practically a state church.

[10] The completest study of this subject in any language is H. C. Lea's *History of the Inquisition of Spain,* 4 vols. His *Inquisition in the Spanish Dependencies* is less exhaustive.

4

UT France and Spain, though they achieved virtual home rule in matters of religion, remained bound in name and spirit to the Roman Catholic Church. It required a land like Germany, where there was no centralization of lay authority, for a definite break to occur. Germany in the beginning of the sixteenth century was a chaos of rival principalities and city-states, and its disorganization made the land a mound of powder waiting for a spark. On no other country had the Church dared to lay such tribute, for nowhere else was the resistance of the lay princes so feeble. In no other country was the peasantry so rebellious, for nowhere else were the heels of oppression so harsh and yet so unsteady. And, save for Holland and England, in no other country were the townsfolk so prosperous or so restive beneath the yoke of Catholic teaching.

With the peasantry and the middle class thus charged with resentment, and no king at hand to police the magazine, an explosion was inevitable. In the year 1517 a pious monk named Martin Luther, who was then teaching in an obscure Saxon university, unintentionally struck the fateful spark. Luther was a peasant-born man who throughout his infancy had been swaddled in that cloak whereof the warp and woof were hunger and piety. Religion had been all around him in the coarse mining village where he was born: not alone the orthodox religion of the monks and nuns, who had nine establishments in the village, but also the far more ancient superstition of the peasants. Many of the miners practiced sorcery down in the shafts below the earth; and there had been at least one witch in the neighborhood. And these memories left their mark on Luther. From childhood he had known the fear of the Lord, for even in the village church, where he had earned his lodging as a choir boy, he had seen Jesus the vengeful Judge frowning down on him from the great stained-glass window, a flaming sword in his hand. Of tenderness and love he had heard hardly a whisper; the sermons were all of hell and purgatory. And the soul of the lad had been made dark with dread of the other world.

Luther's father, an energetic and thrifty man, managed to improve his lot as the years passed, and when the boy grew up there was money enough to send him to the university. His parents, ambitious for his future, destined him for a career in law, and for four years he wrestled with the scholastic casuistry which was the groundwork of jurisprudence in that day. But then, quite without warning, he dropped his studies and impulsively entered a monastery. Despite the intense unpopularity of the hierarchy, there was still an alluring quality in certain branches of the Catholic system. Quite a number of students apprenticed to the world were breaking away and resorting to the cloister just then. It was an age of violent transition, and sensitive youths, shaken by the sudden shifts and changes, found it hard to keep their feet. A strange spirit of inquiry and individualism had been let loose in the world. Having begun with the exploration of ancient knowledge, men had gone on and were acquir-

ing a knowledge that was new. They were peering into
the skies, clambering over mountains, and setting sail on
uncharted seas. A new world had just been discovered in
the West, and a new path by water had been found in the
Far East. It was as though the very roof and walls of the
world had of a sudden been taken away, and man was
left out in the open. The old assurances had disappeared,
and new ones were slow to take their place. And, though
some men were exhilarated by the challenge, others recoiled in dismay.

Martin Luther in his twenties seems to have been one of
those who recoiled. He became overwhelmed by what was
called a conviction of sin, and sought refuge in an Augustinian cloister. And there he was cured of his disquiet. Invested with that poise, that spiritual self-assurance, which
men call salvation, Luther was able after a time to
stand up to life and strike out almost with berserk
vigor. Deep reading in the epistles of Paul, and in the
writings of Augustine, the later Scholastics, and the German mystics, all had their part in the young man's "conversion"; but what contributed far more was his own
religious predisposition. Though he studied theology with
diligence, took the degree of bachelor and doctor of divinity, and became a professor of Biblical Exegesis at the
University of Wittenberg, the final belief to which he
came was one that a plowman might have acquired. In
essence it was this: man is a sinner, but God is merciful
and forgives. All a man need do, therefore, is have faith
that God has forgiven him, and straightway he is saved.
No matter how earnestly he strives after righteousness,
or how piously he performs the Christian sacraments,

unless a man *believes* in God's grace he is lost. Justification in the last analysis is the reward of naught save faith.

It was this enormous emphasis which he put on "justification by faith "that led Luther to touch off the Protestant explosion. The incident occurred, like almost everything else in Luther's life, quite suddenly and without intention. An Indulgence-seller had come to the neighborhood of Wittenberg to sell those "papal letters" which were supposed to assure men of pardon for their sins and

ON THE EVE OF THE REFORMATION

of commutation of their sufferings in Purgatory. He was a Dominican monk named Tetzel, a very eloquent man who, were he living to-day, would be described as a "high-pressure salesman." The money he drained out of the country was supposed to go toward the building of the new church of St. Peter in Rome; but it was known that half the proceeds were going to the local archbishop, to reimburse him for the price he had paid the papacy when acquiring the three episcopal benefices which he held.

But it was not Tetzel's manner, or the disposition of the money he collected, so much as the whole institution of the Indulgence that moved Luther to protest. In the primitive Church a man who had lapsed into serious sin was deprived of the right to take Communion until such time as he publicly confessed and performed certain visible "satisfactions" prescribed by the congregation. But long since then the hearing of Confessions and prescription of penances had been made prerogatives of the priests. The change yielded no small profit to the priests; but it also profited the sinners. The churchmen were tractable, and when the penances were particularly severe—for the crimes were often of a most heinous sort—the sinners were allowed to make atonement by proxy. Rich penitents might appoint hungry peasants to fast for them, or pay homeless beggars to go on pilgrimages in their behalf.

And thus had developed a complex system of trafficking in pardons. The clergy had begun to teach that sinners need no longer go to their poor neighbors to purchase merit; they could buy all they wanted of it directly from the priests. The Church claimed to possess a treasury containing not alone the infinite merit of Christ, but in addition the almost as infinite merit of the saints past and present! Drafts on this treasury were called Indulgences, and, when countersigned by none other than the Vicar of Christ, were guaranteed to be honored in the hereafter.

By Luther's time, the sale of Indulgences had become one of the most obnoxious of papal abuses, and there were certain regions where the local rulers would not permit the papal agents to show their faces. Wittenberg itself was in one of these closed principalities, its ruler being the elector of Saxony, who had his own building schemes to finance, and his own very famous collection of relics to attract the offerings of the faithful. But the electoral lands were scrambled up with the lands of other princes, and Tetzel, the Indulgence vendor who was exploiting Saxony in 1517, was able to take his stand on the outskirts of Wittenberg with impunity. This he did, and the town flocked to him with its sins and its money. The professors at the university were most of them monks, and therefore direct vassals of the pope; but they were also men of learning and character, and—incidentally—employees of the elector, who was both founder and patron of the university. They were therefore incensed at Tetzel's activity, and they appealed to Luther, who was one of the most pious and respected men on the faculty, to make some protest. He hesitated at first, and then ventured to suggest an academic disputation on the question of Indulgences. He prepared a statement containing ninety-five points for discussion and, quite in accordance with academic etiquette, posted the document on the door of the castle church, which was the university bulletin board.

And that quite innocent gesture started the bitterest and bloodiest revolution in Church history. The *Ninety-Five Theses* ran the length and breadth of the empire, and almost overnight Luther became a world figure. No one was more astounded than he at the sudden uproar. His theses had not denied the right of the pope to grant Indulgences. They had simply posited that such Indulgences could neither remove guilt, nor remit punishment in Purgatory, and were therefore quite unnecessary for salvation if one were truly a repentent sinner. Such assertions had already been made by several enlightened men, most conspicuously by the great Dutch humanist, Erasmus; and besides, in posting them on the chapel door Luther had not committed himself either for or against them. Yet in the tenseness reigning in Germany at that particular moment, the *Ninety-Five Theses* took on the character of a declaration of war.

Luther was summoned to Rome, but fortunately his protector, the elector of Saxony, was able to intervene and get the summons recalled. The agitation did not subside, however, and Luther, pilloried by the papal supporters as though guilty of the foulest heresy, was goaded at last to real revolt. Luther was, after all, the product of a mining village, and once he was aroused he did not stop to consider the proprieties. As he once said of himself: "I am rough, boisterous, stormy, and altogether warlike." He began to pour forth a flood of vehement and outspoken pamphlets in which he committed himself to increasingly radical doctrines. He wrote these pamphlets not in Latin, but in the language of the people, using the simple, vigorous, even vulgar expressions familiar to the common folk. He raised the cry that the pope had no warrant to interfere with the churches in Germany, nor any right to interpret Scripture contrary to its plain meaning.

And the people flocked to his support. They loved, as Heine put it, "the divine brutality of Brother Martin." The monk was one of their sort. Though learned, he yet seemed one of the "foolish of the world," believing in God and virtue, and fearing Satan and Hell, like the simplest charcoal burner dwelling in the woods. And he was absolutely fearless. In 1520 he was excommunicated in a decree which described him as a fox wasting the Lord's vineyard. (Had he not ruined the sale of Indulgences in Germany?) But Luther, far from being daunted by the condemnation, took a copy of the decree and burned it in the central square in Wittenberg. He was called to justify his conduct before a parliament of princes and prelates summoned by the emperor, the great Charles V; but even then he was not overawed. He obdurately refused to recant what he had written, or beg forgiveness for what he had done. "Here I stand," he had cried, "I can no other. God help me. Amen!"

Had there been a strong central authority in Germany at the time, Luther's career would have ended then and there. But, with the land divided into numerous principalities and free-cities, the monk was able to escape. The populace was very largely on his side. As Cardinal Wolsey's agent wrote home: "A hundred thousand Germans are ready to lay down their lives for Luther." And also a great number of the princes, chief among them the elector of Saxony, were his open or secret supporters. Thus protected, Luther was able to go on with his work. Hidden away in a castle, he continued to fling out his inflammatory pamphlets. What was even more effective, he prepared a new translation of the New Testament which rapidly became the most read and best loved book in the German language.[11]

But then the movement began to get out of hand. All the extravagances of heresy that had been stifled for centuries now broke loose and flooded the land, and Wittenberg, where the banner of revolt had first been raised, became the capital of frantic dissent. Not alone in its university, but even in the local Augustinian cloister, men began to denounce Confession, the Mass, the adoration of images, the fasts, and the clerical vows. The priests took wives unto themselves, and the town council confiscated the monastic lands. Foaming evangelists began to flock in from other places, hysterical men who claimed to be divinely inspired; and the town was deafened with shrill announcements that the world was coming to an end.

That was more than had been bargained for, and certain elements began to grow uneasy. The elector of Saxony had invested heavily in a collection of holy relics which was one of the sources of his income, and he did not like the iconoclasm that was being preached in Wittenberg. The other princes, too, were disturbed, for they did not know how far the agitation might be carried. Luther, enjoying the protection of those nobles, saw that he must quit his hiding place and take charge of the situation in person. Returning to Wittenberg, he swiftly suppressed the more radical preachers and restored the old ritual and institutions. Some of his erstwhile colleagues turned on him then, for his conservatism seemed to

[11] Most of Luther's writings have been translated into English. For the flavor of his style and way of thinking, Smith's translation of *Luther's Table Talk* is especially recommended. Smith's life of Luther is likewise recommended, as is also Lindsay's *Luther and the German Reformation*.

them arrant treachery; but the princes were highly grati-
fied.

Luther was still a fugitive from justice, but those princes
saw to it that he was well protected, for they needed him.
He was a most convenient tool in their hands, being a man
of courage, power, zeal, sincerity, and a perfect incapacity
for knowing that he was being used. With the appre-
hensiveness characteristic of the educated peasant, Luther
could not be made to go to extremes, but had to be
dragged forward step by step. At first he would commit
himself to no more than a repudiation of the supremacy
of the pope and a denial of the efficacy of Indulgences
and other such papal inventions. Then with apparent
reluctance he went on and denied the validity of certain
of the sacraments, especially that of Ordination. Unable
to resist the demands of the new evangelical congregations
which were now springing up all over Germany, Luther
began to agree that these associations of believers had full
right to appoint their own priests or depose them, and
might conduct their services in German instead of Latin.
He even began to teach that the wine as well as the bread
should be given the laity in Communion, that Confession
was not obligatory, and that Masses for the dead were
"heathenish." But he still held out for certain of the
Roman institutions such as the use of candles, the crucifix,
and pictures.

Such concessions were not enough, however. Luther
had let loose a beast that would not wait on his reluctant
pace. By the year 1523 the reformer found himself left
far behind, the leader now of no more than a small party.
The enlightened scholars in the Church, the Humanists,

had withdrawn from him in intellectual revulsion. Led by the brilliant and sardonic Erasmus—whose satire they believed far more damaging to the pope than Luther's angry ravings—they had begun to insist that what Christendom needed most was not revolution but education.[12] And, at the other extreme, the real radicals had decided that Luther was a craven.

Worst of all, even the princes were beginning to turn against Luther, largely because his anticlerical agitation was stirring up a far graver revolt. From the attack on the pope the masses were going on to an attack on the princes. The South-German peasantry had long been restive—they had already broken out in bloody rebellion in 1476, 1492, 1512, and 1513—and now they were putting forth demands they had never before had the wit or courage to frame. They had been reading Luther's translation of the New Testament, and it had quickened them to a new realization of their grievances. If it was true that Christ had redeemed them and made them free, why then were they still serfs? If it was true that all were equally the children of God, why were some on earth so rich and the rest so hungry? A whole horde of toilers began to march through southern Germany and ask these questions with bludgeons and scythes in their hands.

Luther, terrified lest his cause be blamed for the uprising, hastily published a pamphlet entitled *Against the Murderous and Thieving Rabble of the Peasants,* in which he urged the princes to "knock down, strangle and stab"

[12] See P. Smith, *Erasmus: a study of his life, ideals, and place in history;* and R. H. Murray, *Erasmus and Luther,* which contrasts the attitudes of the two great men toward toleration, etc.

the rebels, and declared: "in such times a prince can merit heaven better by bloodshed than by prayer." Evidently the strain of eight years of strife had begun to tell on Luther's disposition. No doubt ill-health also had something to do with the change. From about the age of thirty he had been suffering from dreadful noises in the head, incessant banging, whistling, thumping, and crashing. These were accompanied frequently by horrid attacks of giddiness which sometimes caused him to fall from his chair, and which rendered work impossible. His own interpretation of these afflictions was that they were the work of the Devil, and it is said that once he threw a pot of ink at the fiend. (The marks are still to be seen on the wall of the room he occupied while in hiding.) More plausibly, however, the trouble had its origin in a disease of the inner ear—a theory which seems borne out by the fact that later in life Luther became temporarily deaf.[13]

But the peasants against whom Luther launched that vituperative broadside could not be expected to inquire into the reasons for his savagery. They turned on him in immeasurable hate, and spurned his whole movement.

With the Humanists aloof, the peasants alienated, and a number of the rulers still suspicious of the movement, there was no chance for Lutheranism to spread very far. Its program was adopted by about half the princes in Germany, probably because they stood to profit by the change.

[13] See MacLaurin, *Post Mortems of Mere Mortals,* p. 122. "What a difference a course of salicylates and bromides might have made to Luther, and possibly through him to the whole Reformation," comments this learned physician.

They confiscated the wealth of the monasteries, subjugated the priests, and succeeded in making religion a mere branch of politics. But the rest of the rulers in the land—and these were mostly in the southern portion, where the agrarian uprisings had been most menacing—remained loyal to the pope. Most of them may have had little love for the Catholic hierarchy, but, having seen the fruits of heresy in the Peasants' War of 1525, they had a positive hate for Lutheranism.

The emperor, Charles V, who was a Spaniard and a devoutly orthodox man, was mortified that some of his vassal princes should dare to espouse a heresy. But, ironically enough, the treachery of the pope made it impossible for the emperor to drive the recalcitrants back into the fold. Charles, who had inherited the thrones of Germany, Austria, Burgundy, Spain, and the Netherlands, and had in addition made himself virtual ruler of Italy, was far too powerful for the pope's comfort. The one menace within the empire was the dissension in Germany, and, had Charles been able to put an end to that, his power would have been overwhelming. So the pope and the Catholic king of France secretly encouraged the Lutheran princes to hold out and defy their overlord. Finally the emperor had to give up the struggle. Distracted by the encroachments of the Turks in the East, betrayed by the pope, harassed by the French, Charles could not possibly root out the heresy flourishing in his realm. By the terms of the Treaty of Augsburg (1555) each prince in Germany was allowed to decide whether his state would be Catholic or Lutheran. If a subject found that his religion was not the one chosen by his

ruler, he had the choice of conversion or of moving elsewhere.

And thus, in a smolder of compromise, the German
conflagration was halted for the moment.

5

PARKS leaping from the blaze had
fallen in other lands, however, and
Luther lived to see his movement
spread far beyond the confines of
Germany. A former Wittenberg
student named Hans Tausen began
to fan the flames in Denmark in
1524, and in 1537 Lutheranism
was made the state religion there.
About the same time Norway,
Sweden, Iceland, and Finland likewise abjured subjection
to the pope. In all these lands, significantly enough,
the change was brought about almost entirely by the
kings. They liked Lutheranism—not altogether for spiritual reasons, either—and they established it by fiat as the
religion of their lands much as their Barbarian ancestors
had once made Catholicism the religion of the tribes.

England, too, was led by its king to establish an anti-
papal religion much like Lutheranism. The history of
that defection from Catholicism is worth recounting in
some detail, for it throws a lurid light on the whole spirit
of the Reformation accomplished by the princes. Henry
VIII of England was a shrewd, able, and enormously
energetic man whose one ambition seems to have been

to make himself the absolute despot in his kingdom.[14] He was, by the standards of that day, a pious man. Indeed, he received from the pope the title of *Defensor fidei,* "Defender of the Faith," as a reward for the attack on Luther's doctrines which the king published in 1521. But not long thereafter Henry was himself at odds with the pope. Like the run of ambitious princes in that age— or in any other—he was ready to believe in the Church and support it vigorously so long as it lent itself to his purposes; the moment it refused, however, his loyalty was at an end. And the Church did refuse at a certain juncture. Henry had been married to Catharine of Aragon, a Spanish princess, for over twenty years, when he decided to take another wife. Had he been prompted merely by lust, there would have been no trouble, for then he might have taken one or a dozen more mistresses; but Henry's real motive was dynastic, for his controlling desire was for a son and heir. Accordingly he appealed to the pope for an annulment of his marriage to Catharine, alleging that it had never been religiously valid because she had once been betrothed to his deceased brother.

Under ordinary circumstances Henry's appeal would have been readily granted, for the Roman Curia was inclined to be tractable when dealing with powerful personages. But in this particular case there were complications because just then the pope was virtually a prisoner of the emperor, Charles V, who was none other than a

[14] For literary distinction as well as biographical understanding there is no book on this subject that is comparable to Francis Hackett's *Henry the Eighth.*

nephew of the wife Henry wished to put aside. Under such circumstances it was impossible for the pope to accede to the English king's request. Henry pleaded and blustered for fully ten years, and then resorted to drastic measures. Assured that the people were on his side— for nationalism was already a potent force in England, and there was no little hostility to the foreign pope—and with Parliament well in hand, the king prepared for what might be termed a *coup d'eglise.* On May 23, 1533, the archbishop of Canterbury, after having held proper ecclesiastical court, formally declared as primate of England that the marriage of King Henry VIII to Catharine of Aragon was null and void. And less than four months later the new queen, Anne Boleyn, bore a daughter, the princess Elizabeth, who later became the "Virgin Queen"!

Thus originated the Anglican Church. The pope, incensed at Henry's insubordination, prepared a decree excommunicating the king, interdicting his realm, forbidding his subjects to obey him, or other states to hold commerce with him, dissolving all his treaties with foreign princes, commanding all the clergy to depart from England, and ordering his nobility to rise up in revolt.[15] But fulminations of that sort had lost their potency. Henry simply turned about and abjured all allegiance to Rome. In 1534 the English Parliament passed the famous "Act of Supremacy" which declared Henry and his successors to be unqualifiedly "the only supreme head on earth of the Church of England."

[15] Burnet, *History of the Reformation of the Church of England,* 1816, Vol. I, pt. 1, p. 409.

Having broken completely with the papacy, Henry's next move was to suppress the monasteries. The king was afraid of the monks and nuns, for, being bound by vows to the pope, they could not but be hostile to the schismatic church. In addition, Henry coveted the monastic lands and treasures. Accordingly he commissioned Thomas Cromwell, a layman who had been appointed vice-regent in ecclesiastical affairs, to make a visitation of the monasteries and report on their condition. The report was very dark, not alone because the monasteries were actually corrupt—though not nearly so corrupt as on the Continent—but also because the inspectors were prejudiced. Burnet assures us that the monks and nuns

> "were all extremely addicted to idolatry and superstition. In some (monasteries) they found the instruments and other tools for coining. . . . The lewdness of the confessors of nunneries, whole houses being found almost all with child; the dissoluteness of abbots and other monks and friars, not only with whores but married women; their unnatural lusts and other brutal practices: these are not fit to be spoken of, much less enlarged on, in a work of this nature. The full report of this visitation is lost; yet I have seen an extract of part of it, concerning one hundred and forty-four houses, that contains abominations equal to any that were in Sodom." [16]

These "abominations" were the excuse used by Henry for the suppression of the monasteries throughout his realm. The "liquidation"—to use the term applied to the

[16] Burnet, *op. cit.*, Vol. I, pt. 1, p. 347.

same process in Russia during the Bolshevik Revolution —took three years, and when it was over Henry was the wealthiest monarch the land had ever known.

But it must not be imagined that England had ceased to be a Catholic country. Its Established Church was still practically orthodox in all save its attitude toward the pope; its bishops could and did still boast direct "succession" from the Jewish fisherman who was said to have been the first bishop of Rome. Transubstantiation, clerical celibacy, Masses for the dead, Confession—these were all part of the faith and order insisted upon by the king and passed by his Parliament.

But what else could be expected? The Church of England was the handiwork of a prince filled with pride and greed, not of a people hungering for salvation.

6

 GENUINE reformation of the religion was impossible among men who put their trust in princes. Christianity had had its origin in a brotherhood of peasants, and for generations it had been followed only by the "foolish of the world." Necessarily, therefore, it was solely among peasants that a real return to the pristine faith could be instituted. The appearance of a Francis of Assisi was an anomaly in the upper strata of Christendom; only among those already stripped by society did it seem necessary "in

nakedness to follow the naked Christ." During the later Middle Ages the attempts to make Christianity once more a prophetic faith had been supported almost entirely by the lower classes. The clerics and nobles had sought only to crush such attempts, knowing well how they menaced their privileges. But even though the movements were indeed suppressed, the hunger which had bred them endured. Stifled by the rulers, the protest of the masses became an inward groan, an ominous rumbling in the deepest bowels of society.

And now in the sixteenth century the protest was able to make itself heard once more. The clerics and the princes had fallen out among themselves, and the mailed hand had been lifted momentarily from the lips of the populace. And a roar went up such as had not been heard since the days of the early Christians. Throughout Europe, but most especially in the northern lands, wandering preachers began to excite the populace with mad warnings and madder hopes. They were for the most part untutored men, and therefore unbounded in the violence of their sentiments. Luther, though no less honest a man, was restrained by his learning and affiliations. Most of the other educated reformers, having been trained to walk with the goosestep of the Scholastics, could only slightly free their gait. But these peasant agitators careered along like madmen. They had picked up a little knowledge and it had made them dangerous. They had learned to spell out the words in the Bible, and now they thought themselves inspired. Simple men heard the "call," left wives and children, and wandered off to preach the good tidings. They went about in rude homespun garments, often barefooted, their heads covered with rough felt hats. Some preached aloud in the market places, or else strode into the churches and started disputes with the priests. Others begged hospitality in the remote farm-houses, and, after supper, produced fragments of the Bible, read and expounded, and then vanished again before dawn.

There was no uniformity among these preachers, yet almost all of them were agreed on certain fundamentals. They were one in their loathing of the pope, and of all for which he stood. In their Revelation-ridden minds they could not think of him save as the Antichrist, or of Rome save as the "Whore of Babylon." They were one also in their hostility to clericalism, monasticism, the images, the veneration of the saints, the Masses, and all the other inventions of priestcraft and relics of heathenism with which the Catholic faith had become encumbered. And almost all of them were united in an opposition to infant baptism. They insisted that baptism was a seal upon one's personal faith and must be earned. Administering it pro-miscuously to infants robbed the rite of all significance, and made Christian fellowship an involuntary inheritance instead of a hard-won privilege. Jesus, they declared, had called his followers the *salt* of the earth, not the earth itself; the first churches had been communities of saints, not haphazard aggregations of human beings.

It was their unanimity in opposing infant baptism that won for these heretics the nickname of Anabaptists, or "rebaptizers." The designation was inaccurate, for they did not believe in *re*baptism save for those who had al-ready received the sacrament at birth. (In the next century, when the movement came to life anew in England, its followers called themselves more correctly the Baptists.) They seem to have first emerged as a distinct sect in 1525 in Zurich, where a former priest named Huldreich Zwingli was leading the Reformation. Driven from the city by the supporters of Zwingli, the dissenters gathered in a near-by village and instituted "believers' baptism" at first by sprinkling and later by total immersion. Zwingli and the other Reform pastors who now dominated Zurich, were as intolerant of dissent as the worst Catholic clerics, and they lost no time in pouncing upon the radicals. The town council ordered that the Anabaptists be given their fill of immersion and drowned—and the sentence was actually carried out. Several of the leaders of the sect were put to death, and others were imprisoned and tortured.

But such persecutions only intensified the zeal of the dissenters, and they began to carry their teachings to other places. Anabaptist congregations soon sprang up in Germany, Poland, Austria, Hungary, and the Netherlands. The agitators even got across to the east coast of England. Certain of the founders of the movement—for instance, Hübmaier and Hans Denck—were men of fair scholarship as well as piety, and the Anabaptism they preached was altogether a noble and ennobling doctrine. But now the heresy began to draw to it coarser advocates, good men but very ignorant, and at their hands the doctrine achieved a mighty appeal to the lower classes.

Many of its popular preachers declared that the world was at last coming to an end, that Christ was about to return and establish his Kingdom. And the disinherited of the earth, elated at the tidings, flocked to the river banks where these preachers held forth, and flung themselves frenziedly into the waters to receive the baptism of faith. Thus consecrated, they knew they belonged to the saved "remnant"; that they were chosen ones who would not fail of reward when the great hour came. They banded themselves together in devout brotherhoods and forswore all interest in civil government, repudiated violence, refused to serve in the armies, would not take oaths, and generally decried most of the institutions considered sacrosanct among men. Pure and holy they tried to keep themselves while they waited impatiently for the Return.

As was to be expected, the rulers, both Protestant and Catholic, looked on these extremists much as had the Pagan authorities on the early Christians; and they persecuted them even more cruelly. The Anabaptists were tortured on the rack, scourged, drowned, buried alive, or crushed into coffins too small for their bodies. In Holland a special form of execution was invented for them: instead of being burned alive they were chained to a stake at some distance from a huge fire, and were slowly roasted to death.[17] But, as with the early Christians, persecution only helped the movement. Spite is a far greater incentive to fanaticism than love, and those downtrodden toilers, already goaded to desperation by their hunger and social abasement, became quite mad when denied the right to their faith. They did not strike back at their persecu-

[17] Lindsay, *History of the Reformation*, Vol. II, p. 236. For a detailed account, see Heath, *Anabaptism*.

tors, for that was forbidden them by their religion. But they persisted in their beliefs and suffered martyrdom with a courage more provoking than the most violent retaliation. What buoyed them up was their utterly unshakable conviction that it was but a matter of weeks, perhaps even of days, before this whole wicked world would be no more. Some among them even prophesied the exact hour. For instance, a certain man named Melchior Hoffman won a great following in the Netherlands by going about and declaring that Strassburg had been divinely appointed as the New Jerusalem, and that after he had suffered imprisonment there for six months the Advent would occur. Nor was he afraid to test his prediction. Marching up to Strassburg in 1532, he began to shout aloud in the streets until the first part of his prophecy was fulfilled and he was flung into prison. But the six months passed and nothing occurred. Hoffman pleaded a miscalculation and set a later date for the Advent. Month after month he kept setting later dates until finally, after almost eleven years in the dungeon, he died.

But while Hoffman lay waiting for the Kingdom in Strassburg, other preachers set out to *force* its coming. They gathered in the city of Münster in 1534, drove out the bishop who was both lay and clerical ruler of the domain, and made themselves masters of the place. Led by a Dutch baker named Jan Mathys, a tall lean man with piercing eyes and a splendid black beard, they decided that here, not in Strassburg, the New Jerusalem would arise; and they proceeded at once to live the perfect life. All adult inhabitants were commanded either to receive bap-

tism and become "saints," or leave the city; and all food
and other necessities were communized.

News of the wonder spread swiftly, and thousands of
Anabaptist refugees from Holland and all the other lands
where there was persecution, came flocking to the city. At
the same time the prince-bishop of Münster gathered an
army of Catholics and Lutherans and encamped outside the
walls. The Anabaptists, utterly mad with zeal for the
"Kingdom of God" which they had established, prepared
to resist the enemy. Sure that God was on his side, Jan
Mathys picked twenty men and with them marched out
of the city gate to scatter the bishop's army. He was, of
course, cut down at once; but his followers within the city
remained undaunted. A new leader arose, another Dutch-
man, Johann Buckholdt; and the "saints" got themselves
ready to withstand a long siege. Johann, a handsome
young man of twenty-five, had once been a tailor by trade
and a bit of a poet and actor on the side; but he was a born
leader and had no difficulty in assuming control of the beleaguered city. He knew very little save the Bible, and
that was enough for his needs. Following Biblical precedent he declared himself king of the community and
appointed twelve princes to serve as his counselors. Then
he settled down to rule his subjects precisely as had the
monarchs in ancient Israel.

Almost a year and a half this strange "Kingdom of
God" was able to sustain itself in Münster. As the months
passed the privations of the "saints" grew unendurable, for
food ran low and the besieging army cut down every soul
that sought to escape from the place. What added to the
distress of the community was the abnormal sexual situation in its midst, for the women outnumbered the men

more than four to one, and, though the quarters were close
and the emotions were at fever heat, there was absolutely
no relaxation of the Old Testament moral code. Something had to be done to end the intolerable tension, and
the "king" himself at last suggested a solution. Calling a
council of the elders and chief preachers, he proposed to
them that they make polygamy the law of the city! The
others were shocked, of course. For eight days they held
out stubbornly against the "king's" eloquence and Bible
proofs. But finally they were won over. When the decree
was made public, however, there was a roar of protest from
the scandalized citizens, and a mutiny was started. But
the women strongly favored the new law, and, outnumber-
ing the men as they did, they were able to suppress the
opposition. Every marriageable man was compelled to take
as many wives as were available—handsome Johann Buckholdt himself took sixteen—and not a woman was left
without at least a share in a husband.

And thus, with every man a latter-day Solomon, and
every woman a pale Sheba, the "saints" managed to withstand the besieging army for still another year. But the
struggle, though maintained with incredible heroism, was
hopeless. At last, in June 1535, the bishop's soldiers succeeded in penetrating into the city and the "Kingdom of
God" in Münster collapsed amid carnage and fire. The
population was put to the sword and the leaders were
executed with terrible tortures. And that was the end of
Anabaptism as a militant movement.[18]

[18] Kautsky, *Communism in Central Europe in the Time of the
Reformation*, recounts this whole episode in detail, as does also Bax,
Rise and Fall of the Anabaptists.

A SUCCESSFUL proletarian movement was impossible in the sixteenth century. The toilers, being still very ignorant, and as unable to follow enlightened leaders as to espouse coherent ideas, were quite incapable of more than futile rebellion. Success was reserved for the efforts of the higher folk, for the kings riding the wave of nationalism and the burghers swimming with the tide of trade. During the very weeks when the tortured and dismembered body of hapless "King" Johann Buckholdt hung rotting in a cage atop Münster's walls, King Henry VIII of England was drafting articles of faith for his own national church, King Gustavus Vasa of Sweden was making pawns of his bishops, King Christian III of Denmark was negotiating with Wittenberg for a Lutheran coronation, the Protestant rulers in Germany were winning new allies in Kurland and Esthonia, and a young French heretic named John Calvin was beginning to preach in Geneva. From then on the skirts of Protestantism were held high above the peasant gutters, and adventism, communism, and all the other extravagances of the lowly folk, were forgotten. Thenceforth the Reformation remained very largely staid and sober.

A new leader now emerged to dominate the movement —that young Frenchman, Calvin.[19] By training he was a

---

[19] Audin's famous biography of Calvin is unfairly critical. Williston Walker's *John Calvin, the Organizer of Reformed Protestantism*, is less detailed but more just.

lawyer, but at the age of twenty-two some mysterious religious experience which he himself could speak of only as a "sudden conversion," turned his thoughts to God. Thenceforth he began to devote himself altogether to theology, and the more he studied the literature of Christianity, the more was he drawn to the new religious teachings which were then seeping through from Germany. Before long his critical attitude toward the Catholic Church brought him into conflict with the French government, and, after a brief period in prison, Calvin fled to Protestant Basle. There he sat down and wrote a treatise entitled *The Institutes of the Christian Religion,* a work which was at once recognized as the most coherent exposition of Protestant doctrine that had yet appeared. None of the older Protestants, neither Luther nor Farel nor Zwingli nor Butzer nor even the very learned Melanchthon, had been able to produce such a treatise, for no one of them had had much time for collected thought. They had developed their theologies, as it were, under fire, and doctrines maintained one year had been repudiated the next. But Calvin, entering the field when the first smoke of battle was already clearing, was able to work out a comprehensive strategy. In a later day he came to be spoken of as "the only gentleman among the Reformers"; but already in 1536 he was seen to be almost the only clear thinker.

Soon after the *Institutes* was published, John Calvin chanced to pass through the city of Geneva, where a zealous pastor named Farel was furiously trying to advance the evangelical cause. Seizing hold of the youthful author, whose repute was already well known to him, Farel insisted so vehemently on his remaining in the city that the other could not refuse. The town council, largely for political and economic reasons, had already cast off obedience to Rome, but the populace was—to quote a contemporary writer—"very imperfectly enlightened in divine knowledge, and as yet hardly emerged from the filth of the papacy." [20] Accordingly Calvin was impressed into service as a teacher of Protestant theology. He was able to make but little impression on the community at first, for he was frail-looking, reserved, not very eloquent, and a foreigner. Before long, however, his quiet power and profound learning began to assert themselves. The Protestant cause was still being fought with the tongue rather than the sword, and Calvin was found to be a most redoubtable champion in the great public disputations then being held in Switzerland. The evangelical teachers were still insisting that theirs was not an heretical religion, but the only true orthodoxy. It was necessary, therefore, for them to be thoroughly versed in the ancient Church literature, for on that alone could they base their arguments. And Calvin, studious from childhood and blessed with a phenomenal memory, could outquote his opponents with an ease that soon made him the darling of his side.

But the need of the hour was for more than a debater, as Calvin was the first to realize. "The idols had been sought out and burned," he wrote, "and there was much preaching; but that was the extent of the reformation; everything was in disorder." [21] Accordingly he began almost at once to draft a program for the complete reorganization of the life of the community. Informing it from start to finish was the conviction that religion was not a part but the whole of life, and that therefore the Luther-

[20] Beza, *Vit. Calvin, an. 1536.*
[21] Bonnet, *Lettres francaises de Calvin,* Vol. II, p. 544.

ans, who made the Church subject to the State, and the Anabaptists, who sought to separate the two, were both wrong. Calvin insisted that all must be rendered to God and nothing to Cæsar—that the Church must be utterly insuperable in its power. Such a teaching would probably have cost Calvin his head had he dared to voice it in Germany. But this was Switzerland, a land of semi-independent republics, and there was no ruling caste to resent his theocratic doctrine. Control of the churches had already been vested in the town council in Zürich, through the influence of an earlier reformer named Zwingli; and the idea had spread thence to Basle, Berne, and other cities in and around German-speaking Switzerland. But Calvin wanted to reverse the situation and vest control of the town council in the churches. All life in the municipality must center around the Lord's Supper, he insisted, and all the inhabitants must keep themselves pure so as to be worthy of receiving the sacrament as often as once a month. He even suggested that "men of known virtue dwelling in different quarters of the town" should be appointed to watch and report those in their neighborhood who had sinned, and that the church authorities be empowered to excommunicate those transgressors who persisted in their wickedness.

The program was, of course, bitterly criticized when first laid before the Genevan government. No one questioned the right of the municipality to legislate concerning private life. Geneva, like every other medieval town, had always had its laws against extravagance in dress, in eating, and in drinking, against cursing and swearing, against gaming, dances and masquerades. Laws prescribed the number of guests to be invited to weddings and parties, when the pipers were to play, when they were to leave off, and what they were to be paid. They even declared how a man should part his hair and when he must go to bed.[22] But there had never been much effort to enforce those laws. Occasionally the civic fathers had found such statutes useful. A particularly brazen kitchen-wench could be flogged for wearing a silk apron, or an unpopular shopkeeper could be fined for doing his books on Sunday. Otherwise, however, the restrictions went unheeded, for most of them had been passed as gestures of feudal paternalism rather than earnests of Christian devotion.

But Calvin's program gave a totally new meaning to those sumptuary laws. It sought to make their puritanism not an onerous convention which was endurable only because rarely observed, but a precious privilege to be assumed voluntarily and fulfilled with righteous joy. That was much more than the Genevan burghers were prepared for, and some of them tried to have Calvin driven from the town. But he was already a power there, and with the aid of his fellow-pastors he actually succeeded in getting a large part of his program adopted. Had he been satisfied with that, all might have gone smoothly; but Calvin was no man for half-measures. His colleague, Farel, had drawn up twenty-one articles as the creed for this regenerated community, and Calvin now ordered that all the inhabitants come in parties of ten and accept these articles under oath as the confession of their faith. Such high-handed conduct intensified the opposition, and soon there was bitter dissension in the city. Calvin did much that was

[22] See section on "Sumptuary Laws" in Preserved Smith, *History of Modern Culture,* Vol. I, pp. 508ff. For the parallels in England see F. E. Baldwin, *Sumptuary Legislation and Personal Regulation.*

unchallengeably admirable in founding schools for the young and laying the foundations for a university; but that was forgotten in the hostility to his despotic puritanism. Finally there was a rebellion, and both Calvin and Farel had to flee from the city.

Calvin was still under thirty, and he seems to have suffered no great dejection at thus being expelled from Geneva. Taking refuge in Strassburg, he proceeded to devote himself once more to study. He revised and enlarged his great work, the *Institutes,* and did some preaching in the local churches. But before three years had passed he was being implored to come back to Geneva and take charge there again. He was at first most reluctant to obey, for he liked the quiet and studious life he was able to lead in Strassburg. But his friends in Geneva insisted it was his duty to return, and Calvin, who had the utmost respect for duty, gave in.

The young reformer returned to Geneva in the year 1541, surer now than ever of the rightness of his ideas. From then until his death, some twenty-three years later, he continued unflaggingly to seek by pious teaching and harsh correction to make Geneva perfect. His official position was merely that of a pastor; but his influence dominated all life in the city. Repeated attempts were made to overthrow him, but none succeeded. Having control of the Consistory, a body of pastors and lay elders which had the right to excommunicate sinners, he was able to control everything. Geneva was made the capital of puritanism—a city where grim virtue stalked in every street and intolerance choked the air. When a Spanish physician named Servetus, an erratic genius who had discovered that the blood circulated in the body because of the action of the heart, and that the whole notion of the Trinity was an invention of superstitious priests, came fleeing to Geneva for protection from the Catholic inquisitors, Calvin had him burnt to death as a heretic. Calvin had many people burnt to death: heretics, witches —thirty-four in a single year—and anyone else whom he thought offensive in the eyes of the stern God he served. His spy system turned Geneva into a city of glass houses, and the Consistory was provided with an endless queue of sinners to judge at its weekly sessions. The rare insurgents who dared to refuse to go to Church or who would not conform to the rigorous regulations concerning dress, were kept imprisoned till they agreed to walk barefoot and in sackcloth through the city and make confession on their knees in the public square.

Thus did John Calvin seek to return to the teachings of him who cheered the wedding guests at Cana.

8

E live in an age so hostile to puritanism that it is difficult for us to be fair to the man who gave puritanism its charter. Actually Calvin was the most influential figure in the whole Reformation movement, and was one of the founders of what we call modern civilization. Luther, whose name is far better known, accomplished far less. The German monk was swept into revolt almost as a man on a hulk is swept along by a flood; but Calvin started out in a trim and well-

caulked vessel, and steered his course with unfaltering de-
liberation. As a consequence, while Lutheranism fell a
prey to piratical princes, Calvinism caught the trade winds
and sailed off to conquer a world. Whereas the one was
brought to shore and made, as it were, a pleasure-boat for
lordlings, the other became a freighter for merchants. Or,
to view the difference in another light, Lutheranism exhausted itself as a protest, whereas Calvinism, which came
later, was able to go on to affirmation. And in that profound contrast lay the enduring distinction between the
Lutheran and what came to be distinguished as the Reformed churches.

A partial explanation of the success of Calvinism lies
in the fact that it was to commercialism and the ambitions
of the middle-class what Catholicism had been to feudalism and the usurpations of the lords. In its theology, morality, and organization it was at once the sanction and
inspiration for the burgher's way of life. Its most distinctive doctrine, Predestination, had quite curious implications. In the first place, it blasted all those worldly caste
distinctions which were built into the very foundations of
Catholicism. By maintaining that each man's eternal fate
is decided in advance by the inscrutable will of God, it
made a mockery of all those mundane superiorities upon
which the aristocrats had so long prided themselves.
Birth, prestige, apostolic succession—these were mean and
shriveled claims in the light of the supernal honor of
"election." A penny-pinching shopkeeper, whose father
had been a serf, was yet infinitely better off if he was of the
elect than a duke if he was of the damned; for whereas
the latter might dwell in his castle for a brief moment here
on earth, the former would have his throne in Heaven

throughout eternity. Calvinism was therefore obstreperously democratic. It gave legitimacy to the claims of the rising bourgeoisie, and, wherever these claims were challenged, gave impetus to the most furious revolutions. Calvinism made necessary a complete reorganization of church polity. Respecting neither priest nor prince, it had to vest the government of its churches entirely in the worshipers. It had to set up consistories of elected presbyters and pastors who were accountable neither to bishops nor to princes, but only to God and the congregants.

Belief in Predestination had another effect on conduct, in that it intensified the believer's individualism. Each man felt that he must take his separate trail to God, for he had been elected to Heaven as an individual, not as a member of society. Bunyan, in his *Pilgrim's Progress,* thinks it quite right that his hero, Christian, should forsake wife and children in his frantic effort to reach the Heavenly City; for Bunyan, a true product of Calvinistic teaching, believed firmly that each man must be for himself in the pursuit of salvation, and let the Devil take the hindermost.

And there was a third unsuspected consequence of the belief in Predestination: it goaded its adherents to activity. That may sound paradoxical, but its truth is established by history. The Calvinists were, as a group, extraordinarily energetic and self-reliant, accomplishing revolutions, conquering wildernesses, developing industries, and amassing wealth with incomparable aggressiveness and courage. Why this should have been is not quite clear. One suspects that Calvin, with his teaching that a man's everlasting fate was predetermined by God's will in Heaven, gave the middle-class of the sixteenth century an assurance much like that which Karl Marx gave to the working-class three hundred years later when he told them that society's development was predetermined by economic factors already present. The Calvinists knew well that each man's election or damnation was settled in advance, and that no amount of labor or prayer could affect the issue. But they knew also that they themselves happened to be of the elect, and, to prove it, they conducted themselves in a manner becoming to the elect. To have done otherwise would have been to confess themselves damned. . . .

The index to Calvinism's real character is furnished by its notion of the conduct becoming to the elect. Its ideal was not the perfectionism of the first believers, for that seemed feasible only as an interim code. The insistence on an abnegation of wealth and suppression of the self could be endured only so long as one reckoned on the imminent return of the Lord; and the men to whom Calvinism appealed were highly skeptical of any such reckoning. They had a feeling that this world might yet last a long while—perhaps because they wanted it to—and they were most unwilling to sacrifice everything when the reward was still so far out of sight.

Nor was Calvin's ideal the asceticism of the Catholic Church, for that, too, could not fit the needs of his following. Asceticism had flowered when Europe was reduced to a howling wilderness, and life had become beyond bearing. But in Calvin's day Europe was flush with sudden prosperity, and life for at least one group in society, the bourgeoisie, was just then becoming quite glorious. The idea of fleeing the flesh could have no appeal for the burghers. They preferred to believe it was far more to

God's liking that they strive to use the flesh for the profit of the soul. It was characteristic of John Milton, the epic poet of Calvinism, that after describing how Adam and Eve were expelled from Paradise, he should say:

"Some natural tears they dropped but wiped them soon;
The world was all before them, where to choose
Their place of rest, with Providence their guide;"

The world was indeed at the feet of these middle-class men, and they were not content to let it go to the Devil. On the contrary, they were determined to conquer and use it—for the greater glory of God, of course. Thus, in the place of the reckless perfectionism of a frantic peasantry or the profligate asceticism of a sated aristocracy, Calvinism set up a provident puritanism for ambitious shopkeepers. The whole world was made a secular monastery in which each good man had his "calling" to fulfill—to work hard, advance himself, save money for the sake of saving, and thus prove himself to be of the elect. The religion put no store by voluntary poverty or bootless self-mortification; on the contrary, it insisted on prudence, thrift, industry, diligence, and sobriety. These secular monastics spoke of themselves not as Christ's soldiers but God's stewards. Their favorite text—Calvin quoted it repeatedly—was Paul's fiat: "If a man will not work, neither shall he eat." Calvinism was above all else a provident religion, praising virtues which, though ostensibly evidences of heavenly election, were actually guarantees of worldly success.

Catholicism, as we have already seen, was still hostile to emergent capitalism. So, too, in a measure, was Lutheranism. Both were controlled by the land-owning class, and, though Lutheranism did suppress the monastic orders and oppose the indolence and mendicancy which they encouraged, and though it did lay emphasis on Predestination, it was as bitter as Catholicism in its denunciation of money-lending. But Calvinism, a purely urban movement started by a lawyer and supported by tradesmen, took a different stand. In the first place, it saw nothing dishonorable in business. As Calvin himself declared: "Whence do the merchant's profits come, except from his own diligence and industry?" [23] In the second place, Calvinism insisted that there was a distinction between usury and a fair rate of interest. The first it condemned unsparingly, but the second it considered quite proper. Calvin himself dismissed all the oft-quoted denunciations of money-lending in the Bible and the Church Fathers, on the ground that they had no bearing on present conditions. In the new society which had sprung up in Europe, the payment of interest for capital was, he insisted, as reasonable as the payment of rent for land.

It was no calculated opportunism that led Calvin to teach as he did. Like Paul, the man was quite without guile, and if his doctrine happened to conform to the needs of the hour it was probably because he was a genius and could sense those needs intuitively and make adjustments to them unconsciously. The rise of the middle-class had created, as it were, a magnetic field in the social atmosphere, and when Calvin sent a charge of new energy

[23] Quoted in R. H. Tawney, *Religion and the Rise of Capitalism*, p. 105—a most illuminating discussion of economic elements involved in the origin and progress of the Reformation. See also Harry F. Ward, *Our Economic Morality*.

through the loose wire of Predestination, dynamic consequences were inevitable. Calvinism made all Europe vibrate. It set the tone for the entire Protestant movement, making over Anglicanism almost completely, and profoundly influencing Lutheranism as well. In France it gave rise to the Huguenot movement, which, even after a hundred and fifty years of intermittent persecution, could still count more than half a million followers who preferred to go into exile rather than abjure their faith.[24] In Scotland, largely through the influence of John Knox, it integrated the national spirit and created a Presbyterian Church which became in time one of the most vigorous sectarian influences in Christendom. And in Holland, England and North America it effected such revolutionary changes, and gave such impetus to trade and learning, that those lands were soon able to become the leaders in the commercial expansion and intellectual advancement of the whole race. Above all, Calvinism gave sanction to certain attitudes which in their zealous expression by increasing multitudes of men made for the revolutionizing of the basic character of society. Its doctrine of election made for democracy, its individualism encouraged the competitive spirit, and its emphasis on relentless industry and incessant thrift helped bring into being this whole capitalistic civilization we live in to-day.[25]

[24] Smedley, *History of the Reformed Religion in France* (3 vols.) is a very full account. Browning, *History of the Huguenots* is briefer.

[25] For the extended argument on this point see Max Weber's epoch-making essay *Die Protestantische Ethik und der 'geist' des Kapitalismus,* and Troeltsch's elaboration of the thesis in his *Protestantism and Progress,* N. Y., 1912. See also J. I. Good, *The Reformed Reformation,* 1916, p. 140ff. The whole argument is well summarized in Moehlman's comprehensive syllabus, *The Story of Christianity in Outline,* Rochester, N. Y., 1930.

NLY belatedly, very belatedly, did the heads of the Church awaken to what was occurring all around them. Tucked away behind their fortifications of ancient prestige, and surrounded by a wide moat filled with superstition and awe, the churchmen imagined themselves secure forever. So for long they refused to be exercised over the uprisings north of the Alps. With the exception of unhappy Adrian VI, who reigned but a single year, the popes remained quite blind to the gravity of the Protestant revolt. Indeed, some of them seem to have looked on the disturbance with secret delight, seeing in it naught save a source of vexation to their hated rival, the emperor.

Not until 1542 did the Vatican become genuinely apprehensive, and then, characteristically enough, its first move was to reorganize the Inquisition. The curse of the hierarchy was that it could remember more easily than it could learn. It recalled with what success violent measures had stamped out dissent in the thirteenth, fourteenth, and fifteenth centuries, and it could not understand why like measures should not succeed now.

But there were those outside the Vatican who did understand, and, being supported by none other than the emperor, they were powerful enough to impress their opinion on the hierarchy. In 1544 Charles V was able to compel the pope to call a general council of the Church. It met at Trent, was moved to Bologna, returned to Trent, adjourned for ten years on account of the religious wars which were then at their height, and met again for a year in 1562. Covert hostility between pope and emperor, rivalries between different Orders, jealousies of individuals— all these evils were present to edge the deliberations. There was intrigue, spying, backbiting, and all the other mean accompaniments of professional politics. But also there was a hard zeal and high-hearted devotion, for the plight of the Church was plain now, and desperate measures were imperative. And the miracle of it was that this zeal was able to triumph in the Council and effect a house-cleaning of the entire Church. The reforms were far from realizing the wishes of the most advanced thinkers in the Church, but they nonetheless were of profound importance. In the first place, they put an end to that ignorance and apathy on the part of the clergy, which had allowed the religion to become rigid and so largely mechanical in its operations. Catholicism was made lively once more, full of appeal to the individual and compelling because of its own innate attractiveness as well as the prestige of its ancestry and the weight of its tradition. Provision was made for public interpretation of the Scriptures, and seminaries were established where the clergy could be prepared to preach and teach as well as perform the ritual. A new character was given to the priesthood: it was to be a privilege, not a means to privileges. Clerical celibacy, which had long been little more than a hypocritical pretense, was once more insisted upon. And this time there were signs that the command would be enforced. The taunts of the Protestants had had their effect: the "Papists," though they would not confess to having been bad in the past, were yet determined to be better in the future.

Together with this overhauling of the machinery came a
restatement of the belief. The tradition of the Church was
put on a plane with the Word of God—the *Summa* of St.
Thomas Aquinas and the Bible rested side by side throughout the deliberations—and every moot point was settled
on the basis of both. All the teachings and institutions
rejected by the heretics were redefined explicitly and re-
affirmed with fresh vigor. All doctrinal compromise and
modification were contemptuously thrust to one side: the
Church settled itself foursquare on its medieval foundations. And, to protect the "true believers" from the wiles
of the heretics, provision was made for the compiling
of an Index of all the books which impugned the "true
belief."

The enactment of these measures marked the beginning
of a new era in the career of the Church. Thenceforth the
apathy of the later Middle Ages and the cynicism of the
Renaissance were no more. Rome became a more somber
city, and, beginning with Paul IV in 1555, the popes,
though still temporal princes and much concerned with
Italian politics, were prevailingly men of strict life, religious earnestness, and strenuous Catholicism. Throughout
the clerical ranks the new spirit made its way, endowing
the Church with a vigor such as it had not known since
the early centuries. And therewith the Protestant tide was
checked; even more, it actually began to recede. Fifty
years after Luther's revolt, Catholicism was left clinging
precariously to the shores of the Mediterranean; a hundred
years after that revolt, Protestantism was left clinging no
less precariously to the shores of the Baltic. The Catholic
Church, which the Protestant evangelists had been wont to

picture as a decrepit and dying "Whore of Babylon," had suddenly become young again.

The one man who more than any other was responsible for this enormous change was a certain maimed Spanish soldier named Ignatius Loyola.[26] He was an aristocrat by birth, and he spent his boyhood years at the royal court in preparation for the cavalier life which was his due. From his youth until he was thirty he lived in camps and garrisons, fighting, gaming, drinking, and wenching in a manner worthy of a knight. But then his leg was shattered by a cannon-ball, and, after lying a while at the point of death, he recovered only to find that his soldiering days were apparently over. Impetuous by nature, and with a mind filled with those chivalrous fantasies which Cervantes was soon to caricature in *Don Quixote,* Loyola was tormented as he lay bedridden in his father's castle. What was he to do with the rest of his days? Maimed, it seemed, for life, he knew he could nevermore go to war or cut a figure before the ladies. Barely able to read, and not given to chicanery, he could not hope to advance at court. What should he do? . . . For weeks he tossed in agony, and then suddenly a wondrous thought fell into his mind like a star into a dark sea. He would become a Knight of the Blessed Virgin! Unable to live the hard life of a warrior, he would live the even harder life of saint. He would go as a pilgrim to Jerusalem (what an adventure *that* would be!) and practice such austerities there that all Heaven would ring with his praise.

[26] Innumerable biographies have been written of this extraordinary man, but the best in many respects is his own work translated into English under the title, *The Testament of Ignatius Loyola,* London, 1900.

And thus were Loyola's limping feet set on the path which was to lead him to immortality. Arising from his bed, he went to a near-by abbey and laying his sword and dagger on the Virgin's altar he kept a vigil all night long. The next day he departed a penniless wanderer, and thenceforth until his death, thirty-four years later, he never ceased to be the champion of his Blessed Lady. He made his way to Jerusalem in a pilgrim ship, but there his demonstrative piety led to an altercation with the Turks which forced the Franciscan provincial to order him from the Holy City. Returning to Spain, he determined to obtain an education, and at the age of thirty-three took his first lessons in Latin. Two years later he entered the university at Alcalá to study philosophy; but there, for the second time, he came into conflict with the authorities. He had become the leader of a group of devout students who affected beggars' clothing and who submitted themselves to severe austerities. The Inquisition, always suspicious of nonconformity, hailed Loyola to court, and, after finding no heresy in the man, dismissed him with a warning that he dress properly and wear shoes. Four months later, however, he was once more brought before the tribunal, accused now of offering spiritual advice though not yet ordained. (In those days unordained men were prohibited from dispensing religion much as unlicensed healers are prohibited from prescribing medicines to-day.) Loyola was held in prison almost two months, and then released with a warning not to instruct others till his four years of study were ended.

He moved on then to Salamanca, taking his companions with him; but there, too, he came under suspicion and was flung into prison. Thereupon he moved to Paris, for, though most eager to complete his course of studies, he wanted to be free at once to give comfort to others. There was some inexplicable thorn in the man's spirit which goaded him continually to seek combat with the Devil. It was not enough for him that he had saved his own soul; he ached to save every other. And there was that about the Spaniard which made him a welcome savior. Certain of the more devout students were drawn to him in Paris, even as they had been in Salamanca and Alcalá, and before long he became the leader of a curious sort of brotherhood. His followers were of a cast of mind much like his own. They were most romantically pious, and cherished all sorts of holy ideals which they yearned to fulfill in dramatic ways. It was characteristic of them that they should seal their fellowship with solemn vows taken at the altar. Gathering one day in the crypt of a church on Montmartre, six of them swore by all that was holy that henceforth they would remain chaste and poor all their days, and that at the first opportunity they would go to Jerusalem as missionaries.

And thus was founded the society destined to save the Catholic Church. Unable to go to Jerusalem because war was on with the Turks, the little band of holy knights decided to devote themselves to missionary work at home. They began to labor in the hospitals and preach in the market places, attracting increasing attention to themselves from the leaders in Rome. At first the attention was none too cordial, for Loyola had begun to regard his little fraternity as the nucleus of a new order of knighthood. His notion was tainted with originality, a trait highly suspect in the eyes of the Church, and it required three years of incessant pleading and intriguing before he could win Rome's approval of his labors. But at last in the year 1540 Pope Pius III condescended to authorize the establishment of a "Society of Jesus," and therewith Loyola's dream was realized.

The express purpose of the new Society was to help the pope fight his battles against heresy, infidelity, and indifference.

> "Without equivocation or excuse," ran one of its declarations, "with all possible promptitude, we must fulfill all that the present pope and his successors, shall command us to do for the good of our souls and the propagation of the faith, in whatever countries he may wish to send us—whether to the Turks or other infidels, or to the regions called India, or to the lands of the heretics, schismatics, or faithful Christians."

The Society was organized along strict military lines. Loyola was appointed its "general"—an office which he held till his death sixteen years later—and he in turn appointed "provincials" to direct the units garrisoning the various lands of the Church or deploying in the lands of the enemy. The one ideal governing the whole movement was that of absolute discipline. Loyola, a soldier born and bred, insisted that each man must obey his superior implicitly, and must never presume to question or complain. Room was left for individuality in that each member was assigned to do the work for which he was best fitted; but there was to be utter conformity in thought. As Loyola's "Rule of Thinking with the Church" explicitly stated: "To arrive at the truth in all things, we must always be ready

to believe that what seems to us white is really black if
the hierarchical Church so defines it." In externals there
could be variety, and no one form of dress was ordained,
or fixed schedule of worship; but that was only so that
each soldier might move about the more freely in the pursuit of his allotted task. So far as the inner attitude was
concerned there was to be absolutely no divergence. Each
novitiate was to be drilled in Loyola's manual of arms
entitled the *Spiritual Exercises;* and, after having thoroughly mastered its contents, the disciple was to be sworn
to lifelong service in the Society. Thenceforth he was to be
not a man but "as a corpse, or as a staff in the hands of an
old man."

It proved a superb instrument, that Society of Jesus—
indeed, the most effective of its kind in the whole history
of civilization. Its advantages over the other orders were
immediately apparent. Unlike the secular priests, the
Jesuits were educated, disciplined, and sworn to poverty;
unlike the monks, they were not confined to cloisters or
compelled to devote half the day to prayer; unlike the
friars, they were not obliged to wear a uniform or go begging from door to door. An army of such men, each picked
and trained for a specific task, yet all responding to a central authority, could accomplish miracles. And it did. The
Society of Jesus accomplished a thousand miracles in one,
for it saved Catholicism from what seemed an immediate
doom. The Jesuits terrified the lax priests, spied on the
corrupt bishops, and dictated even to the popes. They set
up schools for the sons of the nobility and the rich burghers;
they penetrated to the remotest hamlets and into the most
noisome slums to preach and hear confessions. They ven-

tured out into the newly discovered lands and organized
a missionary movement such as Christendom had not
known since the early centuries. Above all, they crept
into the lands that had adopted Protestantism and there intrigued for the restoration of the orthodox faith.[27]

10

A RESORT to arms became inevitable.
Protestantism, which had been allowed to develop unchecked for
almost a generation, had intrenched
itself far too solidly to be dislodged
by mere intrigue or argument. And
Catholicism, now renewed in spirit
and renovated in body, could not
reconcile itself to the existence of
the heresy. The Church had never
been really Catholic, for it had never commanded the fealty
of the Orthodox Christians in Russia and the Levant, or
the Monophysite Christians in Egypt, Armenia, and Abyssinia, or the Nestorians in Persia and India. But at least in
Europe it had enjoyed a virtual universality, and the persistence of the Protestant sects was a taunt which the
Church could not endure. Apparently there was no one
who saw how barbarously absurd it was to seek to restore
the hegemony of the "true faith" by resorting to violence.
Men felt then about theological dogmas as they did later

[27] There is a vast literature on the Jesuit order, but almost all of it—
not excluding the histories by Crétineau-Joly and Joseph McCabe—are
either extravagantly eulogistic or defamatory. Rene Fülöp-Müller's recent
work is one of the least unfair.

about political theories: they had to *force* them on their neighbors if they could not impose them by gentle means.

The first of the many wars which followed on the Reformation broke out in Switzerland as early as 1529. Somewhat later France, too, became the scene of religious conflict, and so did Holland and Germany. But the real contest did not occur until early in the seventeenth century, for not until then did the Church feel itself prepared for Armageddon. Peace had been declared between the two sides at Augsburg in 1555; but as the century wore on the precariousness of that peace became increasingly manifest. Rumors of conspiracies and reports of local riots kept flying about like gulls before the storm. Both sides began to gird themselves, at first secretly and then in the open. The Protestant princes banded themselves together in an Evangelical Union, and their enemies formed a Catholic League. And then all was in readiness.

The contest was ushered in by a quite absurd incident which has gone down in history as the Defenestration of Prague (1618). Some Protestant politicians forced their way into the old palace in Prague, seized hold of the three Catholic counselors gathered there, and threw them out of the window. No one was hurt—a fact which the Catholics attributed to the miraculous intervention of angels, and the Protestants to the lucky presence of a heap of refuse right beneath the window. But though the counselors escaped injury, Christendom did not. The thud on that refuse heap behind the imperial palace in Prague was heard all over Europe, and in its train came a cannonading that did not cease till all central Europe lay wasted.

The first phase of this Thirty Years' War lasted until

1629 and closed with the Protestant cause in a state of collapse. The emergence of a new Protestant champion in the person of Gustavus Adolphus, king of Sweden, brought on a renewal of hostilities, and this time the Catholics suffered defeat. The third phase, lasting from 1635 to 1648, was not so much a contest between Catholicism and Protestantism as between the Hapsburgs of Austria and the Bourbons of France. It dragged on until both sides were exhausted, and terminated at last in the Peace of Westphalia in 1648. To go into further detail would lead us afield to no purpose. It was a religious war—at least during its first two phases—and it was waged with thoroughgoing religious passion. The sack of Magdeburg in 1631 reveals in all its ghastly ruthlessness the spirit which pervaded the whole conflict. When the Catholic troops, commanded by General Tilly, were able at last to storm their way into the city, there was enacted a scene for which, as Schiller has put it, "history has no speech, and poetry no pen." Young and old were cut down without pity. Wives were violated in the presence of their husbands, and daughters at the feet of their fathers. Women were beheaded in a church; infants were speared at their mothers' breasts. "Come again in an hour," was Tilly's only reply when some of his officers besought him to halt the carnage: "Come again in an hour and I shall see what I can do." The horrors continued unchecked till at last smoke and flame made further plundering impossible. The city had been fired in several places, and a wind spread the flames with rampant speed. In less than twelve hours the town was in ashes; only two churches and a few huts remained undestroyed. And when the smoke cleared at last, living men came crawling out from under corpses, lost children ran shrieking for their parents, and babes, their starved faces black with soot and tears, sucked desperately at the breasts of dead mothers. More than six thousand bodies were thrown into the Elbe before the streets could be made passable. It is said that, in all, some thirty thousand persons perished in that sack.[28]

And that was only an incident. No war was ever carried on with more violence. When it drew to a close all Europe was spent, and its central lands lay utterly desolate. The population of Bohemia had been reduced from two million to seven hundred and eighty thousand. Only one-fiftieth part of the inhabitants of the Rhinelands were left alive. Saxony had lost almost a million of her citizens within the brief space of two years. In 1646 alone Bavaria saw more than one hundred of her thriving towns laid in ashes. Between one-half and two-thirds of the entire population of Germany and Austria was destroyed.

Yet when at last the Catholic kings had to give up the struggle, and sought to treat with the Protestant rulers, the pope in Rome became furious. He sent his nuncio to Westphalia to plead and protest and fulminate against any dealings with the heretics; and when these remonstrances proved of no avail, the pontiff sat down to prepare a bull. The Peace of Westphalia guaranteed "a peace Christian, universal, and perpetual, and a friendship true and sincere" between the two sides, and furthermore pledged each to be zealous for the "service, honor, and advantage of the

---

[28] Dowding, *Life and Correspondence of Calixtus,* pp. 153-154. For the history of the whole Thirty Years' War see S. R. Gardiner's excellent volume by that title.

other." To every ruler was granted the right to choose the religion of his realm; and whether he chose Lutheranism, Calvinism, or Catholicism, none had the right to brook his decision. The Holy Roman Empire was practically dismembered. Switzerland and Holland were recognized as free and independent countries. Indeed, all the purposes for which the war had been started seemed definitely surrendered.

Little wonder that the pope was mortified. He seemed not to care that so many millions had been slain and that the labor of centuries had been reduced to débris. All that counted with him was that Protestantism still existed, and that by this treaty its existence was guaranteed forevermore. And he, the Vicar of Christ, Bishop of Bishops, Pontifex Maximus, and successor of Peter, would not stand for that. At once he made public his bull, declaring therein that the treaty was "perpetually null, void, accursed, frivolous, iniquitous, ineffective, contemptible, and without any influence or meaning for the past, the present, or the future."

But the man might as well have flayed a dying ox for all the response he received. A murderous spear whose head was religious fanaticism and whose shaft was dynastic greed had been thrust by Christendom into its own side; and there was no strength left to thrust it any deeper. The pope could kick the carcass all he cared; Europe could only turn over and moan.

BOOK SIX

The Ordeal of Survival
A. D. 1648-1931

THE ORDEAL OF SURVIVAL: 1648—

1: Catholicism Marches On. 2: Catholicism Falters. 3: Protestantism Disintegrates. 4: Denominationalism Reaches America. 5: Credulity Triumphant: the Witch-Hunt. 6: The Emergence of Rationalism. 7. The War of the Church against Science. 8: The "Age of Reason." 9: The Reaction Called Pietism. 10: Methodism. 11: The French Revolution. 12: The Reaction. 13: The Ordeal of the Church. 14: The Ordeal of the Sects. 15: Then Came the War.

THE face of Christendom had changed forever. The Catholic Church—which had never been really catholic either in the world or in Christendom—was nevermore to be catholic even in Western Europe. Only the lands which it had not itself converted—for instance the Latin lands which were already Christian when the pope was still a mere bishop, and Ireland, which was Christianized without the help of Rome—these alone remained loyal. The rest, though sprung from the womb of the Mother Church and nurtured by her for centuries, had revolted. Shooting out the lip and calling her the "Whore of Babylon," they had broken away and set up churches of their own. And Rome, utterly powerless to cajole or coerce them back into subjection, was constrained to live on without them.

The loss was grave but profoundly salutary. We have already seen how the shock of the Reformation galvanized the ancient Church into a new liveliness. Had the Counter-Reformation halted at violence and contented itself instead with quiet intrigue and missionary attrition, it might even-

tually have won back almost all that had been lost. But
even the Thirty Years' War, perhaps the ghastliest blunder
Rome ever committed, failed to prove fatal. When the
disastrous interlude was ended, and the vicious effort to
crush Protestantism by might was given up as vain,
Catholicism was still able to creep along. Indeed, for a

AFTER 1648 A.D.

time it was able to move more surely than before, for it
had been sobered by adversity and no longer blustered and
lunged. Resigned for the moment to its losses in Europe,
it set out to recoup them by making gains in other regions.
Once the religious wars were ended, the full stream of
Catholic zeal was turned into this new channel. A Congregation of Propaganda was established in Rome as early

as 1622 to foster and guide a concerted missionary movement; and later the various Catholic governments began
to give their own support to the work. It is true that much
of this governmental support was proffered for other than
strictly Christian reasons, for the occasional murder of a
missionary could be made to serve as a most excellent
pretext for new raids and colonizing invasions. Besides,
Christianized natives were easier to rule (and exploit)
than natives still addicted to their own ancient beliefs.

Only in ignorance, however, or else against their will,
did the missionaries lend themselves to such imperialistic
schemes. They were themselves, for the most part, men of
indubitable sincerity who served usually as merciful inter-
cessors between the helpless natives and the rapacious con-
quistadors and traders. To what extent they succeeded in
making true converts to Christ remains dubious. At most
they were able to win new adherents to Rome, and even
in that direction they seem to have enjoyed greater success
among the Eastern Christians than among the heathens.
For the Catholic missionaries did not confine their labors
to the infidel; on the contrary, they gave themselves almost
as generously to the more grateful labor of winning over
the Eastern heretics. "Uniate" churches were established
in Poland, Rumania, and Armenia, and great numbers of
Orthodox believers, while still observing their old Eastern
rites, were persuaded to desert their patriarchs and ac-
knowledge instead the authority of the pope.

The gains made among the non-Christian races were
accomplished only at the cost of the most egregious concessions. Like the apostles in the early centuries, the
Jesuits and other missionaries in this later age found that

the tribesmen would adopt Christianity only if they were permitted to adapt it. So the permission was given. Indeed, the missionaries themselves helped make the adaptation. So eager were they to swell the number of their converts that certain of the Jesuits actually perpetrated pious frauds and forged documents to prove the identity of Christ with the native gods. Their first concern was to get the natives baptized, for the sacrament was still believed to exercise some sort of magical influence. It is reported that some of the missionaries in the excess of their zeal would actually try at times to administer the rite by stealth, resorting, for example, to some subterfuge like spilling holy water on infants under pretense of giving them sweetened water to drink! [1]

What was accomplished by such devious means was not impressive in the end. Most of South and Central America became Catholic, but only because Catholic colonists came over from Europe and settled there. In only one uncolonized country, Japan, did the missionaries succeed in making deep inroads; but even there the results of their labor did not endure. More than a million converts were made in Japan during the sixteenth century, and for a time it seemed likely that the entire land would turn Christian. But then the Franciscans and Dominicans fell out with the Jesuits who dominated the mission; and Dutch traders, jealous of the Catholic Portuguese who were crowding in the wake of the missionaries, began to arouse the native rulers. In the end the whole lot of them were driven out, and after forty years of intermittent persecution, hardly a trace was left of all that the Catholic missionaries had accomplished. Japan had apparently had more than

[1] Creighton, *Missions*, p. 45.

[342]

enough of Christianity. Thenceforth for another two hundred years the land was closed not alone to missionaries, but to any person coming from the Christian world.

But even though the Catholic missions accomplished little objectively, they had a profound subjective effect. Especially was this true of the home missions which made their appearance during this period. Devout men and women went into the slums and sequestered hamlets to bring comfort and healing to the poor, the sick, and the fallen; and though they were able to do little that was not superficial for the objects of their mercy, their very will to be helpful gave a new tone to the Church. Gone was the arrogance and complacency of former days; now the clergy seemed almost panically eager to prove itself worthy of its hire. Ebullitions of zeal were no longer frowned upon by the authorities in Rome and new monastic Orders or reforming sub-Orders were organized one after the other. And these new companies were devoted to ideals strikingly unlike those of their medieval predecessors. They urged their members to embrace the world rather than flee from it, to find God by seeking out his children rather than deserting them. As a result, the Catholic Church produced men in the seventeenth century who would have done honor to any religious body in any land or age. There was, for instance, the sainted Francis de Sales, whose piety can perhaps be best gauged by the resolution he himself made at his ordination: "to remember all day long that he was preparing to say Mass the next morning." Sent to be a priest in Savoy, where the bulk of the population was Calvinist and only the dissolute soldiery represented Catholicism, he preached with such winning gentleness that before long he had converted almost all the inhabitants in the district. Or there was the dramatic Vincent de Paul who, having once been captured by pirates and held a galley slave for two years, spent the rest of his life executing the most amazing philanthropic schemes. He worked among the prisoners condemned to the galleys in Marseilles and Bordeaux, founded the Congregation of Missions to train preachers for the working-class, established hospitals and foundling homes, and—most valuable of all—organized the Sisters of Charity to minister to the people in the slums.[2]

2

 HE revival spent itself before long, however. The spirit became flesh, and then—as was inevitable—it languished. The many Orders which had been founded to do good did well, and their growing prosperity betrayed them. The first to succumb was the Society of Jesus, which, being the most efficient, was the least able to resist the blight. The most valuable accomplishments of the Society were in the field of education, where it plowed and seeded with unprecedented thoroughness and intelligence. The Jesuits established schools wherever they could find pupils and manned them with better trained teachers than were to be found

[2] There is no adequate life of Vincent de Paul in the English language, despite the fascination of the subject. A biography by de Broglie in French has gone through several editions. For the life of St. Francis de Sales see Leigh Hunt's delightful essay entitled *The Gentleman Saint.*

in any other schools in Christendom. But even in this work the Jesuits were not above reproach, for their primary purpose as educators was to develop loyal followers of the pope rather than tolerant comrades of men. Dogma and tradition loomed large in the curriculum, and a type of thinking was encouraged which could not but make for mischief in a world that seemed determined to remain prevailingly non-Catholic.

That sin was slight, however, considering the value of Jesuit example in setting up a widespread and organized system of popular education in the Christian world. The graver transgressions of the Society were committed in the many other fields which it invaded. No one can gauge the full extent of its guilt in precipitating the outbreak of the religious wars of the seventeenth century; nor is there any calculating its responsibility for the political intrigues which kept embroiling the nations during the centuries that followed. But if the nature of its political activities remain a matter of dispute, none can question the sort of influence the Society exerted in the moral sphere. In their frantic desire to increase the Catholic fold the Jesuits were prone to open the gate to sheep of every hue. So notoriously lax were they in judging guilt that they came to be taunted with the cry: "Behold the fathers who have taken away the sins of the world."

Morality had long been a codified thing in Catholicism, and the Jesuits had found a way of interpreting the codes so as to justify almost any crime if necessary. Unlike the "rigorists," who insisted that an act was sinful if a single one of the Church Doctors judged it so, or the "probabiliorists," who called it sinful if such was the opinion of at least the majority of the authorities, the Jesuits were ready to declare an act innocent if they could find no more than two or three "grave doctors" who held that view. The Society had committed itself to this "probabilist" type of interpretation in 1577, and its members had become the most popular of confessors, especially in the higher strata of society. In judging sexual sins their indulgence was exceeded only by their prurience, and the lubricity with which they discussed erotic matters—one famous Jesuit treatise, *De Matrimonia,* has been characterized as "an Iliad of impurity written at the foot of the cross"—made them the favorite authors in court circles. In their writings one could learn "how the bankrupt without sinning mortally might defraud his creditors of his mortgaged goods; how the servant might be excused for pilfering his master; how the gay young noble might justly kill his rival in a duel; and how the adultress might rightfully deny her sin, even under oath." [3]

By the second half of the seventeenth century these abuses had aroused such resentment that open attacks began to be made on the Society in certain Catholic circles. In 1656 the French scientist, Blaise Pascal, one of the most brilliant and devout men of the Age, was goaded into writing a series of pseudonymous articles entitled *Letters to a Provincial Friend,* which stripped and flayed Jesuit hypocrisy and craftiness with surpassing wit and eloquence. Not until a century later, however, when the secular rulers entered the lists, did the position of the Jesuits really become precarious. Awake at last to the power and presumption of the Society, the temporal princes began then to hinder its work and harass its leaders. The head of

[3] Preserved Smith, *History of Modern Culture,* Vol. I, p. 367; a most stimulating survey of the underlying factors in the history of the era.

the Jesuits in Portugal was brought to trial before the Inquisition and burnt in 1759, and all his followers were expelled from the land. A similar fate was meted out to the Jesuits in France in 1764, and in Spain in 1767. Finally such pressure was brought to bear on Rome that, in 1773, the entire Society was suppressed by the pope himself.

And what happened to the Jesuits happened also to many of the other Catholic Orders. Once the wave of enthusiasm receded and the excitement of reviving the spirit of the Church gave way to the drudgery of conserving its body, the monastics lost their savor. Many of them forgot their calling and thought only for themselves or for their houses. And then the laity turned on them as it had already turned on the Jesuits. For by that time, the end of the eighteenth century, the acids of skepticism had begun to dissolve the awe that had so long coagulated the minds of men. A new day had dawned by then. . . .

3

HILE all these things were occurring in the Catholic Church, even more striking happenings were taking place among the heretics. Protestantism had developed into what a Catholic writer has described as "Christianity on the road to disintegration with only half a mind to follow it." Once the first phase of the Reformation was ended and the authority of the Church had been supplanted by the judgment of the individual, there seemed to be nothing left

to hold the rebels together. In vain had Luther struggled to stem the flood of dissension which came in the wake of his own great dissent. In vain had he cried that if the pope was dethroned, it was only that the Bible might be made the universal authority in Christendom. The Bible was no adequate substitute for a human autocrat, for it could not speak for itself. It had to be read, and in the reading of it all sorts of divergences were possible. It was all very well for Luther to insist that the Bible be interpreted "according to its simplest meaning." Who was to decide just what was the simplest meaning?

Therein lay the chief cause of Protestantism's progressive disintegration. Though all the reformers started from the same Bible, each was able to deduce from it a different meaning. Puritanism, licentiousness, celibacy, polygamy— these were all to be found in the Holy Writ. Quite mad vagaries, too, were to be found in it—if only one looked hard enough. For instance, some demented creature named Serles went up and down England in 1543 and won adherents to his belief that, according to Scripture, the Virgin Mary was the moon and Christ was the man in the moon!

A century after Luther's death a contemporary named Thomas Edwards was able to list one hundred and eighty different sects! Very few of these were of any importance. They were like so many particles in a storm of meteors: each burned brightly for an instant and then became part of the night. But though most of the sects were of small significance individually, all of them collectively caused such confusion and turmoil that it looked for a while as though Protestantism would soon tear itself to shreds.

Such sectarian dissensions grew particularly rife in England. Even the despotic Henry VIII was incapable of smothering all "perverse opinion," and his successors finally gave up the attempt. After almost a century of incessant religious strife, during which there were two revolutions costing one king his head and another his throne, England at last surrendered all hope of stamping out sectarianism. Toleration was apparently indispensable if there was to be any peace in the land, and in 1689 a law was finally passed granting freedom of worship to almost all types of Protestant dissenters. The official religion was still the episcopalianism adopted by Henry VIII, though with a ritual far less Catholic than of yore, and a creed which had grown almost completely Calvinist. But no one was compelled to accept this religion. The toleration was not complete, for Unitarianism, Roman Catholicism, and all other forms of non-Protestantism were still prohibited in the kingdom; but at least the many varieties of Protestantism were allowed.

The sectarians paid heavily before that partial victory was achieved.

A most significant development had occurred, however, during the century preceding the adoption of that Act of Toleration. Many sectarians unable to endure the persecutions yet unwilling to forsake their beliefs had arisen at times in whole congregations and taken refuge across the seas. The first of these flights of which there is any record was one led by a certain dissenting clergyman named Robert Browne. He was a Cambridge man of good family who, in 1581, after taking orders in the Anglican Church, went out and founded a separatist congregation at Norwich. Whence Browne derived his inspiration is not known, but it may well have been from the Anabaptists, who had always insisted—save when in power as in Münster—that

Church and State should be kept scrupulously separate.[5] But to pray to God without employing the rites sanctioned by Parliament was regarded then as both treason and heresy, and once Browne's activities were discovered he was thrown into the lock-up. On his release there was no recourse left to him but to leave the country, and this he did do, taking with him part of his congregation. They settled in Holland, which was the least intolerant land in Europe at the time, and there they sought to worship as Browne thought proper. It so happened, however, that the leader soon fell out with his followers, and in disgust —or, as some say, while out of his mind—he returned home and rejoined the Anglican Church.

But if Browne recanted, others did not. Congregationalism, as this separatist movement came to be called, continued to crop out in England, and a statute was passed in 1592 decreeing that all who questioned the ecclesiastical authority of the throne should be banished from the land. That was the signal for more migrations, and several companies of English dissenters sought refuge in Amsterdam and Leyden. It is possible that economic need as well as religious nonconformity was responsible for their willingness to go to foreign parts, for we know that many of these fugitives were destitute folk who left little but their debts behind them. Yet religion undoubtedly played the major rôle in their lives, as is plain from the way they comported themselves in their new home. They began almost at once to quarrel over doctrinal differences, and before long there were four distinct denominations in their midst. One element held fast to the fundamental Calvin-

[5] Walker, *History of the Congregationalist Churches in the United States*, pp. 30ff.

ism in which the whole movement had had its origin. Another, led by an earnest but unstable preacher named John Smyth, went over to that gentle survival of Anabaptism called Mennonitism and began to aspire to the unworldly perfectionism of the first Christians. A third element, the General Baptists, struck a compromise between Mennonitism and a milder form of Calvinism known as Arminianism. And a fourth element, the Particular Baptists, tried to compromise between Mennonitism and strict Calvinism.

4

INABILITY to live together in harmony, added to the other difficulties attendant on their life in Holland, finally drove many of the refugees to look for some other place to settle. They were unable to follow their regular crafts in Holland, for the native guilds excluded all foreigners. They could keep alive only by doing manual labor twelve to fifteen hours a day. So finally one group picked up and left. By virtually indenturing themselves to a group of London merchants for a period of seven years, a number of these stout-hearted dissenters secured their passage to the New World across the seas. It was, as a contemporary assures us, no "new fangledness" or other such "giddie humour" that prompted these expatriates to start out for the strange continent. They knew well that "the grimme and grislie face of povertie" would confront them there.

But they were urged on by the hope that it would not confront them for long—a hope they could hardly entertain in the Old World.

Swept out of their course, the Pilgrims landed far north of their destination, in a forbiddingly sterile region now known as Cape Cod. It was in December, 1620, and by the time the snow melted at the end of that winter "out of 100 and odd persons, scarce 50 remained." But there was no retreat. With bodies inured to hardship, and wills tempered by the stern Calvinism which was their faith, the Pilgrims took up their spades and set to digging furrows for seed.

The colony did not thrive. Not until a decade later was a promising settlement made in that region, and then it was founded not by dissenters but by "gentlemen." The disturbed conditions in the mother country had led a group of small proprietors to dispose of their lands and other holdings and set sail for Massachusetts Bay. They were for the most part conscientious Calvinists and belonged to the Puritan party in England; but they were not at all like the earlier colonists, who were, in the language of the Bishop of London, "contemptible troublemakers instructed by guides fit for them: cobblers, tailors, feltmakers, and such like trash." These respectable burghers and petty noblemen had left their homeland with regret. As one of their leaders had cried: "We will not say as the Separatists were wont to say at their leaving of England, 'Farewell Babylon, farewell Rome!' but we will say, 'Farewell dear England! Farewell the Church of God in England and all the Christian friends there.'" [*]

[*] This and other quotations in the present section are cited in Beard, *The Rise of American Civilization*, 1927, Vol. I.

But once they settled in the New World these staunch Anglicans could not possibly keep from drifting toward ecclesiastical independence. Far removed from the bishops at home, and with their own tiny churches separated by miles of primeval forest, it was inevitable that they should be driven at last to outright Congregationalism. But though they did tend to change thus in church polity, they remained inflexible to matters of doctrine, and showed no more tolerance of "perverse opinion" than did their brethren in the Old World. Nor were the poor refugees who settled on Cape Cod any better in this regard, for they too regarded all dissenters from strict Calvinism as rank infidels. As someone has said, the Puritans came to America to worship God in their own way and make everyone else do likewise!

But it was impossible to enforce rigid conformity where each man was allowed to read the Bible for himself. Five years after the founding of the Massachusetts Bay Colony a devout man named Roger Williams rebelled against the religious as well as political constraint exercised in the settlement. Crying aloud that "persecution for cause of conscience is most evidently and lamentably contrary to the doctrine of Christ Jesus," he caused so much disturbance that he finally had to take flight. Surviving a dreadful winter in the forests, he found his way with five of his followers to a place called Rhode Island, and there founded a new settlement in 1636, which he named Providence.

Williams believed that religion and politics should be kept apart, for he had come under the influence of Anabaptist thought, and maintained that whereas the Church could accept only the voluntary "saints," the State had to include all the living. As a consequence he had to write the principle of religious toleration into the very charter of the new colony—an unprecedented act in Christian history, and one destined to mark the beginning of a new age.[7]

Williams and his fellow Baptists were by no means the only sectarians to be expelled from the Puritan colony. In 1656 there arrived in Massachusetts two women who belonged to a new cult called the Friends, or more popularly the Quakers or the Ranters. It had been founded in 1652 by an English shoemaker named George Fox—a man whose mysticism verged at times on the psychopathic, but whose courage and simple sincerity were beyond questioning. The cult had succeeded almost at once in attracting a few men and women of education and means in England; but its widest gains from first to last were made among the lower-class folk. The express aim of the Quakers was to take the Gospels literally and live the life of the early Christians. They looked on all ecclesiasticism as an abomination, and insisted that only the Spirit should be one's guide in following Christ. They called churches "steeple-houses" and had no use for pastors or theology. When they gathered for prayer they sat in silence till one of them, either man or woman, was moved to arise and speak. If none was thus moved, they continued to sit in silent meditation, and then in silence departed. They refused to bow or remove the hat to anyone—were not all men equal in the eyes of the Lord?—and addressed high

[7] For a brief account of the development of religious toleration see J. B. Bury's comprehensive little *History of Freedom of Thought*, ch. 5. Ruffini's *Religious Liberty* (Eng. tr. 1912) is more detailed and exhaustive.

and low with the same unpretentious "thee" and "thou." They would not fight, for that was contrary to Jesus's express command; nor would they take oaths, for they insisted that they spoke the truth always. They spurned all pleasures, abhorring even hymn singing; and they shunned all luxury. In a word, they sought to be perfect, even as Jesus had commanded. And they were reckoned most abominable by all the respectable folk in England.

So it was hardly with gladness that the two Quaker women were greeted when their boat reached Massachusetts Bay. They were at once arrested and put into a prison, the window of which was thoroughly boarded so that none of the colonists might see or address them. The tracts they had brought with them, about a hundred in number, were burnt in the market place by the hangman, and the women were denied paper, pens, and ink. They were stripped altogether naked and subjected to an outrageous examination to see if they were witches. Finally, after five weeks of torment, they were put on board again and shipped back whence they came.[8]

But two days later another boat brought eight more of the ecstatics, and though these too were sent back, other Quakers did finally succeed in worming their way into the colony. They were treated with the utmost barbarity—four of them were actually hanged—but nonetheless they continued to come. Their persistence was due in part to their irrepressible missionary zeal; but it was also due, and perhaps in larger part, to sheer need. Hounded unmercifully

[8] Thomas, *American Church History*, Vol. XII, p. 206. George Fox's *Journal* is well worth reading (the two volume edition by Rufus M. Jones is especially recommended). For the history of the whole movement see Edward Grubb, *Quaker Thought and History*.

in the Old World, they had no otherwhere to go save to the New. And since Rhode Island and Maryland, where they could worship unmolested, were too small to contain them, they were compelled to seek entrance to the other colonies.

In 1682, however, they were able to found Pennsylvania, a settlement of their own, and thenceforth they were better off. One of their leaders in England was a certain William Penn, an admiral's son, who, despite the blows of his irate father and repeated arrests by the authorities, had persisted in avowing the Quaker belief. Coming into his father's fortune, this man purchased from the throne what was virtually a feudal estate in North America; and thither he invited his brother Quakers and all the oppressed sectarians in Europe.

5

THE example of tolerance set by Rhode Island, Maryland, and Pennsylvania, was followed only reluctantly by the other Protestant states. Indeed, it was not until well into the nineteenth century that complete freedom of worship was legally guaranteed even in relatively enlightened countries like England and Germany. The Reformation, though itself an assertion of private judgment, had by no means established the right to religious liberty. No one of the great reformers had believed that one denomination might be as good as another; on the contrary, with the possible exception of Zwingli, they had all reiterated the old hierarchical teaching that *extra ecclesiam nulla salus* —"there is no salvation outside the Church." The reformers had fought not for freedom but the "truth"— and the "truth" had been as definite, unique, and absolute to them as to the Jesuits. In its essential ideology Protestantism had remained very largely medieval. If it had dethroned the pope, it had only been to set the Bible in his place. If it swept away a whole host of Pagan superstitions, it was only to restore older Hebrew ones. It is true that the Protestants—with the exception of the more conservative Lutherans and Anglicans—refused to believe in the miraculous nature of the Eucharist. (It was probably among them that the formula *hoc est corpus*— "This is [my] body"—was first corrupted into "hocus-pocus.") But they continued to hold fast to so many other irrationalities that the gain was hardly appreciable.

There was, for example, the rooted belief in Protestant circles that special providences were not merely possible but quite common. Obvious miracles were no longer expected, but all classes and all sects continued to look for heavenly signs and portents. If a battle was won, that evidenced God's approval; if it was lost, then—to quote the state papers of Massachusetts—"God spit in our face" to teach his people a lesson. God was no mere inward illumination; rather He was a very objective presence who did not hesitate to reorder the stars in their courses just to help a loyal servant or embarrass a treacherous one.

He it was, for instance, who sent the fair wind which carried the Swedish army across the Baltic to save the Protestant cause during the Thirty Years' War! He it was also
who drove the clouds across the moon to cover the sortie
of Cromwell's hymn-singing army at Dunbar! On the
other hand, according to the Dean of Windsor, it was God
who sent the unseasonable heat to England in January
1662 as a sign of His wrath, because the Puritan regicides
had not yet been punished! In one of the many religious
controversies in Massachusetts, "God himself was pleased
to step in with his deciding vote," declared Governor
Winthrop, by causing two women of the dissenting party
"to produce from their wombs . . . such monstrous births
as no chronicle, I think, hardly ever recording the
like!" [9]

The Protestants believed that not alone God but the
Devil, too, could intervene in that fashion. The dread of
the Evil One was quite as intense throughout Christendom
after the Reformation as it had been before. If anything,
the hysteria engendered by the religious wars, and the
persecutions accompanying the revolt against Rome, made
that dread even more intense. Protestantism was successful in abolishing the veneration of saints, but not the fear
of the demons.

The culmination of this fear was an epidemic of witch
hunting toward the end of the seventeenth century that
was without parallel in the whole history of mankind.
There had been considerable persecution of supposed
necromancers throughout the Middle Ages, but then it

[9] See Preserved Smith, *History of Modern Culture,* Vol. I, p. 433.

had been conducted by professionals and according to set rules. The Inquisitors, in the course of their investigations, had convinced themselves of the existence of a regular cult of Satan-worshipers who gathered on certain nights in remote glades or subterranean caves to practice "black magic" and indulge in weird, obscene, blasphemous rites. Since the female sex was notoriously less proof than the male against the wiles of the Evil One—could not the very word *femina* be derived from *fides* and *minus,* proving that females had *"less faith"?*—it was deduced that most of the Satanists were women. The campaign against Satanism had therefore always been largely confined to the persecution of widows, wives, and maidens. Time and again helpless women of every age and station were dragged to the Inquisitorial chambers, tortured till they confessed whatever was suggested to them, and usually burnt or hanged.

The medieval Inquisitors had developed a most elaborate technique for detecting witches. If torture could not drag confession from the lips of the accused—which was rare—other tests were employed. Sometimes the victim's thumbs and large toes were tied fast together and she was flung into a pond. If she sank she was innocent, and if she floated it meant that the waters declared her guilty by refusing to receive her in baptism. A commoner test was to look for the "devil's mark" on the body of the victim. If she had supernumerary nipples—which meant she was equipped to suckle demons—or any other abnormality, the woman was unmistakably a witch. If no other evidence was to be found, the Inquisitors looked to see if any spot on her was anæsthetic. Having stripped her and shaved the hair from her body, they pricked her all over with needles. The examination was almost always conducted by men, and the Inquisitors do not hesitate to report how women who did not quail before the cruelest pain, begged on their knees for a cloak to protect their modesty.

And this whole ghastly phobia, with all its attendant barbarities, was carried over into Protestantism. The pastors were perhaps slightly less sadistic and prurient in conducting the trials than were the celibate Inquisitors; but that was in part because they had less time to devote to each case. For once the witch-hunt spread to the lands of the Protestants it ceased to be an esoteric occupation followed by professionals, and became the sport of the mob. The Reformation, having made every man a priest, had made him also an inquisitor. The witch-hunt became literally epidemic after the Thirty Years' War. It would break out in one place, reach a climax, burn itself out, and then leap to another. If there was drought in a region, or famine, or plague, or a catastrophic fire, invariably the preachers would recall the Biblical injunction, "Thou shalt not suffer a witch to live"; and immediately the populace would go searching for suspects. The epidemic never became so intense in the Catholic lands, for the Church, even if it did restrain the thinking of scholars, also restrained the bigotry of fools. But in those lands, too, there was no lack of atrocities. In a group of little villages near the city of Trier no less than three hundred and six persons were executed for witchcraft between 1587 and 1593; in each of two villages only two women were left alive. In the district of Würzburg some nine hundred persons were put to death for the imaginary crime during the years 1623-29. "Children of three and four confessed sexual intercourse with devils; boys and girls of nine and ten were burnt alive; among the wretched women who perished one was noted as the fairest and purest maid in the city." [10]

Naturally enough the mania was most virulent in Germany, where religious warfare had exacted the greatest toll in life and sanity; but it made its appearance also in Switzerland, France, England, Scotland, Hungary, Scandinavia, and the New England colonies. Did not our records of the atrocities come from the pens of the persecutors themselves, we should find it impossible to give them credence. For instance, in 1669, in the district of Delacarlia in Sweden, some children told strange tales of having been carried off to distant wilds. A commission was appointed to investigate the matter, and, by ample use of the rack, succeeded in extorting confessions which led to the burning of eighty-four adults and fifteen children, and to the infliction of a weekly whipping to one hundred and seventy-eight children during one whole year! In France one judge named Nicholas Rémy boasted that he had sentenced nine hundred witches to death between 1676 and 1691. He had even condemned some children of six and seven to be put to death, but later relented and allowed the babes to get off with no more than being stripped and scourged while walking around the stake at which their parents had perished.

[10] Smith, *History of Modern Culture*, Vol. I, p. 442. Much of the rest in the present section is taken from this volume.

6

OT until the beginning of the eighteenth century did the witch-hunt subside, and the change then was wrought by agencies quite unblessed by the clergy. Had the pastors and priests been given their way, the madness might have continued forever. It was the emergence of reasoned skepticism, an attitude altogether foreign to the churches—indeed hostile to them—that finally destroyed the mania. Regarded from our point of vantage, the ghastly outbreak of superstition in the late seventeenth century can be seen to have been something like the final flare of a guttering candle. It had leapt up in the dawn-wind of a new day; but once the young sun came out and the dawn-wind fell, the wretched flame was doomed. Thenceforth the belief in witchcraft could linger only as a spark, a malevolent, reeking, noxious spark that could glower but could nevermore burn.

The new day had been very slow in coming. It had been heralded, though very faintly, as early as the thirteenth century by a certain English friar named Roger Bacon. The distinction of this man lay in the fact that he was apparently the first to reveal a skepticism as to the very fundamentals of medieval knowledge. Though he lived in what a recent Catholic writer has hailed as "the greatest of centuries," Roger Bacon never ceased to complain of the unrelieved ignorance in his world. Even the most learned men of the time were, he insisted, the helpless slaves of custom, vulgar superstition, pretentious stupidity, and unworthy authorities.[11]

But Bacon was several hundred years in advance of his day—which was part of the reason why he was so hounded while alive and so slighted when dead. Not until the Renaissance in the fifteenth century did Europe catch up with him; but then it came sweeping along at such a rate that within a little while that truculently far-sighted monk was left far behind. The characteristic quality of the Renaissance was its insatiable curiosity. It refused to accept pontifical prohibitions or be put off with benign evasions: it insisted on finding out for itself. At first it seemed content to find out about the past, and its most earnest apostles, the Humanists, devoted themselves altogether to uncovering and expounding the wisdom of the ancients. In course of time, however, these same Humanists went on from the recovery of the past to a discovery of the present and the future. It was at this point that the Humanists became scientists. As the brilliant physicist, Professor A. L. Klein, has phrased it: "The new day dawned when the word 'classic' ceased to connote the perfect and began to mean the obsolete or obsolescent."

It was at this point, too, that Humanism and Protestantism parted company. The latter never ceased to be reactionary in its ideals, whereas the former became progressive. The titans who brought on the new day in the

[11] For a many-sided discussion of this man's life and work see *The Roger Bacon Essays*, edited by A. G. Little. Lynn Thorndyke, *History of Magic and Experimental Science*, Vol. II, pp. 616-687, is inclined to minimize Bacon's originality. For the opposite view, see E. Charles, *Roger Bacon*, perhaps the best full-length biography.

world of thought were of the stock of Erasmus, not of Luther. Social conditions had much to do with this signal change in thought. In earlier centuries, when Europe was still semi-barbaric, men could not but consider it futile to concern themselves with the things of this world. But by the sixteenth and seventeenth centuries conditions were enormously improved. The remorseless want and disease and strife of the Middle Ages had been relieved somewhat. Gold had come pouring in from the West, and luxuries from the East. Life, which had so long been a hateful burden, began to take on now the character of an adventure. As a consequence, those who had leisure—and they were more numerous now than ever before in Christian history—were no longer content to sit in dark cloisters and brood over their sins. They preferred to go out into the world and see what was astir. Introversion gave way to a lusty curiosity. Men began to travel the earth, and explore the seas, and search all through the heavens. And with their ardor, their energy, and their happy faith in life here on earth, they were able to drag the sun above the horizon and scatter the mists of night.

This is not the place to chronicle the individual achievements of the scientists. Beginning early in the sixteenth century with Leonardo da Vinci, who was naturalist, anatomist, engineer, and artist all in one, a great succession of titans gave themselves to this labor of bringing the new day into being. They belonged to all the lands, for science, like Catholicism in the early days, was a movement recognizing no frontiers. Among the great astronomers and physicists there were Copernicus the Pole, Tycho Brahe the Dane, Kepler the German, Galileo the Italian, and later, Newton the Englishman. In all the other sciences there were men drawn from every end of the continent. And through their researches not merely more knowledge but rather a *new kind* of knowledge was brought into the world.

It was the eventual spread of this new kind of knowledge that put an end to the epidemic of witch hunting. Science changed the intellectual atmosphere, scattering those gases on which the fires of superstition could thrive. The change was not thoroughgoing, and even centuries later the vapors of ignorance were still thick in the corners of Christendom. But by the eighteenth century the cruder manifestations of superstition were already being banished from at least the centers of what was called the civilized world. Not the scientists themselves but the popularizers of science were immediately responsible for this precious accomplishment. Some of the keenest and most energetic investigators were themselves quite unconscious of the import of their labors. Many of them were men in orders, and they imagined themselves quite orthodox, despite that their work was productive of the most novel results. It was Sir Francis Bacon, a publicist far more than a laboratory worker, who seems to have been the first to appreciate the significance of the new knowledge. He made no specific discovery in the field of science; rather he discovered science itself. As Preserved Smith has put it with characteristic felicity:

"Science had been the Cinderella of the world's youth, doing the humble and thankless chores of mankind while her haughty sisters, Theology and Philosophy, had danced at the court balls. Once again the ancient fable came true: the cinder-wench married

the prince and became queen;—and Francis Bacon
was her fairy god-mother."

There was no way of yoking the new way of thinking
with the old. The method of science was investigation,
not introspection, and it was furthered by skepticism, not
credulity. Not that most of these scientists were in any
conscious sense anti-Christian, or even anticlerical. On
the contrary, in so far as they had any time for religious
concerns, the majority of them were quite observant, and
some were even devout. God was as indispensable in
Descartes' system of philosophy as it was in that of St.
Thomas Aquinas; Sir Isaac Newton believed in the Second
Coming almost as implicitly as had St. Francis of Assisi.
Nonetheless science was always foreign, and at some
points directly hostile, to the methods and findings of
theology. Confining itself altogether to natural phe-
nomena, it sought to observe these objectively, classify
them systematically, and finally draw from them general-
ized "laws of nature." As Professor Whitehead has defined it, science became the conscious and organized effort
to relate irreducible and stubborn facts to general prin-
ciples. Necessarily, therefore, it could take nothing on
faith, or on the authority of tradition. The mountain of
Scholastic pumice which had seemed so sure because it had
bulked so large, was swept out of the way with a wave
of the hand, and men set about building a totally new
structure. They came to realize with Francis Bacon that
there remained "only one salvation and health: to begin
the whole work of the mind over again from the beginning."

It was an ambitious program—but ambition was

rampant just then. All manner of new instruments had just been invented, telescopes and microscopes, logarithms and calculus, and men found themselves endowed of a sudden with the eyes and minds of gods. Nothing in the sky above, or the earth beneath, or in the waters under the earth, seemed beyond knowing now. As the philosopher Campanella wrote in almost lyric ecstasy, man was now:

> "a second god, the first God's own miracle, for man commands the depths, mounts the heavens without wings, counts its moving bodies and measures their character. He knows the nature of the stars . . . like a god he determines their laws."

The enthusiasm was contagious and soon spread far beyond the tiny circle of the specialists. It is significant that Shakespeare, who was born contemporaneously with Galileo (1546), makes few allusions to scientific matters, and those few quite inaccurate. But Milton half a century later is full of the new lore, and, though the characters in his epics are biblical, he puts a knowledge of astronomy and geography into their mouths which is distinctly modern. For by Milton's time the love of natural science had become almost the vogue among the cultured. One reads of kings and queens and nobles who built themselves laboratories as their ancestors had once built private chapels. Scientists began to be patronized by the wealthy with much the same mingled awe and condescension once accorded to personal confessors and local hermits.

Even some of the middle-class folk became intrigued—the word is used here literally—and we find a man like Samuel Pepys struggling to learn the multiplication table when already thirty, and thenceforth applying himself so diligently to amateur research as to attain the Presidency of the Royal Society. An illuminating detail is provided by the French playwright, Molière, whose *bourgeois gentil-homme,* Monsieur Jourdain, in his pathetic effort to enter high society, finds it necessary to hire a professor to teach him all about "the nature of the elements, metals, minerals, stones, plants, and animals, and the cause of meteors, the rainbow, comets, lightning, thunder, rain, snow, hail, winds, and tornadoes." Even the ladies took to studying these matters. It became the fashion for them to exhaust their excess emotion not in outpourings to confessors, but in writing letters to scientists. They formed study groups which served—to quote Preserved Smith—"like the women's clubs of our own day, to enable those who were afraid to meet culture single-handed to hunt it in packs."

7

AT first the Church held back in perplexity, not knowing quite what to do about this incursion of strange knowledge. The devout Catholic apologist, Cardinal Bellarmine, after having taken a look through a telescope, wrote in dismay to the mathematicians of the Roman College to inquire whether what he had seen *with his own eyes* was real or only an illusion! Many a good Churchman found himself in like bewilderment, for the new discoveries confounded

all that had been taught concerning the universe. If the Copernican theory was correct, and the earth, far from being the center of the universe, was a mere planet swinging around the sun, what was one to do with the sacred book of Genesis? How could one continue to believe that the whole universe had been created for man's benefit, when it was shown that this earth on which man dwelt was no more than a midge dancing around a candle flame? Where was Heaven now, the Heaven where Christ was supposed to sit on a jeweled throne and receive the souls of the religious? For that matter, where was Hell? . . .

At first the majority of theologians would not even listen to such questions. With a peremptory gesture they forbade the whole business of rational investigation. Martin Luther roared that those who sought to discover their relation to the universe by their own thoughts rather than through Christ, would break their necks. "Thunder strikes him who presumes to examine," was his warning. When word reached him of Copernicus' theory he dismissed it as a shallow paradox born of vanity. Nor were the other reformers less unenlightened. Melanchthon could see only absurdity in the Copernican teaching, and suggested in a letter written in 1541 that "wise rulers ought to suppress such wanton ingenuity." Calvin, too, condemned the heliocentric theory, citing as his final authority the verse in the 113th Psalm which declared: "The world also is established that it cannot be moved."

But the Protestant leaders were impotent to do more than frown and utter warnings. Beset by Rome, and divided among themselves, they were in no position to join battle with the men of science. It was left for the Catholic leaders to take the offensive on this new front; and they did. Of course, the majority of the priests had no part in the campaign, for its issues were quite beyond their understanding. It was the conservative scholars in the Church, the philosophers still bogged in Aristotelian dialectic, who shouted for the suppression of the new thought. No action was taken against Copernicus, for the true import of his teaching was not yet appreciated. The Council of Trent, which was convened in 1544, the year following Copernicus's death, contented itself with the declaration that "he who is gifted with the heavenly knowledge of faith is free from an inquisitive curiosity." Nor was there any persecution of scientists during the succeeding half-century, partly because the Church was then preoccupied with the Counter-Reformation, and partly because the heliocentric theory was still regarded as a mere vagary of unbalanced scholars.

By the end of the sixteenth century, however, both these considerations were no longer operative. The Jesuits and other Counter-Reform forces had effectively checked the tide of Protestantism in the churches; and at the same time Copernicanism had crept up till it was to be detected in many, if not most, of the universities. The heliocentric theory had been corroborated through the findings of Kepler and Galileo, and had been widely popularized through the writings of such men as Giordano Bruno, Vanini, and Campanella. And the Church, no longer pressed by theological heresy, now found it necessary to attend to this more insidious attack.

The first victim was the impassioned Giordano Bruno, who was lured back to Italy, flung into prison, tortured and finally burnt at the stake in the year 1600. The next to be put to death for teaching the Copernican theory was the philosopher Vanini. Condemned to have his tongue cut out and his body burnt, he remained undaunted to the last. "*Andiamo, andiamo allegramente a morire de filosofo,*" he kept saying as they led him to the place of execution: "Let us go, let us go joyfully, as becomes a philosopher about to die!" [12]

But both Bruno and Vanini were philosophers rather than scientists, and their destruction had only slight effect on the production of the new knowledge. To destroy the actual producers of this knowledge was more difficult, for they, having started out with a skepticism as to the old beliefs, remained skeptical even with regard to the new. Being scientists, they knew that a willingness to suffer for a cause by no means proved its objective truth. Therefore whenever they were attacked by the Church, they discreetly recanted. Galileo, the greatest experimentalist of the age, did that twice during his life, for though ready to die in an experiment, he was most reluctant to do so in an argument. The campaign against his disturbing work was initiated by a popular preacher in Florence in 1614, and thereafter he was subjected repeatedly to annoying accusations and attacks. It was almost impossible for him to find a common ground for argument with his opponents, for they were still committed to a type of reasoning from which he had completely freed himself. For instance, one

[12] John Owen, in his discursive *Skeptics of the Italian Renaissance,* ch. 5, offers evidence that Vanini, who was condemned for "atheism" was in reality merely a skeptic. The story of the whole campaign against Copernicanism is told in White's monumental *History of the Warfare between Science and Theology.*

of his learned antagonists in Florence, an astronomer named Sizzi, questioned Galileo's statements concerning an eighth planet on the ground that since there were only seven branches in the sacred candlestick, and since it required no more than seven months to form a perfect fœtus, there could not possibly be more than seven planets in the sky!

But what his opponents lacked in sagacity they more than made up in power, and Galileo, realizing this, did not try to cross them. Having been warned by the Inquisition in 1616 that he must "forsake the opinion he had hitherto held . . . that the earth moves," he kept discreetly silent on the subject for almost sixteen years. But when he broke his silence at the end of that time, he was again brought to book by the authorities. Though almost seventy years of age, and so ill that he had to be carried in a litter from Florence, he was summoned before the Roman Inquisition and put on trial for his life. Whether he was actually tortured is doubtful, but that he was threatened with it is certain. And for the second time Galileo gave in. He confessed himself guilty of teaching that the earth moves, and solemnly signed a recantation which declared, "with a sincere heart and unfeigned faith, I abjure, curse, and renounce the said error." Then, kneeling before seven cardinals and the host of lesser clerics who constituted the court, he meekly received the sentence of perpetual imprisonment and the order to repeat the seven penitential psalms once a week for three years. But—so goes the apocryphal legend—as he got to his feet the broken old man muttered under his breath, *"Eppur si muove"*—"But it does move nevertheless!"

And the world did move. The Church was powerful, for it had the Jesuits for its eyes and the Inquisition for its hands. But science was even more powerful, for it had reason and demonstrable fact on its side. No one was converted by Galileo's recantation, least of all himself. At most the incident persuaded many of his followers to take refuge in hypocrisy. As Gabriel Naudé, the librarian to Mazarin, was wont to advise his friends: "In thought please yourself, but in conduct follow the customs." Such men realized well that the blood of martyrs could never be the seed of science. To them was denied the ecstasy of spectacular self-immolation. Reason taught them that it was infinitely more valuable to live and seek further truth than to die for an hypothesis.

So the new learning kept welling up and spreading. At first its discoveries were confined to the natural sciences, but soon they began to be made in other fields. A secular philosophy arose on the basis of the new knowledge, and men employed the data of science precisely as Duns Scotus and St. Thomas Aquinas had employed the verses of the Holy Writ. And when the religious authorities accused them of contradicting the divine Word of God, the philosophers retorted that that Word contradicted itself at times, and was most fallibly human rather than divine. Such a retort would have been a capital offense in earlier days; but by the eighteenth century it had become possible to utter free-thinking sentiments almost with impunity. The intellectual climate had changed, and the Inquisition, like the witch-hunt, could no longer enjoy the vapors of credulity off which it had thrived so long. By that time the whole idea of sacerdotal authority

in the realm of knowledge had lost its hold on the minds
of at least the cultured.

A century and a half of religious warfare had bled all
sects alike of strength and prestige. Earnest men, hearing
he fulminations which the theologians kept hurling at each
other indiscriminately, were moved to wonder whether
everyone of the theologies might not be false. What
added to the confusion was the discovery that there were
in the world not alone rival sects, but also many rival
religions. In earlier centuries the world of even the most
learned had been confined very largely to Christian Europe. But the voyages of discovery had put an end to that
provincialism, and now even common folk knew that
there were other continents on earth where dwelt other
races with religions of their own. Nor were these religions
without their likeness to Christianity. All of them claimed
to be divinely revealed, most of them had elaborate rituals,
and many possessed hoary scriptures and high moral codes.
And these similarities, once they were pointed out, could
not but cast reflection on the uniqueness of Christianity.
What warrant was there that the Bible was true and that
the holy books of the Hindus, the Chinese, and the other
heathens were false? Regarded critically—which usually
meant adversely—did the Bible really reveal any profounder wisdom than was contained in those other writings? Did it truly teach a higher morality, or promise any
more certain rewards?

Only a tiny minority within Christendom dared to ask
such questions; but it was an articulate minority, and therefore profoundly influential. A totally new type, the free-
thinker, began to raise his voice in the universities and the

salons; and the authoritarians and traditionalists were powerless to anathematize him into silence. Times had changed and the old curses had lost their potency. Heady with pride over their sudden achievements in science, men laughed at the anathemas of the clerics. "Knowledge cannot defile," they argued in the language of Milton. "A forbidden writing is a spark of truth that flies up in the face of them that seek to tread it out!"

8

DARING was the dominant note in the intellectual life of the eighteenth century. The idea of progress, a notion which even the Greeks had never entertained, took possession of the best minds of the age. Instead of conceiving human development to be a retrogression, it was now regarded as a process of gradual improvement. Men ceased to grieve because of Original Sin, or be thankful for the Vicarious Atonement. They had learnt to believe in themselves and in their future, and they were right pleased with themselves.[18]

The cultured refused to believe any longer that God was a person who hovered over the world and capriciously interfered with its workings. Some few refused even to

[18] For the significance of this changed interpretation of history see J. B. Bury's brilliant work, *The Idea of Progress*. For an analysis of 18th century rationalism see Flint, *Anti-Theistic Theories*, and Farrar, *Critical History of Free Thought*.

believe that there was any God whatsoever, and the rest insisted that though He did exist, He was not a Person but a Being—the precise distinction was not always clear —and that though He had indeed created the universe, He no longer governed it. God was pictured as a sort of a Cosmic Clockmaker who, having once wound up the universe, had then gone off and left it to run by itself according to immutable mechanical laws. The whole idea may have been naïve, but it sounded most persuasively rational in that day. It fitted in with current political ideas, for, just as Jehovah in ancient days had been an oriental despot, and Christ in medieval times had been a feudal lord, so this Supreme Being was a sort of constitutional monarch. Like the kings of the more enlightened lands in the eighteenth century, this God ruled His realm but did not govern it.

Something approximating a religion grew up around this novel theology. It had its origin in England, where it came to be called Deism; and thence it spread to France, where it won over men like Voltaire and Diderot, and to America, where it became the religion of Franklin, Washington, Jefferson, Thomas Paine, and many of the other leaders of the American Revolution.

Deism was not a consistent religion, for each of its exponents felt free to make of it what he pleased. Indeed, the Deists were able to agree among themselves only in their criticism of Christianity. They took savage joy in making sport of the irrationalities in the traditional faith, and in pointing out the more flagrant discrepancies in the Holy Writ. But when it came to positive assertions, they were all at sixes and sevens. The trouble was that the

Deists did not realize how little their science had as yet been able to ascertain. They sought to create a "natural religion" when they still knew little, almost nothing, about nature. They were incapable of realizing that the "laws of nature" demonstrated by men like Sir Isaac Newton were in reality only tentative hypotheses. To these enthusiastic disciples, hungry for some new certainty to which to cling, the men of science were priests of an infallible oracle.

What made matters worse was that the apostles of the new religion exercised too little discrimination in selecting their priests. They gave credence not merely to the calculations of sober physicists, but also to the reports of the most romantic explorers. It was largely on the basis of such reports that the Deists developed their contention that all "revealed" religions, most especially Christianity, were corruptions of an original "natural" religion innate in the human race. The underprivileged Christian crawling in his slum was contrasted with the "Noble Savage"; the dull-witted, fox-hunting bishop was set side by side with the "Chinese Sage": and it was not difficult to decide which was the superior. And from this it was argued that the traditional religion had damned the race rather than saved it. Christianity, far from being regarded as a unique revelation from God and the one salvation for all mankind, seemed in this new light to be but a fraud and a source of naught save degeneration.

And the Deists never wearied of flooding the world with this new light. Though few in number, they wrote with such zeal and wit that in time their ideas were the commonplace of conversation in every salon in Europe.

The positive teachings of the new religion attracted only slight attention; what appealed more was the destructive element in Deism. Powerful monarchs like Frederick the Great of Prussia, Joseph II of Austria, and Catherine II of Russia, openly encouraged the infidel philosophers and even tried to impose some of their ideas on the masses. For instance, Joseph II, though head of the Holy Roman Empire and nominally an observant Catholic, passed a law in 1784 restricting relic worship and taxing pilgrimages, another in 1785 removing the side altars with their images from all churches, and still another in 1786 introducing the vernacular into the ritual. Nor did such enactments arouse any fierce protest, for the germs of skepticism had found their way into the Church itself, destroying its powers of resistance. The Jesuits were gone from the scene—their suppression had been made possible in part by that same spread of skepticism—and Rome was left devitalized and helpless.

The peasants still clung to the Church, for the new freedom of thought had not seeped down to them as yet. The Deists and other rationalists had made no attempt to proselytize among the lower classes. For all their protestations of thoroughgoing liberalism, those philosophers remained exceedingly distrustful of the rabble. They did believe in democracy but only for gentlemen, and in freedom of thought, but only for the cultured. They considered the lower orders unworthy of such boons, and they were willing at times even to simulate piety just to keep those orders from becoming restless. Atheistic noblemen like the Duke of Orléans would attend Mass regularly, even though it was only to read a bawdy tale of Rabelais bound as a prayer-book. The great Voltaire built a church at his own expense for the peasants on his French estate, and he did not draw the line even at attending the services on occasion. So the common folk, being unenlightened by their betters and both unable and unwilling to enlighten themselves, continued to believe with a full heart—and an empty stomach.

The situation was somewhat different, of course, in the Protestant realm. The aristocratic tradition had been somewhat weakened there, and what was known in the higher strata of society could not so easily be kept from the lower. As a consequence, Protestantism reacted far more sharply to the new kind of thinking than did Catholicism. At one extreme it sought to accommodate itself to skepticism, developing rationalistic philosophies like those of Bishop Berkeley in Great Britain, and Gottfried Wilhelm Leibnitz in Germany. Starting out with premises which even the radical Deists could accept, these enlightened Protestant apologists sought to prove that Christian theology was still valid and true. They succeeded to a degree, but only by recasting that theology in a totally new mold. As a recent historian has put it: "the Enlightment produced a Christianity without Christ and a Protestantism that still remained Protestant when it was no longer Christian." [14]

Rationalism prompted the development of new denominations as well as new philosophies among the Protestants.

[14] J. W. C. Wand, *A History of the Modern Church,* 1930, p. 178, a most comprehensive and readable outline.

The traditional Christology with its doctrine of the Holy Trinity had been one of the chief targets for the Deists, and there were some among the more liberal churchmen who urged that the target be surrendered. Anti-Trinitarianism, a doctrine which had been declared heretical when Arius was condemned by the Council of Nicea in 325, had been stealthily winning adherents ever since the first years of the Reformation. It had been advocated by that fractious heretic, Servetus, whom Calvin caused to be put to death, and by a number of other radical theologians, most of them Italians, who vainly sought refuge in Geneva. One of these, Fausto Sozzini, found his way to Poland in 1579 and there succeeded in founding a tiny sect of Anti-Trinitarians. The movement, which took the name of Socinianism, could not thrive, however, in the intellectual climate of the sixteenth century. Not until two hundred years later were conditions more favorable, and even then the denial of the divinity of Jesus was able to obtain only limited acceptance.

In 1774 an Anglican clergyman named Lindsay, aided by an eminent scientist, Joseph Priestley—the discoverer of oxygen—founded a Unitarian Church in London. Some eleven years later a similar development occurred in Boston. King's Chapel, the oldest Anglican church in New England, having fallen into the hands of laymen during the disorders accompanying the American Revolution, was made over into a Unitarian institution. The movement won adherents throughout Boston, and later began to influence the other denominations. No fewer than a hundred and twenty-six Congregational churches in New England rejected the Trinitarian doctrine, and in 1805 even Harvard

University, the center of North American culture at that time, went over to the Unitarian side.

At about the same time there arose a second such liberal sect, the Universalists. Its membership, unlike that of the Unitarian churches, was drawn largely from the lower middle-class, and its creed was less rigorously intellectual. Unitarianism, especially in England, had yielded almost completely to the rationalistic spirit and would not adhere to any of the "creeds of human composition." It insisted that Jesus was a man not a god—"unique," of course, but still a man. The Unitarians revered him because of the supernal greatness of his moral teachings, and because he more than any other man had comprehended the true nature of God. But they would not worship him, nor could they, save in figurative speech, invoke his aid. They scouted the possibility of miracles, were skeptical as to the validity of mysticism, and prayed with fast-waning faith in the objective efficacy of their prayer.

The Universalists, being for the most part humbler folk and less sure of to-morrow's bread, were less cavalier than the Unitarians in their attitude toward the old beliefs. They were largely Arians in their Christology, considering Jesus neither divine nor altogether human, but rather a *tertium quid* in between. Their Arianism was a secondary accretion, however. The original point of departure for the Universalists was their belief that all human beings are of the "elect" and destined to be saved. Jesus had died not to appease God's wrath but simply to make manifest His abundant love. Though there might be punishment here or hereafter for the stiff-necked and the wayward, it would not endure forever. The Universalists believed that no man could stand out against God's corrective love forever, and therefore all men would finally work out their salvation and inherit blessedness at the Final Judgment.

9

UT the creation of these liberal philosophies and denominations was only one aspect of Protestantism's reaction to rationalism. That same skeptical eighteenth century witnesssed one of the most fervent evangelical reactions in all of Christian history. The movement had its origin, appropriately enough, in Germany, where the ravages of the Thirty Years' War had left the people far too feeble to dare indulge in freedom of thought. Instead of rejecting the traditional beliefs, the plain folk in that unhappy region clung to them the more tenaciously. Around the year 1670 a Frankfort pastor named Spener organized within his congregation an inner group made up of members to whom religion was more than a convention. This group devoted itself to studying the Bible and to practicing the sternly puritan code of morals advocated in its pages. Spener's innovation was opposed at first, but his example was soon imitated by other pastors. *Collegia pietatis* began to make their appearance all over Germany, and the devoutness which they fostered brought a new vigor into the Lutheran Church.

Pietism as a movement endured little more than half a century in Germany, but its effects lasted for generations. It encouraged popular education by founding parochial schools, helped to systematize philanthrophy by establishing orphanages, and aided the spread of Christian knowledge by creating the still existent Bible Institute for the publication of cheap editions of the Scriptures. Most remarkable of all, it actually initiated a missionary movement that was in no wise connected with imperialistic or commercial interests. So great was its ardor that it even tried to convert the Jews!

The wave of Pietism began to recede before the eighteenth century was a quarter spent; but almost at once a second wave began to rise in one corner of the land. A group of earnest Moravian Protestants had taken refuge in Saxony on the estate of a certain nobleman named Graf von Zinzendorf. They belonged to a sect called the Unitas Fratrum, or Communion of Brethren, and were descended from the radical Hussites of the fifteenth century. Zinzendorf, who was a Pietist by conviction as well as rearing—he was a godson to Spener—warmed to these Moravian refugees, for he saw in their devotion to the Bible, their puritanical life, and their all-engrossing faith, the realization of his own religious ideals. He gave them the land on which to build a village of their own, called Herrnhut, and encouraged them to organize a model commonwealth there. It was in a measure a communist commonwealth, for these Moravian Brethren were typical peasant evangelicals, and, though they might not be realistic, they were exceedingly literal. They tried to live according to what they conceived to be the letter of the Scriptures and surrendered themselves body and soul to the will of the Lord.

Naturally enough they found small favor in the eyes of the Lutheran clerics, for in addition to their strange way of living together the Moravians had an even stranger way of praying. They believed that not baptism but conversion was what made a man truly a Christian, and they further believed that this conversion was most thorough if it came suddenly and in a moment of ecstatic fervor. Consequently they encouraged enthusiasm in their prayer meetings, and the frenzied shouts and seizures which marked their gatherings soon became the scandal of the countryside.

Harassed by the authorities, a company of Moravians, aided by Zinzendorf, set out for the New World in 1735. They found their way after a while to the tolerant colony of Pennsylvania, and there they founded in 1741 a semi-communist settlement which Zinzendorf named Bethlehem. Other Moravians migrated singly or in companies to other lands, and within a generation their prayer halls and missions were to be found scattered throughout the world. Believing that they alone knew the way to salvation, they regarded missionary work as the first of their duties in life. They went exhorting and praying from Greenland to Surinam, and from Norway to South Africa; and wherever they moved they raised the religious temperature. Their doctrine of the holiness of frenzy and the necessity of ecstatic abandon found favor among the masses in many lands. Poor folk, weak with want and cowed by oppression, were elated to be able to fling themselves hysterically into the arms of Jesus. Though the Moravian Church always remained obscure and impoverished, its spirit invaded almost all the Protestant sects and left its mark even on Russian Orthodoxy. Indeed, its spirit is dominant to this day in the hinterland of Protestantism.[15]

10

IT so happened that among the passengers on a boat carrying a company of Moravians to Georgia in 1735, there were two young English clergymen, by name John and Charles Wesley. They were brothers, and John was going out as a missionary to the new colony, while Charles was to be secretary to the governor. Their devoutness, a quality none too common in the Established Church in that generation, had won the Wesleys a certain notoriety while at Oxford. They had been the leaders of a group nicknamed the Methodists because of the methodical way in which they had prayed and practiced righteousness. They and their friends had fasted regularly on Wednesdays and Fridays, had taken Communion once a week, had studied the Gospels in Greek, and had gone about among the prisoners and the sick to give them the consolations of religion.[16]

[15] The Moravian Church is still in existence—it counts about thirteen thousand adherents in the United States alone—and still supports great missionary activities. For the details of its rise, see Hutton, *History of the Moravian Church.* For Zinzendorf's life, see the biography by Bovet translated into English under the title, *A Pioneer of Social Christianity.*

[16] For the details see Fitchett, *Wesley and His Century* and Adam Clarke, *Memoirs of the Wesley Family.* Abram Lipsky's *John Wesley* is an excellent biography in the very modern manner.

It was but natural, therefore, that these two young men, predisposed as they were to religious earnestness, should become interested in their Moravian fellow-passengers. John, the elder of the Wesley brothers, set himself at once to learn German, and within a few days was deep in conversation with the leader of the strange group. And what he learned disquieted him profoundly. Neither he nor his brother had ever experienced that moment of ecstasy of which the Moravians made so much. Neither had felt himself suddenly cleansed of sin and "born again" in the spirit. And, being introspective young men, they were both disturbed.

The Wesleys did not remain long in Georgia. Charles became ill and left after but a few months, and John got himself into unseemly difficulties over a jilting and was compelled to leave two years later. On the journey homeward poor John wrestled much with himself, for he realized all was not well with his soul. Despite that he had titanic zeal and obvious ability, he felt himself frustrated at every turn. He quite obviously suffered from some psychic maladjustment, for his diaries reveal that desires and phobias, appetites and inhibitions, were incessantly at war in his mind. In his own language, of course, what troubled him was the burden of sin. A Moravian missionary, whom John met on his return to London, spoke with terrible assurance on that point. What the young gentleman needed, the peasant declared, was to throw himself on the mercy of Jesus and be saved. He must forget his learning and abjure his pride. Like a child, like one of the "foolish of the world," he must come in penitence before the Lord and be converted.

And John Wesley followed the man's counsel. On May

24, 1738, while attending a workingmen's prayer meeting in some small hall in Aldersgate, the distraught young cleric felt his heart "strangely warmed" and was suddenly overcome with the conviction that he had at last been saved. . . . Thenceforth he was a changed man. After a brief visit to the Moravian center at Herrnhut he returned to England and began to preach wherever he could find a congregation. Charles, who had also become "converted," tried to join in his elder brother's work; but he was far too weak to stand the hardships of itinerant preaching. Instead, he devoted himself to composing hymns, and with such energy that by the time he died he had produced some six thousand five hundred sacred songs, many of them among the most popular as well as the most beautiful in the English language.

John, too, wrote hymns from time to time; but his chief labor was that of preaching. With inexhaustible zeal and apparently a tireless body he kept traveling through England to tell the populace of the wrath to come. When allowed, he preached in churches of the Establishment; when not, he addressed great mobs in the open. Often he spoke twelve or fifteen times a week, employing the hours between sermons to compose hymns, tracts, and letters, or to pay pastoral calls. He was a man after the heart of Paul of Tarsus. Having once seen the light, he could not abide that his fellow-countrymen should remain in darkness. He ached that all Anglicans, indeed all men, should be even as he was himself—sinless by the grace of God, reborn in the spirit, and saved from the toils of the Devil. And that ache goaded him to labor as have few men in all history.

Wesley was not a man of great eloquence, and always

[387]

eschewed what he called "the amorous style of prayer and the luscious style of preaching." Yet such was the force of his personality that he could stir huge mobs and set them a-tremble. Sometimes he was booed and pelted with offal, for he minced no words in denouncing vice, and hooligans often resented his language. But if at times he turned tail before such enemies, it was only to return a second time. Courage was strong in him, for he knew that God was on his side. It was characteristic of his faith that once, when he took flight from a mob and sought refuge in a stage-coach, he saw the workings of God's special Providence when, as he wrote in his diary, "a very large gentlewoman sat in my lap and screened me so that nothing came near me." [17]

Most of the time, however, Wesley was able to do what he willed with his listeners. Swept up in his own holy frenzy, the people would begin to shout and scream hysterically. They would fall to the ground in seizures, and foam at the mouth and writhe while the Holy Ghost wrestled with the demon within them. Wesley's *Journal* records again and again how his listeners would some-times "drop down on every side as [though] thunder-struck," or would be "seized with a strong pain and be constrained to roar for the disquietness of their hearts," or would be "torn with a kind of convulsive motion in every part of their body," and would scream "with the utmost vehemence, even as in the agonies of death."

Most of the respectable clerics of the Establishment frowned on Wesley and his ways. When he assured them that only in such ways could religion be communicated to

[17] Lipsky, *John Wesley*, p. 88.

men, these clerics answered that it might be far better not to communicate it at all. The pompous Bishop Butler—he who sought to confound the Deists with his circuitous *Apology*—lost his temper in a conversation with John Wesley, and cried out: "Sir, the pretending to extraordinary revelations and gifts of the Holy Ghost is a horrid thing, a *very* horrid thing!"

But horrid or no, it swept the country. Other preachers in increasing numbers flocked to Wesley's banner, and what had originated as one man's struggle to master his inner thwartings, terminated in a national upheaval. England was ready for Methodism, for the common folk were in misery and the regular churches could offer them no relief. The development of trade and extension of a broad empire had brought prosperity to the land; but, as always under such circumstances, it was a prosperity enjoyed only by a few. The poor folk were actually not as poor as they had been in former centuries; but, when compared with the newly rich, they seemed poorer than ever before. And there was nothing in the official religion to make them forget their poverty.

The spirit of sincere devotion had largely died out in the Anglican Church; only the forms and doctrines had persisted. It was an age of political prelates, absentee bishops, and fox-hunting parsons; of politely mumbled prayers, soft-spoken sermons, and smugly hypocritical laments. The middle-class folk who had so vigorously favored puritanism while socially and economically on the climb, had but small use for it now that they were on the summit. They no longer favored restrictions as to how one should dress or what one should spend. They felt they had slaved and stinted long enough; now they wanted to enjoy their hoardings. They still believed that leisure and luxury were wicked—but only for the laboring class. For that reason they, as employers, paid the lowest possible wages and exacted the longest hours of toil—they knew that thus they were keeping the workingmen from sinning. So far as they themselves were concerned, however, piety and righteous self-restraint seemed eccentric and in bad form. "Everyone laughs if you try to discuss religion," wrote Montesquieu of English society. Serious-minded men like Lord Herbert of Cherbury, and his successors in the development of Deistic thought, formed a tiny minority even among the cultured of the period. The vast majority, sick of religion after the savage wars it had engendered in the land, preferred to ignore the whole subject.

But the folk down below could not be so cavalier with regard to religion. They still had desperate need for the consolations afforded by faith, for life was hard for them. Science had gone on from abstract theorizing to the invention of machines, and the basic character of British life was rapidly becoming revolutionized. The worst evils of industrialism were beginning to make themselves felt, and none of the later palliatives had yet been thought of. The migration from the farms to the towns had already set in, and the unrest consequent on this change, coupled with the overcrowding and disease inevitable in slum life, had goaded the masses to desperation. Privilege was flagrant all around them, yet they themselves could grasp none of it. Presumptuous wealth flaunted itself before their very eyes, yet they had to live on in need. And their souls became bitter with frustration. Removed from their ancestral villages and the restraints put upon them by village prying, many of them took to lives of crime. "You will hear little news from England," wrote Walpole to a friend abroad, "but of robberies." An underworld had developed in the grimy huddled towns, and increasing numbers of desperadoes sought to wrest by violent means that which the higher folk acquired by craft or guile.

Of course, the majority of the poor folk kept far from overt crime—but in large part only because they lacked physical daring. That they had no moral scruples against robbery and murder is evidenced by the way they made heroes of notorious highwaymen and cutthroats. Mobs lined the streets and cheered the criminals as they were led to prison; they flocked to hangings as the Roman mobs had once flocked to gladiatorial games. The English proletariat, embittered by exploitations and uncomforted by faith, had become brutalized and savage. Bull-baiting, cock-fighting, and prize-fighting had become the favorite sports of the masses; drunkenness was so common that half the wheat produced in the country was consumed in distilling gin, and every sixth house was a grogshop!

And that was why Wesley succeeded. The poor folk resorted to violence and debauchery because they knew no better way of relieving their thwarted souls. Once a better way was shown them, they grasped at it as a famished man will grasp at meat in preference to raw spirits. They relieved their sense of pent-up frustration in "revivals" rather than at hangings. Assured that they could be accepted in Heaven, they no longer cared that they were rejected on earth. They gave up their dram-drinking and other vices, and deadened themselves to the black anguish of life by steeping themselves in faith. The opiate was not altogether compounded of delusions. The converted joined "societies," and in these societies they found a comradeship which destroyed the anonymity that had blighted their lives. They were no longer bits of refuse floating along in the gutters; they were persons now, with names that were known and sins that might be confessed aloud.

And thus the people were quite literally "saved" by Wesley—saved from that very real hell which is suffered by the annihilated ego. That was why his work flourished. Soon he had a small army of fellow-workers, fiery men who ran about and preached in bare halls or at the mouths of coal pits, and earnest women who brought comfort and food into hovels and cellarways. The most famous of his associates was George Whitefield, an unlearned but sensationally eloquent preacher whose first sermon is said to have driven fifteen people insane.[18]

The majority of the Methodist exhorters were, like Whitefield, unlearned men; and even the learned, like Wesley, were steeped in superstition. John himself was a devout believer in witchcraft, and repeatedly lamented because Englishmen had forsaken the belief.

> With my last breath will I bear testimony [he wrote] against giving up to infidels one great proof of the invisible world. The giving up of witchcraft is the giving up of the Bible.[19]

[18] Wand, *History of the Modern Church*, p. 190. J. P. Gledstone's biography of Whitefield is good.
[19] Lipsky, *John Wesley*, p. 187.

But their ignorance and credulity served only to make the Methodist preachers the more effective in their work, for their appeal was primarily to the "foolish of the world." Soon they had won so many converts and had started so many "societies" that Wesley was driven to create a distinct organization with recognized leaders of its own. Originally he had accepted only ordained clergymen as his associates, but circumstances soon forced him to allow enthusiastic laymen to preach. And when the annual conference of the Methodist leaders became an incorporated body in 1784, these licensed preachers were ruled the equals of the ordained men. That year marked the beginning of the break with the Anglican Church. Until then Wesley had thought to do no more than the Pietists had accomplished for Lutheranism, or the Jesuits for Catholicism. Repeatedly he had urged his followers: "Be Church of England men still; do not cast away the peculiar glory which God hath put upon you." But when he found the episcopal dignitaries would not support his movement with adequate readiness, he did not scruple to go over their heads. Needing authoritative leaders for the widespread work that was being done in America, John Wesley with his own hands made one of his helpers a bishop, and sent him across the seas with instructions to do the same for a young exhorter named Francis Asbury, who was already at work in the colonies. Wesley was sharply criticized for his presumption, but as he argued in his own defense:

"I firmly believe that I am a scriptural *episcopos* as much as any man in England or in Europe; for the

[393]

uninterrupted succession I know to be a fable which no man ever did or can prove."

He refused to withdraw from his stand, despite all the complaints that "ordination is separation." Instead, he went further and proceeded to give ordination to men who intended to serve at home as well as to those who went abroad.

And thus was the way paved for the eventual secession of the Methodist party. Even before the final break occurred, the party was already itself divided. Whitefield had fallen out with Wesley over the question of the possibility of perfect sinlessness this side of Paradise, the former adhering to strict Calvinism and the latter taking the more liberal stand of Arminianism. Two types of Methodists arose: the Calvinistic Methodists, confined largely to Wales, and the Wesleyans who spread out everywhere. Later the Wesleyans fell out among themselves over questions of church polity, dividing in the course of time into some twenty-three distinct denominations, of which the Methodist Episcopal Church of the United States—itself divided into North and South—grew to be by far the most important.[20]

But though thus divided, Methodism remained for long a most virile force in Protestantism. It was to the proletariat what Calvinism had been to the middle-class, and Catholicism had been to the feudal lords. Evangelicalism turned their thoughts from the torments of this life to glories they would inherit in a life hereafter.

[20] For the details see Townsend, Workman and Eayrs, *A New History of Methodism*, 2 vols.

Its preachers kept repeating the Gospel promises that the mournful would rejoice and the hungry would be filled—in the Kingdom of Heaven. And they that hearkened being eager to believe such things, did believe them.

11

IT was a fortunate thing for the peace of England that Methodism did succeed so signally. Conditions in England were ripe for a revolution in the last years of the eighteenth century, and the spread of this new fervor seems to have been one of the primary factors which helped prevent the catastrophe. The evangelical movement distracted the masses. It turned their thoughts to their sins instead of to their sufferings, and set them fighting against the Devil instead of against their employers. It restrained them from drinking and similar vices which, though stupefying for the moment, would have made the poor folk all the more ferocious when they broke loose at last; and it filled them instead with faith.[21]

The potency of Methodism as a deterrent to revolution in England is perhaps best attested by what occurred in France. The plight of the populace in the latter land was only slightly more terrible, yet the closing years of the eighteenth century witnessed an uprising without prec-

[21] See Lecky, *History of England in the Eighteenth Century,* Vol. II, ch. 1.

edent for sustained violence. Had an evangelical movement been able to take hold of the proletariat of France,
as it did that of England, not impossibly the cataclysm
might have been averted. But France had remained
Catholic, and a corrupt clergy working hand in hand with
a dissolute bureaucracy had made all attempts to revitalize
the official religion impossible. Lack of faith was permitted; indeed it had become the fashion among the cultured. But excess of faith—*that* was forbidden. As a consequence the populace, unable to drown its woes in religious frenzy, brooded over them until at last it went mad.
On July 14, 1789, a Parisian mob broke loose and stormed
the Bastille, and within another twelve-month the whole
rotted structure of feudal privilege was no more.[22]

The Church drew the fire of the revolutionists from the
very start. Four weeks after the storming of the Bastille
the insurgent Assembly abolished the system of tithes and
prohibited all levying of contributions by the pope. It was
a straw in the wind, and the clerics were well aware of
the direction in which it pointed. Taking alarm, they hur-
riedly tried to throw a sop to the dogs by selling all the
superfluous ecclesiastical plate in the kingdom and donat-
ing the proceeds—about twenty-eight million dollars—to
the government. But the people could not be bought off
so easily. The wealth of the Church was fabulous. It
owned half the landed property in the country, controlled
some three hundred thousand serfs, and consumed or
hoarded a fifth of the total national income. The commoners in the Assembly were moved to grim laughter at

[22] For an eccentric Catholic interpretation of this dramatic period,
see Belloc, *French Revolution.*

the pathetic efforts of the hierarchy to save the Church possessions. Nothing would satisfy those commoners save the confiscation of all clerical property; and they showed signs of getting their way.

The terrified prelates hastily offered eighty million more, but again they were laughted at. On November 2 the entire wealth of the Church was commandeered by law and placed "at the disposal of the nation." Three months later, in February 1790, all the monastic houses were closed on the ground that they were the abodes of tyranny and the lurking places of lewdness and crime. On March 10 a Protestant was elected chairman of the Assembly, and when a Carthusian monk a few days later dared to arise before that body and urge the recognition of Catholicism as the state religion, there was almost a riot. Not that the revolutionists were Protestants; they were simply anti-Catholics. In July 1790, the Assembly adopted a "Civil Constitution of the Church," which ruled that all Church offices were thenceforth to be filled by popular local election, and without any deference to the wishes of Rome.

The pope, though thoroughly incensed by now, hesitated to speak his mind. His advisers were divided, some urging immediate denunciation of the wicked and sacrilegious French Assembly, and others counseling patience and compromise. Several more months elapsed before the pontiff could screw up sufficient courage to publish a bull condemning the Civil Constitution, and by then it was already too late to intimidate the revolutionists. A Paris mob paraded through the streets bearing the grotesque image of the pope seated on an ass, and the Assembly took advantage of the opportunity to confiscate Avignon and another province in France belonging to the Roman See. In vain did the clerics try to organize some resistance. Six hundred priests were massacred in Avignon alone, and scores were attacked and put to death in other parts of the country. The first phase of the revolution was over, and now the violent Jacobins were in command. On August 13, 1792, the same day on which the king was taken prisoner by the revolutionists, all priests were ordered to leave Paris. Several hundred were thrown into prison, and a month later some three hundred of these were murdered by a mob.

The Reign of Terror had commenced, and the clerics, ancient allies of the aristocracy, were shown no mercy. The heads of the government, Robespierre, Danton, Marat, and their confrères loathed the Christian ecclesiastics much as the Early Church Fathers had loathed the Pagan philosophers. Their great prophet was Voltaire, and one of their first acts, once they got into power, was to exhume the bones of the old skeptic and give them the sort of funeral that could not but impress a populace accustomed to venerating saints. These Jacobins had a religion of their own, a sort of evangelical Deism; and their intense devotion to it made them incapable of any tolerance.[23]

Convinced that Christianity was a rank imposture foisted on the race by the kings and priests, these Jacobin rulers bent every effort on rooting it out of the land. They revised the calendar so as to abolish Sunday, and passed laws militating against Catholic worship on other days.

[23] Brinton, *The Jacobins*, 1930, chs. 6 and 7, is most illuminating on the religious element in the movement.

And finally a company of extremists in the Paris Commune actually ordered the total suppression of Christianity. Led by a fanatical atheist named Hébert and his wife, who was a former nun, these radicals arranged a pompous celebration in the Cathedral of Notre Dame, at which the Cult of Reason was proclaimed the new religion of the land. A pretty actress with a reputation which had long ceased to be questionable was seated on the altar as the personification of the Goddess of Reason, and a drunken mob worshiped the new deity with adequately unreasoned fervor.

But that was too much for the majority even of the Jacobins. The excesses of Hébert and his fellow worshipers of Reason revolted Robespierre, who was a Deist and believed in a Supreme Being. "Atheism is aristocratic," he cried. "The belief in a Supreme Being who watches over the oppressed innocent and punishes triumphant crime—that alone can be the belief of the people." The argument was conclusive. To brand a thing "aristocratic" in France in 1793, was like calling a thing "bourgeois" in Russia in 1917. Hébert, his wife, and a number of other members of his party were dragged off to the guillotine, and the Goddess of Reason was made to abdicate in favor of the Supreme Being. In June, 1794, Robespierre himself led in the celebration of a festival of the Supreme Being. Arrayed in dazzling vestments and bearing a huge sheaf of wheat-ears and flowers—it is said he was going mad at this time—the old zealot strode at the head of a procession to the Champs de Mars in Paris. Papier-maché figures representing Vice and Atheism were ceremoniously burnt, and then a statue of Wisdom was lamely hoisted out of the flames and set on high. And thus was Deism proclaimed the official religion in France.[24]

But the worship of the Supreme Being lasted no longer than that of Reason. Within a month of the celebration at the Champs de Mars, Robespierre was no more. His jaw shot away in the scuffle at the time of his arrest, the wretched old man was dragged to the guillotine and beheaded. And that was the end of Deism in France, even as it was the end of the Terror. Catholic worship was restored to legality in 1795 and the priests began to flock back to their parishes.

Napoleon, who soon became dictator of the land, gave impetus to the reaction, for he saw that he could make use of the Church. With the populace restrained and distracted by religious devotion, he knew he would be less hampered in his effort to dominate France. He himself made no pretensions to devoutness. When he raised himself to the imperial throne in 1806 he asked the pope to officiate at the coronation, but only because he wanted to adhere to the imperial tradition. Napoleon had no reverence for the pontiff, and had already threatened and bullied him into a position of resentful subservience. The Corsican was very careful during the ceremony to put the crown on his head with his own hands; to the pope he relegated only the secondary office of anointing him and blessing the coronation.

But whatever may have been Napoleon's reasons for restoring the Church, the effect was the same. The people began to attend Masses and go to Confession as of yore, and the priests again became a power in the land. And

[24] See F. A. Aulard, *Le Culte de la raison et de l'être suprême,* 1892.

thus terminated the first great effort in modern times to stamp out Christianity by violence.

12

WITH the fall of Napoleon the tide of reaction became a flood, and not alone in France but also in all the other lands, Protestant as well as Catholic. Europe had been in bloody turmoil for more than a decade, and the populace was exhausted. Men no longer cared to doubt and seek freedom; they yearned only to have faith and be content. The past took on a new glamor and both the art and thought of the period took to reeking delicately with the pleasant mustiness of a romanticized medievalism. And with this nostalgia for the past came a renewed interest in Catholicism. It was very comforting after a generation of bewilderment to return to the calm and quiet of the ancient faith. Men were weary of striving to puzzle things out for themselves. They preferred to believe that all problems had long been solved and that the priests knew all the solutions. As a consequence, the hierarchy, after years of oppression in France and neglect in the other Catholic lands, began to regain its ancient prestige.

So changed was the attitude of the laity that it even seemed safe for Rome to let the Jesuits loose again. The ban on the Society was rescinded in 1814 and its members were again sent out into the world to advance the Catholic cause. A vigor faintly reminiscent of the Catholic Revival of the late sixteenth century crept into the Church, and Rome began once more to dream of ruling all Christendom. In 1816 the pope published an encyclical letter branding Bible Societies "a fiendish instrument for the undermining of the foundation of religion." In 1824 a second attack was launched, this time against rationalism as well as evangelicalism. The following year a great jubilee was held in Rome to celebrate the anniversary of the suppression of the Revolution. Three new saints were canonized, and the miraculous flight of a half-roasted bird from the spit in St. Peter's gave plain proof of God's delight in the ceremony. Indulgences were promised to all who would pray for the extirpation of heresy and infidelism, and, as though to anticipate the inevitable effect of these prayers, one hundred and fifty Protestants and Jews were converted there and then.

There were not many, however, who showed signs of following the lead of those converts and a year later the pope, apparently in the hope of stimulating the sluggish tide, let it be known to the whole world that:

> Whosoever is separated from the Roman Catholic Church, however unblamable his life may be in other respects, because of the sole offense that he is sundered from the unity of Christ, has no part in eternal life. God's wrath hangs over him!

It was vain, however, for the pope to try to frighten the Protestants back into the Catholic fold. A few of the cultured in England did go over to Rome, most notably John Henry (later Cardinal) Newman; but their conversion was quantitatively of small significance.[25] Protestantism had sufficient resources to enjoy its own revival during the reaction following on Napoleon's fall, and its war-shocked and world-weary communicants had no need to resort to Catholicism for comfort.

A new wave of evangelical enthusiasm swept across England during the second quarter of the nineteenth century. It had but slight influence on the gentry, for the Established Church with its decorous services seemed quite sufficient unto the needs of men well-fed and soft-bedded. But among the disinherited and the woebegone it mounted like a flood. The movement was stimulated in part by an eloquent Presbyterian minister in London named Edward Irving, who went around preaching that the "gifts" of the apostolic age could easily be restored if only the people would have enough faith. Deposed from the Presbyterian ministry in 1832, Irving began to organize a new denomination, which later called itself the Catholic Apostolic Church. Ruled by twelve apostles who claimed to be the mouthpieces of the Holy Ghost, the new cult soon developed an elaborate ritual of its own and eventually succumbed to the blight of stagnation. But while its spirit flourished the volatile movement exercised widespread influence not alone in England, but also in Germany and in the United States.

A second manifestation of the Protestant revival was the rise of the "Brethren" movement in England. Pious Christians who believed that faith and love were the only fundamentals in the teaching of Jesus, began to band them-

[25] For the history of this much publicized movement see S. L. Ollard, *The Anglo-Catholic Revival,* and R. Church, *The Oxford Movement.*

selves together in brotherhoods and seek the conversion of their neighbors. They had no thought of organizing a new denomination. On the contrary, one of their express purposes was to destroy all denominations and unite the whole human race in one great fellowship of faith in the loving Christ. For that reason they strenuously opposed all professional ministries and established rituals, for in these things they recognized the root cause of religious divisiveness. They maintained that all true believers were priests and that all alike were guided by the Spirit.

They failed of their purpose, of course. Led by an indefatigable exhorter named John Nelson Darby, the movement grew not alone in Plymouth, where he began his labors in 1830, but also in Switzerland, France, Germany, and especially North America. And then it became a denomination unto itself. The Plymouth Brethren, now multiplied in number and widely scattered, were compelled by sheer force of circumstances to organize themselves, establish a discipline of worship, and submit to the rule of chosen officers. The Spirit by itself had been found wanting as a governing agency even in the relatively simple society of the ancients. How then could it possibly be effective in the complex world of the nineteenth century?

Indeed, these Plymouth Brethren did not merely become a separate denomination. Before long they fell out among themselves over questions of belief and organization and eventually divided into six distinct sub-denominations!

The Irvingites and Plymouth Brethren were but two of many contemporary movements within the Protestant ranks which sought to restore the religion to its primitive fervor.

No one of them succeeded to any conspicuous degree, but all of them together managed to exert a profound influence. Especially was this true in the United States, where a population largely of humble origin lived a chronically unsettled life in an atmosphere as full of paralyzing terror as of intoxicating hopes. Existence in such an environment was almost unendurable without frequent indulgence in religious frenzy. Outbursts of adventist hysteria could occur only in time of crisis in Europe, for ordinarily the populace there felt rooted and secure. But in America, where life for most men was a succession of sudden, bewildering, and unusually unprecedented experiences, the feeling that the world might come to an end at any moment was in the air continually.[26]

As a consequence the wandering exhorters enjoyed a wider and steadier popularity in the United States than anywhere else in the world. Men like Jonathan Edwards, George Whitefield, and Herbert Asbury, had kept the colonists in a state of almost uninterrupted religious excitation until the outbreak of the American Revolution gave the populace a new vent for its overwrought nerves. And once the reaction set in after the Revolution, devotional frenzy became more intense than ever. A conflagration of faith broke out in the forest of Kentucky, spreading thence until the whole frontier was aflame.

One of the characteristic expressions of the revival of faith was the Adventist movement started in 1831 by Wil-

[26] See Davenport, *Primitive Traits in Religious Revivals.* A very vigorous journalistic account of the whole subject is to be found in Loud, *Evangelized America.* See also the pertinent chapters in William Warren Sweet's very recent work, *The Story of Religions in America,* New York, 1930.

liam Miller, a Baptist farmer from Vermont. On the basis
of calculations from the book of Daniel this ingenious yet
very naïve man arrived at the conclusion that the world
would come to an end in 1843. Such prophecies had been
made before in Christian history, and though they had all
failed of fulfillment the poorer folk were still ready to
take one more chance. Such folk were relieved to think
that the End was in sight, for, as has already been said,
they had everything to gain and nothing to lose by a
change. They went as wild with trembling expectancy at
the approach of the year 1843 as they had at the approach
of 1666 or 1000—or Passover of the year 29 A.D.

For more than ten years William Miller kept running
about the countryside and sounding the alarm, and thousands were won over to his belief. They were, for the
most part, simple folk whose intelligences were so strained
by the task of checking William Miller's arithmetic that
they had no energy left to inquire into his exegesis. Once
they saw that the prophet had made no mistake in his
additions and subtractions, they were sure he could not
have erred in his Bible interpretations. So they let the
spades fall from their hands, perhaps returned the things
they had stolen, or had borrowed and had hoped to keep,
drained the whiskey kegs, forgave their enemies, and sat
down to wait for the End.

The year 1843 arrived, dragged out its days, and went;
but still the world continued. Miller was appalled, but
only for a moment. On reëxamining his calculations he
discovered that he had erred by one year and that the
Second Coming of Christ was really scheduled for 1844—
October 22, to be precise. And the people took the

prophet's word this second time as credulously as they had the first. When time proved even the revised prediction erroneous, they still continued to believe in Miller's mathematical scheme, though many now ceased to believe that he knew how to employ it. The Adventist Movement persisted somewhat like a fiery nebula in the Protestant firmament, waxing in heat and waning from time to time, breaking up and coalescing at intervals, but all the while radiating long waves of fervor to the other nebulæ in the region.

Some of the Adventists went off and started little communist colonies like the Adonai Shomo ("The Lord is Here"), which endured until the beginning of the twentieth century. Others sought to prove themselves of the "chosen remnant" by observing Saturday as the Sabbath rather than Sunday. Still others insisted that only those baptized by total immersion were eligible for salvation. But all were agreed, at least, that the Lord was on His way, and that at any moment now this wicked world would come to an end. At the present time there are approximately one hundred and fifty thousand men and women in the United States alone who belong to various Adventist denominations, and no one knows how many millions more who are more or less influenced by the Adventist idea!

But an even more striking revelation of the religious hysteria in the early nineteenth century is afforded by the rise of Mormonism. In 1827 a farmer named Joseph Smith suddenly arose and proclaimed that he had dug up near Manchester, New York, a supplement to the Bible inscribed on gold plates and entitled the Book of Mormon.

Smith had translated the mysterious characters in this book by means of a pair of magic spectacles, and this translation he now began to hawk about in the neighborhood. (The original, he averred, had magically disappeared after he completed the translation.) According to this Book of Mormon, the American Indians were the Lost Ten Tribes, and the New Jerusalem was destined to arise in their land. The miracle had been postponed so long because the Indians had fallen into sin. Now, however, the time was ripe for a generation of "latter-day saints" to inherit the legacy of the tribesmen; and Joseph Smith had been divinely called to show how this was to be accomplished.

To inquire into Smith's motivations would be futile. As is not uncommon in men of peasant stock, his mind was an irreducible compound of naïve credulity and shrewd craft, complicated in his case by epilepsy or perhaps paranoia. That he himself believed what he said is almost certain. And largely because of this conviction which flared in his eyes, he was able to convince others. Soon he had a following; and the first church of the Latter-Day Saints was founded in Fayette, New York, in 1830. Driven thence by the "gentiles"—for the Mormons reckoned themselves the only true Israelites and applied the term "gentiles" to all who disagreed with them, even the Jews—these zealots moved on to Ohio, where they gained many more converts. Meeting with persecution there, too, they wandered farther West and laid the foundations of the New Zion at a place in Illinois which Smith named Nauvoo.

The commonwealth appealed strongly to a certain element on the frontier, for it was completely paternalistic and relieved the followers of the need to think for themselves. Joseph Smith was supposedly an avatar of God and was guided at every turn by "visions." The followers had need only to obey his commands, to work hard at whatever tasks he assigned them, and the rest was assured. They received not alone their food and shelter in the present, but were guaranteed an eternal reward in the future.

The company of the Saints waxed mightily, and Nauvoo might have prospered had not the prophet, like "King" Johann Buckholdt at Münster in the sixteenth century, suddenly received a "vision" restoring the institution of polygamy. The dispensation seemed to be required by Mormon theology, which taught that God, who was continually creating souls, counted those men and women most virtuous who produced the largest number of bodies to contain the souls. Polygamy may also have seemed desirable because Mormonism, like every other such cult, had attracted a preponderance of women converts.

The majority of the "saints" did not dare question the propriety of the innovation, even though polygamy was prohibited by the law of the land. But the "gentiles" in the neighborhood were aroused to uncontrollable rage and put Smith to death. Brigham Young, one of Smith's lieutenants, now took charge, leading the "saints" through the wilderness to distant Utah. There, thanks to his extraordinary abilities and to the pathetic faithfulness of his awed followers, the Mormon community flourished exceedingly. Only a frenzied belief in glories to come could have moved a peasant population to do what the Mormons did

[409]

in Utah. By incessant toil and abstemious living they changed a wasteland into an orchard and built up one of the most prosperous states in the West.

But only in its success was Mormonism unique. In its essential character it was but one more attempt on the part of the peasantry to attain the Kingdom of Heaven in haste. The nineteenth century witnessed the rise of several such movements: for instance, the Amana Society and the Koreishan Ecclesia in America, the Doukhobors in Russia, and similar communistic cults in England and Germany. If Mormonism was able to thrive as did none of the others, it was in large part because Brigham Young set up his New Zion in far-off Utah, whence there was almost no escape for the recreant or the faint-hearted. As soon, however, as the railroads penetrated the Rockies and the "gentiles" were able to crowd in on the Latter-Day Saints, the movement ceased to wax in might. Thanks to its vigorous start, and to the redoubtable system of hierarchical domination which Young had established, the Mormon Church was able to prosper materially. But there was no keeping its spirit from flagging. Even the importation of fresh drafts of converts from the peasant population of Europe proved of little avail. Once those converts or their children were relieved of the need to bend all day over their plows, and could look up and see the world, there was a swift waning of the credulity which had made Mormonism possible.

It was the same with all the other cults and denominations created or reinvigorated by the wave of reaction in the first half of the nineteenth century. Those which had failed to win large followings or establish themselves on a sound material basis, were wiped out; and the others began to crumble and lose ground. For the spirit of re-action could not endure. The world had faltered for a moment in its march toward freedom—but only for a moment.

13

HERE was no restoring the old authoritarianism, neither in religion nor in politics. No sooner had the prelates and princes clambered back onto their thrones, than the fires of revolution began to flare once more. The years 1830 witnessed bloody disturbances in France, Belgium and Poland. In 1832 popular disaffec-tion in England compelled the pass-ing of the democratic First Reform Bill. In 1835 the word "Socialism" came into currency in connection with the novel economic theories of a Manchester cotton spinner named Robert Owen. In 1848 there were more uprisings throughout Europe. In 1856 even Russia, until then almost unaffected by the changes in Europe, began to yield to the new spirit and grant emancipation to its serfs. And in 1861 an anti-clerical movement in Italy confiscated most of the Papal States and established Victor Emmanuel as the constitutional ruler of a united land.

Necessarily this fresh surge of revolution could not be confined to the political sphere. Men who dared to deny the divine right of kings were not prone to bend the knee

before priests. Skepticism returned to the offensive and
religious authority began to give ground as never before.
What most weakened its resistance was the mutiny within
the ranks of the authoritarians themselves. More and
more theologians became infected with the virus of rationalism, and even the Bible, the very corner stone of Christian belief, began to be subjected by them to scientific
scrutiny. The verbal inspiration of the Old Testament
had already been challenged on textual grounds by
Spinoza in the seventeenth century, and more systematically by two Frenchmen, Simon and Astruc, in the
eighteenth century. Now a whole battalion of scholars
began to train their critical armaments on the Holy
Writ, and not on the Old Testament alone but also on
the New.

The assault was most vigorous in Germany, where the
increase of national prosperity had brought with it a revulsion against the Pietism that had been born in the times
of distress. The "Enlightenment" (*Aufklärung*) which had
flamed up in the late eighteenth century, began to flare as
never before in the middle of the nineteenth. A professor
at Tübingen named Ferdinand Christian Baur, a scholar
of indisputable standing, became persuaded that the entire
religion called Christianity had first come into being not
as a sudden revelation but as a result of a strained process
of evolution. He discovered that at least two widely discrepant types of belief ran through the New Testament:
that of the original Brethren gathered in Jerusalem, who
had believed in Jesus the Son of Man, and that of Paul's
converts, who had worshiped Christ the Son of God. One
of Baur's students, David Frederick Strauss, went further

and published a work in 1835 to show this Pauline Christ to have been the product of sheer myth.[27] A generation later, Ernest Renan, a brilliant French scholar, popularized Strauss's theory in a beautiful though somewhat melodramatic *Life of Jesus;* and then the havoc that was being wrought in the foundations of Christian tradition became a public scandal.

In the interim new discoveries in other branches of knowledge had done much to undermine those foundations. The severest blow came with the publication of Darwin's *Origin of Species* in 1859, for the theory of evolution which that work expounded seemed to discredit the very first chapter of the Bible. If Darwin was right— and the fundamentals of his theory seemed irrefutable— then the whole story of Adam and Eve became a fable. And if Adam and Eve never existed, what became of the doctrines of Original Sin and the Atonement? The traditionalists had somehow been able to swallow Copernicanism. Even the Catholic Church had given the heliocentric theory tacit approval when it quietly dropped Galileo's books from the Index in 1832. But Darwinism was beyond assimilation, for its theory of how man came into the world was quite irreconcilable with the Bible account. Ingenious conservatives like the English statesman, W. E. Gladstone, did indeed try to effect a reconciliation, but only at an expense of compromises which few clear thinkers on either side were willing to make. The break between the scientific and the traditional accounts was far

[27] For the history of this significant movement see K. R. Hagenbach, *German Rationalism,* Eng. tr., 1864. J. F. Hurst, *History of Rationalism* is unsympathetic and preachy.

too wide now to be straddled. Either Genesis was history or a story.[28]

The Catholic Church, true to its past, had no hesitancy in choosing. It took its stand with the tradition and proceeded to fulminate vehemently against all who presumed to doubt. As though to provoke the freethinkers, the Church actually set up a new target for their missiles by promulgating the dogma of the Immaculate Conception in 1854. Even in the credulous Middle Ages there had been dispute as to whether the mother of Jesus had been conceived without the taint of Original Sin; yet now, in a world rife with doubt and denial, Rome suddenly proclaimed that detail an indispensable dogma of faith! . . . And ten years later the same pope, Pius IX, went further, and in a somewhat promiscuous Syllabus of Errors condemned Pantheism, Naturalism, Rationalism, Indifferentism, Protestantism, Religious Toleration, Socialism, Communism, Secret Societies, Bible Circles, and all other such "pests."

Nor was that the end. In 1869 the pontiff climaxed his reign by getting himself proclaimed infallible in his decisions concerning matters of faith and morals. The act was prompted, one suspects, by bravado rather than confidence. Italy was raging with anti-clericalism, and the pope was threatened with the loss of every last vestige of his territorial possessions. There was even talk among some of the radical patriots of driving him out of the land. And it was perhaps in a desperate effort to save his face

[28] See Otto Pfleiderer, *The Development of Theology since Kant and its Progress in Great Britain since 1825.*

[414]

before the world that the pope had himself proclaimed infallible. Reft of his temporal power, he could at least reiterate that he was still supreme spiritually. Therefore he caused it to be decreed that he, as Roman Pontiff, was "possessed of the infallibility with which the divine Redeemer willed that his Church should be endowed." Moreover, "if anyone (which may God avert) presume to contradict this our definition, let him be Anathema." [29]

But the great day of absolutism was passed. The Catholic masses, anxious to believe that there was someone in the world who knew just what was right and what was wrong, sighed with relief when the pope was proclaimed infallible. But the emancipated either smiled cynically or became incensed. There was widespread murmuring within the Church itself, and certain of the clerics, especially in Germany, made open protest. And when the foremost of them, a distinguished church historian named von Döllinger, was excommunicated for his recalcitrance, a number of the insurgents felt compelled to start a new organization which they called the Old Catholic Church. The majority of the disaffected priests, however, were reluctant to take this drastic step, for they believed they could accomplish far more by agitating from within the Mother Church. Influenced by certain enlightened professors at the Catholic Institute in Paris and other seminaries, they began to demand that Rome reinterpret its teachings in the light of the new knowledge that had come into the world. These clerics had learnt from the biologists that nothing can live without change, and they declared

[29] *Dogmatic Canons and Decrees*, New York, 1912, p. 256.

that even the Church, if it would endure, must evolve. Following the lead of advanced Catholic scholars like Duchesne and Loisy, they began to subject the Bible and the whole history of the Catholic Church to critical examination. And they produced vigorous writers like Franz Kraus and Herman Schell in Germany, Father Tyrrell, a Jesuit in England, and Fogazzaro in Italy, who argued the case for progressive religion with courage and no little ability.

Modernism, as this insurgent movement came to be called, began to assume grave proportions as the nineteenth century drew to a close, partly because the reigning pope, Leo XIII, was himself a man of scholarly tastes and considerable liberalism. But his successor, Pius X, was a man who had begun his career as a parish priest and had never outgrown the parish point of view, and under him Modernism was shown no quarter. In the year of this pope's accession, 1903, five of Loisy's books were placed on the Index; and four years later a papal encyclical explicitly condemned the whole Modernist system. Many of the priests suspected of Modernistic learnings were demoted and scattered to remote parishes, and Loisy and Tyrrell were actually excommunicated.

These measures, however, merely drove the movement underground, and such a flood of anonymous literature began to well up in clerical circles that the pope was forced to take further steps. He ordered that all professors in Roman Catholic universities, and all ordinands, take oath that they adhered unreservedly to the condemnations in his encyclical. The few who refused were forced out of the Church, and a ramifying system of Jesuit espionage saw to it that the rest kept their word. And thus was the Modernist movement stamped out—at least for the moment.[30]

14

THE stubborn resistance to progress set up by the Roman Church was impossible in the Protestant denominations. Not merely did they lack the inner integrity contributed by an unbroken tradition, and the outward solidity produced by a centralized authority, but to boot they had to reckon with a revolutionized order of existence. Life in the Protestant world had come to be dominated by the towns, and the towns had always been the breeding places of heresy. Though millions continued to live on farms, they had ceased to be country folk, for the means of communication had so multiplied that even the rural regions had become suburban. The transition—perhaps the profoundest in the history of civilization—had as yet failed to occur to so grave an extent in the Catholic lands, and the opening years of the twentieth century found the masses there still rooted to the soil. But it had overwhelmed the Protestant regions by then, bringing in its train a whole host of consequences profoundly disturbing to religion.

In the first place, the industrial revolution had begun

[30] For the history of the movement see, among many other works, Loisy's *Modernism*, 1905, and *My Duel with the Vatican*, 1924. For fictional treatments read Fogazzaro's *The Saint*, and an anonymous novel entitled *The Priest, a Tale of Modernism in New England*, Boston, 1911.

to empty man of his age-old awe of the elements. No matter how diligently he had plowed his field and sown his seed while a farmer, without the aid of rain and sun it had all been labor wasted. That was why he had been so prone to worship Heaven in those days: he had been dependent largely on non-human help for his very existence. But now all that was beginning to be changed. Come rain, come shine, the town-dweller could always ply his trade. The forces upon which he was dependent for his bread were largely of his own invention, and as a consequence he was far less apprehensive of the powers beyond his ken. His emancipation was as yet by no means complete. He was, after all, the son of his fathers, and vestiges of the ancient dreads continued to rankle in his breast. Besides, there were still evils a-plenty with which he had not yet learnt to cope. But nevertheless he had indeed made some progress.

It was this radical change in the essential outlook on life that presented the severest challenge to Protestantism. Either the denominations had to revise their creeds and reorient their purposes, or die. The plight of man was not unlike that which had darkened his life in the days when the Roman order fell into decay. The old assurances had crumbled, and new ones were needed to stay him in the whirl which was existence. But these new assurances had to suit the new age. They had to be credible to minds emancipated by science and satisfy souls crushed by the machine.

There was still need for religion; indeed, the need was more bitter and desperate in the late nineteenth century than ever before. Inventiveness had raced far ahead of intelligence, and the machine had developed into a Frank-enstein. The few who had been able to adapt themselves to the industrial order had flourished; but the rest, the vast majority, had gone under. Never in all history had the disparity between the lot of the common folk and that of the masters been so gross. The suddenly swollen cities had become vast slums in which hordes of toilers swarmed in want and woe. They had been somewhat freed of their dependence on the heavenly elements, but only to become thrice as dependent on their human employers. And what they craved was a religion able to relieve them of this dependence. Christianity had once been such a religion. In its very first days it had cried out thunderously against the oppressor; it had declared to the rich that Heaven would never receive them unless they gave away all to the poor. It had been the common man's religion in those generations, and that was why it had so prevailed. And it needed to become the common man's religion once more—if it would endure.

Nor was that all. Protestantism, if it would endure, had to become the emancipated man's religion as well. As we have already seen, the industrial revolution had begun to play havoc with the credulousness which had so long darkened the mind of the race. Popular education coupled with the complex stimuli of a mechanized civilization had brought to the ordinary man's ken all sorts of notions disturbing to his traditional beliefs. Doubts had begun to creep into his mind, doubts which his father could not have even conceived of, but which he, and still more his son, found day by day more tormenting.

The problem confronting Protestantism was thus apparently twofold: to reassert the social teachings once cardinal in Christianity, and to revise the creed in the light of contemporary knowledge. Of the two, though the first was by far the more important task, the second proved for the while the more appealing. Increasing numbers of Protestant scholars not alone in Germany, but also in Great Britain and the United States, began to devote themselves to the critical study of the Bible and the objective analysis of religious experience, and the so-called "broad" church became almost the fashion. With few exceptions those scholars were churchmen, and some held high office in their respective denominations. By and large they were men of genuine piety, and they labored at their tasks only for the greater glory of God. Of course, they encountered considerable opposition, for the bulk of the churchgoing population could not appreciate their motives. The closing years of the nineteenth century, and the opening years of the twentieth witnessed a succession of quite violent attempts to oust those "broad" churchmen and suppress their teachings. But the attempts were futile. By the second decade of the twentieth century the "higher criticism" of the Bible and the evolutionary interpretation of religious history had found their places in the curricula of the better seminaries throughout the Protestant world, and the majority of the pastors in the more influential urban churches were men quite at home in rationalism.

And then—perhaps a little belatedly—concerted efforts began to be made to bring this new understanding to the laity. A widespread educational movement was started in the churches, and rounded religious instruction rather than bibliolatrous recitation became the ideal in the Sunday schools. Much of the zeal which had been devoted for over a century to foreign missions, was turned now in the direction of the universities at home. Earnest and often very brilliant men gave themselves to the task of providing a new devotion to young men and women whom secular education had robbed of their ancestral faith. Student evangelical societies were founded, conventions were held, periodicals were published, and tracts were scattered far and wide. There was a mighty stir in many small circles, a great rushing to and fro, and a vast amount of organizing.

But the other and more imperative task, that of reasserting the pristine social doctrines of Christianity, went largely neglected. The few individuals who did realize its gravity found it impossible to stir the rest in the church councils. Attempts were made to found "Christian Socialist" groups in certain of the universities, and occasional preachers tried to make their churches centers of radicalism in the community. But exceedingly little came of such efforts. The conservative quality inherent in organized religion, buttressed here by the vested interests of many of the dominant religionists, proved an insurmountable barrier in the path of those who sought to make Christianity once more a gospel of social justice. The Socialist movement, by now already a significant element in the spiritual life of the Western world, had to grow without benefit of clergy. Protestantism seemed as committed to an acquisitive capitalistic system as

Catholicism was still fundamentally committed to feudalism.

Protestantism was by no means lacking in a realization of its responsibilities toward society. Indeed, its conscience in that regard was perhaps more keenly developed now than ever before. But even so the bulk of the church-going folk could not be moved to have a share in the work of radical social reconstruction. At most they could be aroused against flagrant but essentially secondary evils. They played a conspicuous part—except in regions where it was economically too disadvantageous—in the movement to abolish slavery, and their initiative was almost exclusively responsible for the crusades against intemperance and commercialized vice. They took an interest in societies for the prevention of cruelty to children and animals, helped agitate for prison reform, and through their very active missionary groups did a little to lighten the miseries of exploited heathen races. But the root evil, the iniquity of the entire acquisitive system, was left untouched. At most, benevolent palliatives received church support. Various of the wealthier congregations set up agencies in neighboring slums to provide food and clothing for the destitute. They founded hospitals, orphanages, and almshouses. On another level, interdenominational bodies like the Young Men's Christian Association came into existence to bring the light of faith and the warmth of fellowship into the bleak life of the "wage-slaves."

But the really indispensable efforts seemed beyond the capacity of the denominations. At most they could offer relief for the sickness of society, but they could not cure.

And this profound impotence, once it became plain to those worst afflicted by the sickness, began to tell on organized religion. Of a sudden the church leaders awoke to realize that they were becoming shepherds without any flocks. The situation appeared less critical in the Catholic communion, for it was integrated, stoutly walled against all doubt, and had its center in lands as yet only moderately affected by the industrial revolution. But Protestantism, torn into unnumbered fragments, open to attack on every side, seemed lost.

15

 ND then all at once the situation reversed itself. The whole bottom of the capitalistic order suddenly fell through, and the world discovered itself plunged into a war without parallel in all its history. The immediate consequence was a galvanic stir in most of the religious establishments. Hysteria took hold of Christendom, and the churchmen, mistaking it for righteous zeal, became full of hope once more. Exceedingly few among them dared cry out against the holocaust, and those few were hounded like felons. The rest, blind to every consideration save that here at last had come salvation for their organizations, seemed almost to rejoice over the war. Young men who had never before thought of Christ were now seeing him lead-

ing their battalions; old men who had long ago forgotten him were now falling to their knees and imploring his aid. And the sight of such wonders moved many of the churchmen to declare that the war was a blessing in disguise. It might decimate the population, they conceded, and shatter the fairest works of man; but, once it was ended, it would leave the race more religious than ever before.

They were not altogether wrong. The World War did bring about a perceptible improvement in the fortunes of the religious establishments. Naturally enough, the Catholic Church profited the most, for in the stress of the war days, and even more in the confusion that came after them, it seemed the one stable thing left in the world. Flames of neo-Catholic enthusiasm began to leap up much as in the period following the Napoleonic wars. Aggressive Catholic missions arose in England and elsewhere, and Catholic writers, many of them recent converts, took to belaying the world with crushing arguments for their faith. The Vatican, never wider awake in its history, took advantage of its sudden popularity to win back a little of what it had lost in 1870. After prolonged negotiations with the reactionary party then ruling in Italy, the pope succeeded in 1929 in becoming once more a temporal ruler. His realm was not extensive: merely the Vatican quarter within the city of Rome. But at least it was a realm. Released at last from his voluntary imprisonment, the pontiff was able to urge the cause of his Church with a new aggressiveness. With the aid of the radio and an efficient press-bureau he was able now to make his voice heard all around the world. What he had to say was in no sense novel. On the contrary, his pronouncements—for instance his encyclical on marriage and morals published in January 1931—might fitly have been made in the thirteenth century. But that only rendered his words the more appealing. The world had grown weary of novelties; it ached to go back to the old ways and rest for a while.

Protestantism was far less well prepared to profit by the wave of reaction. Its tendency for more than half a century had been irregularly but surely toward liberalism, and now that the times seemed to call for retreat many of the denominational leaders were bewildered. Some few kept their heads, insisting that the reaction was only temporary; but the rest became terrified. What edged their fright was the reported chaos that had overwhelmed Russia. The radicals there had had their unrestrained way, and now they were trampling religion underfoot. The Bolshevists, all of them devout apostles of rationalism, were carrying the doctrine to what was apparently its logical conclusion, and were suppressing all belief. The Russian Orthodox Church, for centuries one of the most affluent and stable institutions in Christendom, had been despoiled and brought to shame, and a whole population was being systematically taught to count it accursed. Some of the Protestants who had been even in the vanguard of the rationalist movement were taken aback by that spectacle; and the conservatives were of course thrown into panic. A revolution against all forms of free-thought swept through the denominations. Save in one of the smallest of them, the Unitarian, the one prevailing tendency was toward either a crypto-Catholic sacramentalism or a vituperatively evangelistic obscurantism.

The sacramentalist movement was confined almost entirely to the upper strata in the churches, and showed little sign of enduring. But the sweep toward obscurantism got its support from the masses, and was therefore a far more formidable development. It had its origin, it would seem, in the common man's belated recognition of what the new knowledge had done to his ancient faith. Until then he had not looked to see, for he had felt sure that his faith was safe. But the ordeal of the World War had impelled him to reach out, and lo, he had discovered his faith was no longer there! The new knowledge had taken it away, and he was left now to drift without sign of a mooring. He himself had been reduced by this new knowledge to the status of a mere animal, and his earth to a mere crumb of stellar dust. His familiar God had been banished from the sky, and his virgin-born Son of God from history. What was there left for him to believe in?

It was the shock of this discovery that impelled the "foolish of the world" to throw themselves as they did into the obscurantist movement. Blind with terror, they clutched at the fragments still left of their old religion, made a tower of them, and screamed curses at those who would tear it down. They were finished with science; it was too dangerous. Henceforth they would be "Fundamentalists," believing the Bible from cover to cover, and clinging to every one of the traditional assurances. They would believe as had their fathers—with all their heart and with all their soul and with all their might. And, because their will to believe was very desperate in the terror of that day, they *did* believe as had their fathers.

It was the age-old rythm of shock and recoil repeating itself once more. Man, too sure of himself yesterday, was not sure enough today. His head bloodied and his spirit dashed, he was taking to cover for the moment. But it was only for the moment. One more battle in the war for the mind's liberation had been lost; and lost decisively. But the war—that was still on. . . .

THE END

INDEX

INDEX

Abelard, his confession concerning his own abbey, 195, 196
Act of Toleration (1689), 349
Acts, book of, 22, 61, 85
Adams, Henry, cited footnote page 174
Adonai Shomo, 407
Adonis, a Syrian god, 26, 34, 35
Adrian VI, 323
Adventist movement (1831), 406, 407
Ætius, a celebrated Christian theologian, 130, 131
Against the Murderous and Thieving Rabble of the Peasants, a pamphlet by Luther, 295, 296
Ages of Faith, really Ages of Acquiescence, 238
Alexander VI, his purchase of the papal throne in 1492, 276
Amana Society, 410
Ambrose, a consummate statesman, ultimately made a saint, 141
Anabaptists, 304-309
Anglican Church, 300, 349, 350, 389-391
Angus, S., cited footnote page 32
Anthony, the first historic character to go into the wilderness, 152, 153
Antioch, 24, 31, 35, 39, 41, 46, 56, 80, 120, 124, 130, 142
Anti-Trinitarianism, 380
Antonio, St., of Florence, 239
Apocalypses, 6, 77
Apollinaris, Bishop of, 133
Aquinas, St. Thomas, 236, 366, 373

Arius, 122-125
Arminianism, 351
Asbury, Francis, an exhorter, 393, 405
Ashley, cited footnote page 271
Asklepios, who raised the dead, 68
Astruc, Old Testament challenged by, 412
Athanasius, 125-127
Attis, a Phrygian god, 26
Audin, cited footnote page 310
Augsburg, Treaty of (1555), 297, 298
Augustine, 137-139
Aulard, F. A., cited footnote page 400
Aurelius, Marcus, one of the sagest rulers in history, 103

Babylonian Exile, 6
Bacon, B. W., cited footnotes pages 25, 61
Bacon, Sir Francis, a publicist, 365, 366
Bacon, Roger, an English friar of the 13th century, 362, 363
Badger, G. P., cited footnote page 135
Baker, G. P., cited footnote page 110
Baldwin, F. E., cited footnote page 314
Baptism, 42, 139
Barbarians, 146, 148, 149, 161, 163, 164
Barbarossa, the Emperor Frederick, 222
Baur, F. C., cited footnote page 23

INDEX

Bax, cited footnote page 309

Beard, cited footnote page 352

Believers in Jesus, 15-18

Bellarmine, Cardinal, a devout Catholic apologist, 368

Belloc, cited footnote page 396

Benedict IX, ascended papal throne at age of twelve, 189

Benedict, St., the man chiefly responsible for monastic reform, 157-160

Benedictines, the chief instruments in the conversion of the Barbarians, 160, 161

Berkeley, Bishop, 379

Bethune-Baker, J. F., cited footnote page 135

Beza, cited footnote page 312

Bible, 240, 254, 257, 258, 281, 282, 303, 308, 325, 348, 353, 374, 412

Bidez, cited footnote page 129

"Black Death" in England, 258

Blake, W. W., cited footnote page 111

Bohemian rulers in 15th century, 273

Boleyn, Anne, 300

Bolshevists, apostles of rationalism, 425

Boniface VIII, 229, 230

Bonnet, cited footnote page 312

Bonosus, a 4th century bishop, 139

Book of Mormon, 408

Borgia, Cæsar, son of Alexander VI, 276, 277

Borgia, Lucrezia, daughter of Alexander VI, 276, 277

Botticelli, 279

Bovet, cited footnote page 385

Brahe, Tycho, a Danish astronomer, 364

Brinton, cited footnote page 398

Broglie, De, cited footnote page 344

Browne, Robert, a dissenting clergyman, 349, 350

Browning, cited footnote page 322

Bruce, cited footnote page 230

Brunneleschi, 279

Bruno, Giordano, a 16th century scientist, 370, 371

Bryce, cited footnote page 187

Buckholdt, Johann, a leader of the Anabaptists, 308

Bultmann, R., cited footnote pages 4, 26

Burnet, cited footnote pages 300, 301

Bury, cited footnote pages 354, 375

Butler, Bishop, 389

Butzer, 311

Calvary, 3

Calvin, 310, 311, 312, 313, 314, 315, 316, 318, 319, 321

Calvinism, 317-322, 351, 352, 394

Calvinistic Methodists, 394

Campanella, a philosopher, 367, 370

Canterbury Tales, Chaucer, 255

Capronymus, Constantine, son of Leo the Isaurian, 177, 178

Caracalla, a degenerate ruler, 103

Carus, Paul, cited footnote page 31

Case, S. J., cited footnotes pages 4, 38

Cassiodorus, a contemporary of Benedict, 161

Cathari, the, history of, 245

Catherine II of Russia, 378

Catholic Apostolic Church, 403

Catholic Church, 190, 208, 246, 272, 339, 347, 413, 414, 424

"Catholic Church," denominated Roman, 145

Catholicism, 190, 298, 317, 320, 324, 325, 330, 333, 343, 345, 364, 394

.INDEX

Charlemagne, 160

Charles, later Charlemagne, 185

Charles. E., cited footnote page 363

Charles V, a Spaniard and a devoutly orthodox man, 297, 323

Cherbury, Lord Herbert of, 390

Christ, 41, 43, 44, 45, 70, 72, 73, 75, 82, 83, 91, 95, 96, 104, 114, 119, 120, 122, 123, 128, 134, 135, 149, 151, 165, 166, 168, 169, 172, 177, 183, 198, 212, 215, 233, 249, 256, 289, 295, 341, 348, 354, 369, 376, 412, 423

Christendom, 74, 77, 143, 160, 152, 183, 227, 228, 229, 245, 250, 253, 254, 281, 302, 322, 331, 332, 335, 336, 339, 348, 365, 374, 402, 423, 425

"Christian Civilization," 280

Christian service, a, in the 2nd and 3rd centuries, 94-96

Christianity, 35, 49, 50, 51, 52, 53, 59, 60, 69, 70, 73, 79, 80, 82, 84, 98, 99, 100, 103, 104, 108, 109, 112, 113, 114, 119, 128, 130, 148, 150, 151, 163, 164, 165, 167, 169, 175, 184, 185, 190, 215, 245, 251, 267, 270, 281, 302, 311, 342, 343, 374, 376, 377, 379, 398, 401, 412, 419, 420, 421

Christians, 52, 77, 82, 89, 100, 101, 102, 103, 104, 105, 106, 107, 108, 109, 110, 111, 112, 114, 119, 120, 129, 132, 142, 150, 151, 156, 161, 166, 174, 176, 210, 212, 224, 281, 283, 303, 306, 354

Christmas, origin of the name, 164

Church, 73, 74, 76, 84, 85, 93, 94, 96, 97, 98, 99, 101, 103, 104, 107, 108, 109, 110, 111, 112, 113, 114, 117, 118, 119, 123, 128, 131, 132, 134, 135, 137, 139, 140, 141, 142, 145, 148, 149, 150, 151, 163, 169, 176, 183, 185, 190, 198, 199, 200, 206, 207, 215, 218, 223, 231, 232, 236, 237, 238, 239, 241, 246, 248, 249, 250, 251, 253, 254, 255, 256, 258, 259, 267, 268, 269, 270, 273, 275, 279, 283, 285, 289, 294, 299, 324, 325, 328, 330, 343, 347, 368, 370, 396, 397, 400, 415, 416, 424

Church, R., cited footnote page 403

Circumcision, 36, 40, 55, 164

City of God, St. Augustine, 149

Clarke, Adam, cited footnote page 385

Cloister, in the Middle Ages, 155

Cluny, the first abbots of, 199

Coincy, Gautier de, excerpt from, on Mary, 174

Colet, John, 279

Communion, 95

Congregation of Propaganda, est. at Rome (1622), 340, 341

Congregationalism, 350, 353

Consistory, the, 315

Constantine, 109, 110, 111, 112, 114, 118, 119, 121, 122, 124, 125, 151, 200

Constantinople, 143, 146, 177, 185, 210, 212, 217, 222, 228, 276, 278

Consubstantiality, 127

Consubstantiation, 127

Conybeare, F. C., cited footnote page 4

Copernican theory, 369

Copernicus, 364, 369

Coptic peasants (Monophysites), 137

Coulton, cited footnotes pages 158, 159, 173, 194, 196, 236, 239, 242

INDEX

Council of Constance, 274
Council of Trent, 370
Covenanters, 14
Cox, cited footnote page 166
Creighton, cited footnote pages 260, 275, 342
Crétineau-Joly, cited footnote page 331
Cromwell, Thomas, commissioned by Henry VIII to visit the monasteries, 301
Cross, the, as a symbol, 110, 111
Crucifixion, 3, 43, 62, 63, 70, 75
Crusades, 215-222; Children's, 225-227
Cult of Reason in France, 399
Cumont, Franz, cited footnote page 33
Cunningham, cited footnote page 271
Cutten, G. B., cited footnote page 13
Cyprian, Bishop of Carthage, his contention that there is no salvation outside the Church, 97

Damascus, a cleric in Rome in 361, 140
Damiani, St. Peter, his belief that "It is easier to convert a Jew than reform a prelate," 193
Danton, 398
Darby, John Nelson, an exhorter of Plymouth (1830), 404
Dark Ages, 147, 148, 162, 163, 236, 240
Darwin's *Origin of Species*, 413
Davenport, cited footnote page 405
Decian persecution, 104
Decius, 104
Decline and Fall of the Roman Empire, Gibbon, 104
Defenestration of Prague, 332
Deism, 376, 398, 400
Deists, 376-380

De Matrimonia, a Jesuit treatise, 346
Denck, Hans, a founder of the Anabaptist movement, 305
Derwacter, cited footnote page 28
Descartes, 366
Diaspora, the, the "scattering of the Jews," 18, 27
Diderot, a convert to Deism, 376
Diocletian persecution, 104
Disciples, the, 3-14
Dobschütz, cited footnote page 96
Döllinger, a distinguished church historian, 415
Dominic, St., 250, 251, 252
Dominicans, 250, 253, 284
Donatello, 279
Doukhobors in Russia, 410
Dowding, cited footnote page 334
Drane, cited footnote page 250
Draper, John W., cited footnote page 120
Duchesne, cited footnotes pages 102, 140, 171
Duchesne, an advanced Catholic scholar, 416
Dupuis, cited footnote page 31
Duruy, Victor, cited footnotes pages 103, 111

Easter, origin of the name, 163
Educational movement in the churches early in 20th century, 420, 421
Edwards, Jonathan, 405
Edwards, Thomas, his list of religious sects, 348
Elements, the three, in Christian feeling, 77
Elexius, Emperor, 219
Emmanuel, Victor, established constitutional ruler of a united land (1861), 411
England, its establishment of an anti-papal religion, 298; the his-

INDEX

tory of its defection from Catholicism, 298-300

Erasmus, 279, 295, 364

Essenes, 14

Eucharist, 95, 137, 167, 168, 357

Europe, its change of life, 268-271; 278, 282, 364

Faith in the early Church, three fundamental elements in, 183

Farel, 314, 315,

Farrar, F. W., cited footnotes pages 25, 375

Fausta, wife of Constantine, 124, 125

Ferdinand and Isabella, their establishment of their own inquisition, 284

Fisher, G. P., cited footnotes pages 89, 192, 385

Fiske, cited footnote page 166

Fitchett, cited footnote page 385

Flick, cited footnote page 268

Flint, cited footnote page 375

Foakes-Jackson, F. J., cited footnotes page 25, 144

Fogazzaro, 416; cited footnote page 417

Fortesque, cited footnotes pages 44, 273

Fox, George, founder of the cult of Quakers, 354; cited footnote page 355

Francis of Assisi, a great reformer, 246-250

Franciscanism, paralleled in the history of Dominicanism, 250

Franklin, 376

Frederick the Great of Prussia, 378

Free thinker, the, 374, 375

French Revolution, 396, 397

Friends, the, 354

Fülöp-Müller, Rene, cited footnote page 331

"Fundamentalists," 426

Galerius, foremost of the imperators, 108

Galileans, 11, 13, 20, 22, 23, 67

Galilee, 3, 8, 12, 39, 82

Galileo, 364, 370, 372, 373

Gardiner, S. R., cited footnote page 334

Gardner, Alice, cited footnote page 129

General Baptists, 351

Germany, its definite break with the Roman Catholic Church, 285

Ghirlandajo, 279

Gibbon, cited footnote page 101

Giessen, cited footnote page 4

Gladstone, W. E., his efforts to reconcile science and tradition, 413

Gledstone, J. P., cited footnote page 392

Glossolalia, the "gift of tongues," 13

Gnosticism, 80-83

Gnostics, theologians rather than philosophers, 82, 83

Goddess of Reason, 399

Godfrey of Bouillon, one of the greatest of the crusaders, 218

Goguel, M., cited footnote page 4

Good, cited footnote page 322

Goodspeed, E. J., cited footnotes pages 21, 61

Gospels, the three, 68, 69

Great Schism, 231, 274

Graetz, cited footnote page 7

Gregory the Great, 165

Gregorovius, cited footnotes pages 228, 275

Grubb, cited footnote page 355

Gwatkin, cited footnote page 120

Hackett, cited footnote page 299

Hagenbach, K. R., cited footnote page 413

Hardy, cited footnote page 101

INDEX

Harnack, cited footnotes pages 89, 91

Hastings, cited footnote page 204

Heath, cited footnote page 306

Hébert, 399

Heliocentric theory, 369, 370

Heliogabalus, a degenerate ruler, 103

Hemerobaptists, 14

Henry IV, 201, 205, 206

Henry VIII, 298-300

Heresies during 2nd, 3rd and 4th centuries, 87; the most important in early times, 137; why they were able to spread and endure, 139

Heresy, how sown in later Middle Ages, 235; spread of, with the appearance of printed books, 280-284

Heretical sects, 241-245

Hermes, idea of, as intermediary between the Logos and mankind, 72

Hermits, 153, 154

Hildebrand, 199, 203, 207, 209

Hoare, H. W., cited footnote page 281

Hoffman, Melchior, how he won a great following in the Netherlands, 307

Holy Ghost, 87, 88, 89, 133, 145, 176

Holy Land, 209, 210, 215, 225

"Holy Roman Empire," 187

Horus, born in a stable, 68

Hübmaier, a founder of the Anabaptist movement, 305

Humanism, the literary phase of the Renaissance movement, 279

Humanists, 363

Hunt, Leigh, cited footnote page 344

Hunter, David, cited footnote page 280

Hurst, J. F., cited footnote page 413

Huss, John, 260-262

Hutton, cited footnote page 385

Ibsen, cited footnote page 129

Images, and image worship, 177, 178; development of, 179

Immaculate conception, 414

Indulgences, 289-291

Inman, Thomas, cited footnote page 111

Innocent III, 227, 228, 229, 251, 276

Inquisition, a body appointed to ferret out heresies, 253

Institutes of the Christian Religion, The, Calvin, 311

Irene, Empress, 178

Irving, Edward, a Presbyterian minister in London, 403

Irvingites, 404

Isaiah, 7, 14, misquoted to foretell the miracle of the virgin birth, 65

Jackson and Lake, cited footnote page 15

Jacobins, 398, 399

Jerome, St., 70, 155

Jerusalem, 3, 4, 11, 14, 18, 19, 20, 24, 28, 31, 39, 41, 42, 43, 55, 56, 60, 66, 79, 88, 212, 214, 217, 219, 220, 221, 222, 224, 225, 326, 327, 328

Jesuits, 341, 342, 345, 346, 347, 373, 401

Jesus, 4, 5, 6, 8, 9, 10, 15, 16, 17, 18, 23, 24, 28, 30, 31, 35, 36, 38, 39, 40, 41, 44, 49, 52, 53, 56, 59, 61, 63, 64, 65, 66, 67, 68, 69, 70, 71, 72, 73, 78, 79, 84, 86, 87, 89, 143, 150, 152, 156, 174, 304, 355, 381, 384, 412

[436]

INDEX

Jews, 6, 7, 14, 15, 18, 19, 23, 33, 35, 40, 41, 45, 48, 52, 56, 62, 65, 66, 67, 217, 220, 240, 283, 383

John, the Acts of, 70

John, the Baptist, 14-15

John, the Gospel according to, 70-73

John, the Revelation of, 74-76

John XI, son of Marozia, 188

John XII, 188, 189

Jones, Rufus M., cited footnote page 355

Joseph II of Austria, 378

Jovian, Julian's successor, 133

Jovinian, heresy of, 139

Judaism, 27, 28, 42, 48, 60

Julian, a nephew of Constantine, 129-132

Julius, II, 275

Jusserand, cited footnote page 277

Juster, Jean, cited footnote page 19

Kautsky, cited footnote page 309

Kennedy, A. A., cited footnote page 32

Kepler, a German astronomer, 364, 370

King, C. W., cited footnote page 80

King's Chapel, the oldest Anglican Church in New England, 380

Klausner, Joseph, cited footnote page 4

Klein, Prof. A. L., a brilliant physicist, 363

Koreishan Ecclesia, the, 410

Kurtz, J. H., cited footnotes pages 145, 163

Lactantius, 113

Lake, cited footnote page 28

Lamb, Harold, cited footnote page 214

Last Supper, 44

Latter-Day Saints, the Church of, 408

"Lay investiture," the contest over, 201

Lea, cited footnotes pages 208, 228, 242, 284

Lechler, cited footnote page 256

Lecky, cited footnotes pages 154, 395

Leibnitz, Gottfried Wilhelm, 379

Leontius, Bishop of Antioch, 126

Lent, a borrowing from Paganism, 163

Leo the Great, 143

Leo the Isaurian, 177

Leo III, 186

Leo XIII, a man of scholarly tastes and considerable liberalism, 416

Letters to a Provincial Friend, Blaise Pascal, 346

Lewissohn, Ludwig, cited footnote page 217

Licinius, 109, 113, 114

Lindsay, cited footnotes pages 293, 306

Lindsay (1774), aided by Priestley, founded a Unitarian Church in London, 380

Lipsky, cited footnotes pages 385, 388, 392

Little, A. G., cited footnotes pages 175, 363

Locke, cited footnote page 230

Loisy, 416

"Lollards," 258

London, Bishop of, 352

Loof, F., cited footnote page 89

Lord's Supper, 43, 44, 55, 94, 95, 119, 145, 313

Loserth, cited footnote page 260

Lost Ten Tribes, 408

Loud, cited footnote page 405

Loyola, 326-329

Luke, the Gospel of, 67, 68

INDEX

Luther, 285-296, 348, 369
Lutheran Church, 382
Lutheranism, 296, 298, 320, 321, 322

Macedonius, installed after a massacre in which 3000 were slain, 140
MacLaurin, Dr. C., cited footnotes pages 134, 296
Magdeburg, sack of (1631), 333
Manicheism, 112
Marat, 398
Marcion, a Gnostic, 83
Marcus Aurelius, one of the sagest rulers in history, 103
Mark, 62, 63, 64, 68, 144
Maronites, the name taken by the adherents of Monotheletism, 136
Marozia, 188
Martyr, Justin, cited footnote page 96
Martyrdom, a "second baptism," 106
Martyrs, the first of the, the saints, 168
Marx, Karl, 319
Mary, 134, 171, 172, 173, 174, 177, 243
Masses, 167, 168
Mathys, Jan, a leader of the Anabaptists, 307
Matthew, 64-68
Maximinus, 110
Mazarin, 373
McCabe, cited footnote page 331
Melanchthon, 311, 369
Melia, cited footnote page 244
Mennonitism, 351
Messiah, 3, 6, 7, 8, 11, 42, 71
Messianic cults, 243
Methodism, 389, 394, 395
Methodist Episcopal Church, 394
Methodists, 385, 393-395

Michelangelo, 276
Middle Ages, 155, 206, 235, 236, 278, 303, 325, 358, 364, 414
Miller, William, started the Adventist movement (1831), 406
Milton, John, the epic poet of Calvinism, 320, 367, 375
Mirandola, Pico della, 279
Missionaries, Catholic, 341, 342, 343
Mithra, a Persian deity, 26; essentially a Messiah, 32-34
Mithraism, a religion restricted to males, 111, 164
Modernism, an insurgent movement assuming grave proportions toward the end of the 19th century, 416
Moehlman, cited footnote page 322
Molière, 368
Monastery, the, 193-199
Monasticism, at first largely an unsacerdotal movement, 156, 162
Mönchthum, cited footnote page 154
Monks, 161, 162, 193, 195, 198
Monophysites, 135
Monophysitism, 135
Monotheletism, 136
Montanism, a cult started by Montanus, 97
Montanus, 97
Monte Cassino, reformed itself along Cluny lines, 199
Montesquieu, 390
Moore, E. C., cited footnote page 61
Moravian Brothers, the, 383, 384
Mormonism, 407-410
Moslems, 210, 220, 223, 224, 249, 283
Munro, cited footnote page 214
Murray, cited footnote page 295

INDEX

Mysteries, the, 32, 35, 44, 52, 54, 60, 80, 111

Nabu, in Babylonian religion the instrument of divine revelation to man, 72

Napoleon, his restoration of the Church, 400, 401

Nasarei, 14

Nash, Henry S., cited footnote page 61

Nationalism, as an integrating force in Europe, 254

Neander, cited footnote page 176

Neo-Platonism, 111

Nestorianism, 134, 135

Nestorius, his theory of the two natures of Christ, 134

Newman, John Henry, (later Cardinal), 402

Newman, cited footnote page 242

New Testament, 21, 70, 74, 85, 86, 231, 412

Newton, Sir Isaac, his belief in the Second Coming, 366

Nicholas V., 276

Ninety-five Theses of Luther, 290, 291

Noetus, a Modalist, 87

O'Brien, cited footnote page 271

Obscurantist movement, 425

Old Catholic Church, the, 415

Old Testament, 83, 309, 412

Ollard, S. L., cited footnote page 403

Orders, new monastic, of the 17th century, 343-347

Orléans, Duke of, 378

"Orthodox" Church, denominated Greek, 145

Osiris, an Egyptian god, 26

Ostrogoths, 147

Owen, John, cited footnote page 371

Owen, Robert, and "socialism," 411

Pachomius, 152, 153

Paganism, 31, 32, 49, 60, 129, 161, 163, 169, 179

Pagans, 41, 55, 65, 72, 80, 87, 100, 105, 111, 118, 128, 129, 132, 152, 177

Paine, Thomas, 376

Palestine, 24, 152, 219, 221

Papacy, 142, 148, 190, 205, 227, 229, 230, 231, 254

Papal Pornocracy, name given period from Sergius III through John XII, page 189

Paper, where originated and manufactured, 281

Pascal, Blaise, a French scientist, 346

Pastor, cited footnote page 275

"Patriarch," title refused by prelate of Rome, 142

Paul IV, beginning with, the popes were prevailingly men of strict life, 325

Paul, Vincent de, founder of Congregation of Missions and organizer of Sisters of Charity, 344

Paulot, cited footnote page 210

Peasants of the Middle Ages, 236-238

Pelagianism and Semi-Pelagianism, heresies of the 5th century, 137

Pelagius, a British monk, 137

Penn, William, a Quaker, 356

Pennsylvania, founded by Quakers, 356

Pentecost, the day appointed for Jesus' return, 11-13

Pepin, 185

Pepys, Samuel, 367, 368

INDEX

Percival, H. R., cited footnote page 171

"Perpetual Virgin, the," 139, 172

Peter, head of the Brethren, 15-17, 62

Peter the Hermit, 211

Pfleiderer, Otto, cited footnotes pages 44, 71, 414

Philastrius, 139

Philip Augustus of France, 222

Philo, the Jewish philosopher, 72

Pietism, 383

Pilgrims, the, 351-353

Pilgrim's Progress, Bunyan, 318

Pirie-Gordon, cited footnote page 228

Pius IX, 414

Pius X, under him modernism was shown no quarter, 416

Plymouth Brethren, 404

Polycarp, Bishop, the heroism of, 106, 107

Polygamy, added to the Mormon faith, 409

"Pope," title taken by the prelate of Rome, 142

Popes, 149, 274, 276, 325

Porter, cited footnote page 76

Power, Eileen, cited footnote page 194

Predestination, the most distinctive doctrine of Calvinism, 317, 318, 321

Prescott, cited footnote page 283

Priesthood, the establishment of a, 90

Priestley, Joseph, discoverer of oxygen, 380

Priests, 91, 191-193

Printing, the first consequences of, 281

Probabiliorists, 345

Protestant revival, second quarter of 19th century, 403

Protestantism, 325, 331, 333, 335, 348, 349, 357, 379, 394, 418, 419, 421, 423, 425

Providence, the founding of, 353

Purgatory, 167

Puritans, 352-354

Pusey, S. B., cited footnote page 172

Quakers, 354-348

Quantum theory, 89

Radin, Max, cited footnote page 19

Ramsay, W. M., cited footnote page 27

Raphael, 276

Rationalism, 379-382

Reformation, the, 339, 347, 356, 360, 380

Reign of Terror, 398-400

Reinach, cited footnote page 32

Relics, 169-170

Rémy, Nicholas, 361

Renaissance, 278, 279, 363

Renan, Ernest, a brilliant French scholar, 413

Reuchlin, 279

"Revival of Learning," 279

Revolutions of 1830 to 1861, 411

Ricci, Father, his concessions to heathen ceremonialism, 164

Richard the Lionhearted, 222

"Rigorists," 345

Robertson, J. M., cited footnotes pages 4, 63

Robespierre, 398, 400

Roman Church, subject to conditions different from those in the East, 185

Rome, 143, 145, 146, 178, 343, 402, 414, 424

Rome, Bishop of, 142

Rosicrucians, 81

Ruffini, cited footnote page 354

Rufinius, Historia Eremitica of, 155

"Rule of St. Basil," 157

INDEX

Sabatier, cited footnote page 246

Sabellianists, their stand on the Trinity, 88

Sacerdotalism, 94

Sacrifices, regarded essential in the worship of the gods, 167

Saints, the first, the martyrs, 168-170

Saintyves, cited footnote page 171

Saladin, a Kurdish adventurer, 224

Sales, de, Francis, 343, 344

Sandon, ancient god of Tarsus, 26

Sanhedrin, the council of priests and rabbis governing the religious life of Israel, 23

Saul, 24-30, 36-51, 55, 60, 61, 69, 80, 85, 88, 89, 90

Schaff, cited footnotes pages 170, 189, 206, 208, 211, 260

Schell, Herman, 416

Scholastics, 231-234

Schweitzer, cited footnote page 4

Science in the 16th century, 364-373; the development of, 390

Scott, Ernest F., cited footnote page 50

Scotus, Duns, 373

Sect of Those Who Wait, 14

Sectarianism, 348, 349

Seljuk Turks, 210

Semi-Arians, 127

Serfdom, supplanted by "free labor," 268

Sergius III, 188

Serles, 348

Servetus, a Spanish physician, his discoveries, 315, 316

Shakespeare (1546) makes few allusions to scientific matters, 367

"Sign," the, from Heaven, 14

Simon, verbal inspiration of Old Testament challenged by, 412

"Simony," definition of, 200

Sisters of Charity, 344

Sizzi, an astronomer of Florence, 372

Smedley, cited footnote page 322

Smith, cited footnotes pages 293, 361, 442

Smith, Gregory, cited footnote page 154

Smith, Joseph, founder of the sect of Mormons, 407-409

Smith, Preserved, cited footnotes pages 295, 314, 346, 358; on Francis Bacon, 365, 366

Smyth, John, 351

"Socialism," in 1835, 411

"Society of Jesus," 329-331

Socinianism, 380

Sozzini, Fausto, a radical theologian, 380

Spanish Inquisition, 283, 284

Speculative Freemasons, 81

Spener, 382

Spinoza, 412

Stephen, a Hellenist, 23

Stephen II, 185

Strabo, a Greek geographer, 18, 19

Strauss, David Frederick, a student of Baur, 412, 413

Streeter, cited footnote page 70

Stückelburg, E. A., cited footnote page 170

Sweet, W. W., cited footnote page 405

Swete, H. B., cited footnote page 97

Synoptic Gospels, the, 68

Tacitus, 101

Tammuz, a Mesopotamian deity, 26

Tancred, a crusader, 218

Tarsus, a center of Hellenist culture, 26

Tausen, Hans, 298

Taylor, cited footnote page 198

Tertullian, 101, 105, 107; cited footnote page 96

[441]

INDEX

Tetzel, an Indulgence seller, 288-290

Theodora, 178, 188

Theologians, dissensions among, of the 2nd century, 88, 89

Theology, how it may be defined, 87; the new, 379

Theosophists, 81

Therapeutæ, the, 14

Thirty Years' War, between Protestants and Catholics, 331-334, 340, 358, 360, 382

Thomas, cited footnote page 355

Thorndyke, Lynn, cited footnote page 363

Thot, considered an instrument of divine revelation to man, 72

Tithes, 93

Torquemada, Thomas, leader of the Spanish Inquisition, 284

Townsend, Workman and Eayrs, cited footnote page 394

Trench, cited footnote page 32

Trinity, 85, 133, 171, 380

Troeltsch, cited footnote page 322

"Truce of God," 200

Type, movable, 281

Typography, history of, 280

Tyrrell, Father, 416

Uhlhorn, cited footnote page 101

Ulfilus, translated the Bible into Gothic in 4th century, 240

"Uniate" churches, 341

Unitarianism, 380, 381

Unitas Fratrum, descendants of the Hussites, 383

Universalists, a liberal sect, 381, 382

Urban II, 209-215

Valentinian III, 144

Vandals, masters of North Africa, 147

Vanini, a philosopher rather than a scientist, 370, 371

Vatican, 275, 276, 277, 322, 323, 424

Vestal virgins, the six, 100

Vincent, cited footnote page 201

Virgins, 65, 120, 172

Visigoths, masters of Spain, 147

Vitry, de, Cardinal Jacques, 195, 196

Vohumano, 72

Volney, cited footnote page 31

Voltaire, 376, 379, 398

Waldenses, sect founded by Peter Waldo, 244

Waldo, Peter, 244

Walker, Williston, cited footnotes pages 310, 350

Walpole, 391

Wand, J. W. C., cited footnotes pages 379, 392

Ward, Harry F., cited footnote page 321

Warschauer, J., cited footnote page 4

Waterman, Philip, cited footnote page 111

Watson, J., cited footnote page 80

Weber, Max, cited footnote page 322

Wesley, John, 385-393

Wesley, John and Charles, leaders of the Methodists, 385-387

Wesleyans, 394

Westphalia, Peace of, 333

Williams, Roger, founder of Providence, 353, 354

Windsor, Dean of, 358

Winthrop, Governor, 358

Witchcraft, 360, 361

Witch hunting, 358-362

White, cited footnotes pages 61, 371

Whitefield, George, an associate of Wesley, 293, 392, 405

INDEX

"Whore of Babylon," 304, 326, 339

Workman, H. B., cited footnotes pages 108, 192, 256

World War, immediate consequences of, 423, 424

Wyclif, an English scholar of latter half of 14th century, 255-257

Young, Brigham, 409

Young Men's Christian Association, an interdenominational body, 422

Zeller, cited footnote page 38

Zinzendorf, Graf von, a Pietist, 383, 384

Zöckler, cited footnote page 154

Zoroastrians, the belief of, in a Messiah, 6

Zwingli, Huldreich, 305, 357